Contemporary Jewelry

Contemporary Jewelry

A Critical Assessment 1945-75

Ralph Turner

VNR VAN NOSTRAND REINHOLD COMPANY
NEW YORK CINCINNATI TORONTO LONDON MELBOURNE

To Angela

Published in the U.S.A. in 1976 by Van Nostrand Reinhold Company
A Division of Litton Educational Publishing, Inc.
450 West 33rd Street
New York, N.Y. 10001

16 15 14 13 12 11 10 9 8 7 6 5 4 3 2 1

Contents

Preface

The original idea of this book came about between 1971 and 1974 through my dealings with the public whilst directing the Electrum Gallery in London. It became obvious that people were relatively well acquainted with creative jewelry from the past and could follow the development of the subject up to the turn of the twentieth century. With recent publications, both the Art Nouveau and Art Deco movements have been adequately covered, but when it came to contemporary work the public in general appeared confused and less informed. A few books have been published on modern jewelry during the past decade but no one publication dealt specifically with the creative aspect, and there was little literature that one could refer to. This then motivated me to produce this book.

My main purpose in writing it was essentially to draw attention to contemporary work, but it became more and more obvious that if the reader was to understand fully the work being produced today it was necessary to look at its immediate ancestry. I decided on a brief assessment of the principal achievements that have been made from 1945. For the inevitable omissions, I will plead that I have tried to be impartial, although my selection of artists for this survey can only be restricted to my personal concept of the subject.

In several instances I have included material from other writers that will give the reader a broader view than my own. In some cases these statements put forward arguments that disagree with my own, the intention being to help the reader draw his own conclusions. My own, sometimes critical judgement, has been given in an attempt to cultivate constructive thought, something which all serious artists and institutions are subject to.

To enable the reader to assess the development of the subject over the thirty years in question, I have divided this period into three chapters — 1945—60, 1960—70, and 1970—75 — the dates being given for the sake of convenience and intended only as a guide. Costume jewelry that imitates precious metals and stones has not been included, neither have I made any mention of fashion, commercial or traditional jewelry. Though fascinating topics, they lie outside the scope of this book. Silver and plate have also been excluded. Most of the work illustrated is unique. If produced in limited-edition, number in edition is given, if known. Only the largest dimension is indicated in the captions, and this only approximate.

I would like to thank the following individuals for their help and advice in my research for this publication. They have given invaluable assistance, but are in no way responsible for any errors, which are entirely my own: Hans Appenzeller, Galerie Sierraad, Amsterdam; Bendix Bech-Thostrup, Editor, Guldsmedebladet, Kolding; Dr Gerhard Bott, Hessisches Landesmuseum, Darmstadt; Sven Botenstern, Gallerie Sven, Paris; Marigold Coleman, *Crafts* magazine, London; Noma Copley, New York; Angela Cottura, Marlborough Galleria d'Arte, Rome; Liesbeth Crommelin, Stedelijk Museum, Amsterdam; Mrs A. P. Dufresne, Art Gallery, Ontario; Dr Fritz Falk, Schmuck-museum, Pforzheim; Susan Hare, Librarian, Goldsmiths' Hall, London; Yasuki Hiramatsu, Tokyo University of Fine Art, Japan; Gian Carlo Montebello, Gem, Milan; Renee Neu, New York; Roy Jameson, London; Patricia Meyerowitz, New York; Jacques Pulvermacher, Gallery at Home, Toulouse; Leslie Rankow, Leslie Rankow Gallery, New York; Judy Scolnik, Toronto; Paul Smith, Museum of Contemporary Crafts, New York; Joan Sonnabend, Sculpture to Wear Gallery, New York. I would also like to thank the BBC for permission to quote from Dr Bronowski's *The Ascent of Man*, Thames & Hudson and the Viking Press for *Objects USA*, and the American Crafts Council, for the conversation between John Prip and Ronald Pearson from *Craft Horizons*.

But it is to the artists themselves that I owe my deepest gratitude. So many have been patient in answering endless questions, and my particular thanks go to Arline Fisch, who gave so much time to my research concerning American jewellers; Marion Herbst, who generously helped in Holland, and Sigurd Persson for his knowledge concerning the developments in Scandinavia.

Finally I would like to give my sincere thanks to Ray Carpenter, who designed the book, and to the staff of Studio Vista, in particular Stephen Adamson as editor.

Introduction

If we try to define the word 'jewelry', we find that it has many more meanings than are commonly attributed to it. We now think of jewelry as being restricted to objects that are worn, such as rings and necklaces, but in the broader sense of the word it means the decorating of the body and embraces far more. Throughout the centuries of recorded time men and women of all cultures have felt the compulsion to adorn themselves. Today cosmetics, millinery, regalia, as well as jewelry, are used as an extension of this urge that links us closely with our primitive ancestors.

What is it that makes us decorate and adorn ourselves? If we forget the commercial properties of jewelry and think of our motivations, then perhaps we will discover a fuller and more realistic explanation. Jewelry's history starts with primitive man, although no one knows exactly when or precisely how jewelry came into being. Historians start their assessment with early man decorating his body by rubbing dung and juices into scored tissues of the skin, thereby arriving at a form of adornment that could be compared with present-day cosmetics, or the current fashion for elaborate body painting, as practised by David Bowie, and artists such as Marc Chaimowitz and Claudio Parmiggiani. One explanation for why this should have been done is that by decorating himself not only with dyes, but beads, shells, bone, and feathers, early man was able to show his neighbour superiority in being able to own such possessions through his skill in hunting, thus promoting his position within the tribe.

The psychological basis for the wearing of traditional jewelry today is surely similar, only now jewelry is worn to denote social instead of tribal status. As in the past, too, the distinctions between jewelry and clothing are often blurred. Where do we place the superb headdresses of the American Indian, Japanese kimonos, or the ostrich feathers of the African chieftain? Is the fact that they are made of perishable materials the criterion that separates clothes from jewels? Clothing's prime concern is with the protection of the body, and is essentially functional, while jewelry is used to decorate and adorn, and yet the world of fashion provides endless examples of clothing where the prime aim is to decorate, for example, the top hat, tail coat, bustle, crinoline, ruff and the fantasies still created by designers. Here civilized society and more primitive people work along parallel lines: their motivation is not dissimilar — to draw distinctions, and elevate the wearer. Even today, the London policeman wears a helmet to make him appear taller and a more forbidding figure, much as the American Indian or the African chieftain did with tall plumage. And jewelry is merely one aspect of this display of status.

Jewelry and decoration of the body are also means to enhance the beauty and sexual appeal of the wearer. But if one were cast away on a desert island with nobody to respond to your appearance, would one then wear jewelry? I like to think so. As small children we have all worn one of the loveliest jewels on long summer days, the daisy chain. We wore this not for social, political, or fashionable reasons, but for the sheer pleasure of it. This simplest of reasons is perhaps one of the strongest.

However, jewelry has other connotations and significance. In his book, *The Ascent of Man*, Dr J. Bronowski talked of how gold became 'the universal prize in all countries, in all cultures, in all ages'. To most people jewelry cannot be divorced from its monetary value, and jewelry, being made out of expensive metals, is a form of investment. Gold, the basis of commerce for thousands of years, is the ideal material out of which to make jewelry which is meant to show a person's place in society. But with this book I hope to show that in creative jewelry materials are of little consequence in this respect, and that the commercial aspect of jewelry is its least important. For if we are to consider jewelry seriously as a free form of man's expressiveness, we have to shake off inhibitions and restrictions engendered by traditional attitudes.

When assessing contemporary work it becomes clear that we are witnessing a renaissance. Traditional attitudes are being questioned, and some contemporary work has reacted strongly against the status significance of jewelry. By the first half of this decade talents had emerged that were to question the entire validity of jewelry and which were to be an active force against the traditional approach. This reassessment has produced jewelry of considerable quality and originality, much as it did at the turn of this century. But unlike the pioneers of the Art Nouveau movement, many jewellers today look at the present for their ideas, although there are some who work from a romantic gaze at the past.

In some work reaction has been so severe that this has produced jewelry that is not intended to be worn at all. Jewelry has in the past been dominated by commerce, and to a large extent this is still true today, but many more jewellers are creating work that shuns pure commercial motivation, and, like their colleagues in other art forms, are now creating work free from such restrictions. It could rightly be pointed out that many other forms of art have had their commercial roots firmly planted in galleries and salerooms for some time now, but this has taken place in most cases outside of the artist's studio, and has had little to do with the actual producing of painting or sculpture, etc. Jewelry, however, has been more hampered, with its limits set before the artist begins to work at all. He has had to produce specifically for a market, conditions which subvert its claim to be an art. But this need not be the case.

Jewelry has often been used merely for its sensual appeal but recent years have seen jewelry with intellectual content, thus raising the subject onto a higher level. In the most challenging work this has resulted from the particular problems confronting the contemporary jeweller, often emanating in a broader concept of the subject.
In some ways the new concept could be thought of as a revolt, both against the traditional ideas and the subject in general. The restrictions and limitations imposed on jewelry in the past have been thrown off and, although commercial jewelry still dominates, it can no longer restrain the talents to which this medium has given birth.

1

The Validity of Jewelry as an Art Form

1] Catherine Mannheim
Brooch
Silver, gold, enamel, Awabi shell
5·3 cm (2⅛ in)
1974

'Freedom equals self-determination equals man . . . Art is at its most effective and scientific when expressed with a question mark.' Joseph Beuys

Many artists today are far less concerned with having titles and distinctions conferred on their work than they were in the past, feeling that they mean little as different media converge with one another. With the growth of concrete poetry, field art, package art, conceptual and environmental art, happenings, etc., the arts can no longer be neatly labelled and dissected as they used to be, and so it may appear strange to attempt to establish jewelry's right to be regarded as an independent art form. Some of the contributors to this book also dissociate themselves from any distinction on them or their work. After all, if you are confident in what you are doing, you don't need labels. These jewellers feel that the well-worn terms of 'art' and 'artist' should be left to those who need their support.

However, jewelry is a many-faceted medium. As it has been exploited fully for its commercial associations, some effort is needed to offer an explanation of what the creative jeweller has achieved and to show that jewelry today can be a valid form of creativity. If there is no differentiation between artistic and merely showy jewelry, the creative jeweller suffers lack of recognition. Most other arts have not experienced this disadvantage, so for these reasons, it is important to establish jewelry's status. There appears to be little doubt as to the validity of historical jewelry as some form of man's expression, but the problem arises when we are confronted with contemporary work. How do we assess it? What differentiates between the fashionable, commercial, or mundane and the true work of art?

A much closer relationship existed between all forms of art until the fifteenth century than does today. Up to that point in time few distinctions were drawn between the arts, so consequently these problems did not exist. But during this period a deliberate separation of the arts came about, starting in Italy with painters and sculptors advocating that their art stemmed from an intellectual knowledge. They maintained that their work was separate in kind from other media, regarding their work as 'fine art' as opposed to 'applied art'. This separation gave the painter or sculptor an improved social status, while others working in different media 'applied' their ideas handed down to them from the 'masters'. In his autobiography, Benvenuto Cellini described this theory in some detail, stressing the intellectual requirements of a fine artist by advocating that in order to sculpt a musician, the artist must be knowledgeable in the art of music, and when painting a portrait of a soldier, he must know the principles of war and familiarize himself with arms and the rudiments of battle. It seems ironic that Cellini's most famous work was to be a salt cellar!

2

In practice this conscious separation of 'fine art' and 'applied art' did not really apply. It was often considered necessary for all artists to undertake an initial training in jewelry, as it taught the student discipline and technical proficiency, and as can be seen from the fine examples of jewelry from this period, an artist's studio would have embraced many forms of art. The distinction was, however, being drawn in theory and a prime example of this separation during the Renaissance is Michelangelo's displeasure at being called 'sculptor' in letters sent to him by the Pope. He was in fact known during his lifetime as 'the divine', separated entirely from lesser artists even in his own field. To be called 'sculptor' was to him to be associated with craftsmen.

This distinction became ingrained in our culture, despite the continuing creativity of goldsmiths. Only with the coming of the Industrial Revolution did people begin to question the separation between the arts, and in the nineteenth century an increasing number of artists and critics became dissatisfied with the decline in both design and craftsmanship of objects. In 1851, Prince Albert, the Prince Consort, brought to London an exhibition which was to provide a forum for many nations to display their talents in the arts, crafts and industry. The exhibits themselves in the Great Exhibition enabled the visitor to assess the skill and imagination of both art and industry throughout the world at that time. The Victorians were renowned for their inventive spirit, and to some extent this also applied to their jewelry. In her book *Victorian Jewellery Design*, Charlotte Gere talks of this period in the history of jewelry and the reaction to criticism at that time. Looking at some examples of Victorian jewelry it is easy to understand the critical views expressed by some artists and writers. For to a large extent the work produced merely reflected other periods in the history of art, and original ideas were few and far between. This applied to the visual arts in general, and jewelry was no exception.

The Industrial Revolution was born in Britain, and so it was that this country was the first to question its effects, not only in the objects that it created, but on the mode of life that it eventually brought with it. One of the most prominent and articulate artists who were to react strongly against the decline in workmanship and design was William Morris. He became appalled, not only at the quality of the work produced, but also by the debasing effect of industrialization on people and their environment. He saw both machines as evil and the entire system whose tools they were. His reaction to the Great Exhibition was quite explicit: 'Tons upon tons of unutterable rubbish'. To paint pictures, or design buildings or objects for an elitist society was to him abhorrent, and he wrote, 'What business have we with art, unless all can share it?' Not least of Morris's achievements was his collaboration in setting up the Arts and Crafts Movement, whose influence could be felt both in Europe and America. Morris advocated a return to medieval conditions and attitudes that were later

2] Gerd Rothmann
Brooches
Steel, acrylic
5·5 cm (2⅛ in)
1970

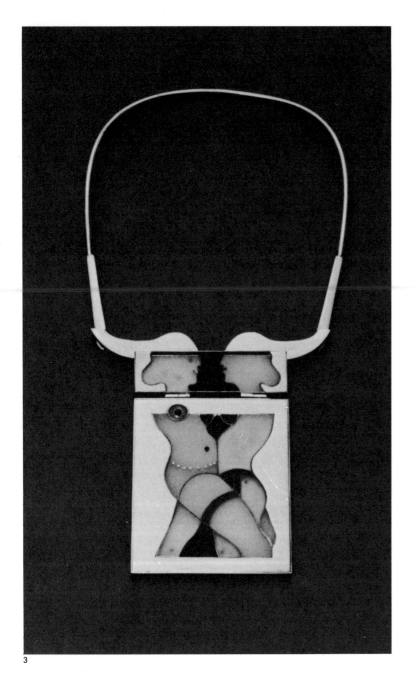

3

3] Ulrike Bahrs
Necklace, 'Two Women'
Silver, acrylic, glass, gold, steel
7·5 cm (3 in)
c. 1970–1

developed by others, including Charles Robert Ashbee, who heeded his call and founded a guild of craftsmen in London's East End. Later this moved to more rural surroundings in Chipping Campden in Gloucestershire, now the workshop of the silversmith Robert Welch. Many fine examples of silver, jewelry and enamel work flowed from Ashbee's workbench. But, like Morris, he was not only devoted to producing good work, but provided a better way of life for the emigrants he brought with him from London.

It was these men and others such as Edward Godwin, Ernest Gimson, Charles F. Annesley Voysey, etc., whose work led eventually to the raising of a 'new art', known now as Art Nouveau. Though this movement was short-lived, it did much to draw together all the arts and, as far as jewelry was concerned, made its mark in no uncertain terms. René Lalique, George Fouquet, Joseph Hoffman, Eric Magnussen, and others, all created jewelry of exceptional quality and originality and, although now seen as typical examples of the movement, their revolutionary jewelry was not at all typical of the work being made at the turn of the century. Most critics would now accept that Art Nouveau did much to blur the old distinctions of 'fine art' and 'applied' art. As far as salerooms are concerned, the price for a fine example of the period could well be compared to a painting of the period, even though it was not the intrinsic value of the materials as precious stones were often not used.

Great changes in attitude in the visual arts developed rapidly between the two World Wars. The distinctions between 'applied' and 'fine' art were being broken down, although they did still exist. The nineteenth century had been a century of revivals: Gothic, Baroque, Rococo, Renaissance and Celtic. The Art Nouveau movement embraced them all but failed to solve the basic problem of how to reconcile art and industry. The Bauhaus in Germany, the Glasgow School of Art in Britain and the Vienna Secession School in Austria — forerunners of Art Deco — attempted to achieve the reconciliation. The examples set by these schools led eventually to jewelry of considerable quality from artists such as Jean Despres, Jean Fouquet, Gustave Miklos and Naum Slutsky.

Even with this acknowledgement of such a close relationship between the arts, there is still the critical question of how to evaluate contemporary jewelry. This distinction exists today and, of course, it applies to art forms other than jewelry. The artist involved with ceramics or weaving is just as prone to these distinctions being made on his work.

Critics and the artists themselves have undertaken to answer the question of jewelry's status as art. In Lee Nordness's introduction to the exhibition Objects: USA, held at the Smithsonian Institute in Washington in 1969 and intended as a survey of various craft media, he asked:

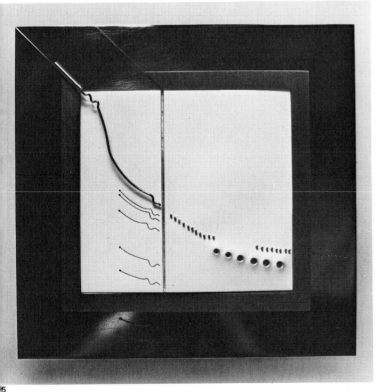

4] Charlotte de Syllas
Bracelet (detail)
Steel, carved amethyst, bronze, silver, silk, amethyst
    beads
c. 1972
Photo: David Cripps, Crafts Magazine

5] Rudiger Lorenzen
Brooch — object
Steel, silver
c. 1972–3

Should non-functional objects alone be candidates for fine art?
An obvious challenge arises for the person working in a functional
expression: the more functional an object is the more difficult for
its presence to overshadow its function. Can a chair ever be a
work of art? Can a teapot? We know a container can be considered an art object; a Chou ceremonial bronze, certainly a vessel
is often displayed in museums juxtaposed with paintings. Or does
one identify the Chou bronze as art because time has erased its
functional aspect from our visual association? . . . There is another
approach to this moot question: intent. This writer maintains that
any person creating an object — whether it be a functional bowl or
a painting — must be called an artist if he creates his object with
the intention that its aesthetic presence be its life. There are
millions of artists creating paintings with this intention whose
works are shallow and lifeless. Artists? Yes, but bad artists. There
are as many potters calling themselves artists making bowls which
will never have any presence beyond their function as containers.
Artists? Yes, bad artists. Let each creative person decide if he be an
artist or a craftsman; let critics and collectors and museum officials
decide if he be a good or bad artist.

David Irwin's *Visual Arts — Taste and Criticism* poses another
interesting question: 'In the last decade, weaving has become more
three-dimensional and pottery has become more like sculpture, to cite
just two of the crafts. Are they therefore trying to become more
"fine", is this a kind of defence mechanism brought about by the
schism, or just a denial that the barrier exists anyway? I leave the
craftsmen to argue that one out.'

Patricia Meyerowitz, now living in America, is an important British
jeweller. In a lecture given by her at the Rhode Island School of
Design in 1972, Miss Meyerowitz explained her beliefs:

Is jewelry art or isn't it? Is jewelry functional or isn't it. That is to
say does it need to be for anything or for anyone. We know that
art has no function. These questions used to be a bother to me.
I worried about them. Wondered about them. Did I have to make
my jewelry for anyone? Did I have to worry about whether anyone
could wear it to any particular social function or was it something
that had no relevance whatsoever?

Well one day I read something in a book by Gertrude Stein called
The Making of Americans, and then suddenly they were no longer
questions that needed an answer and if a question doesn't need an
answer then there is no use in asking it. 'This is the only way I can
do it. Everybody is a real one to me, everybody is like someone
else too to me. No one of them that I know can want to know it,
and so I write for myself and strangers.'

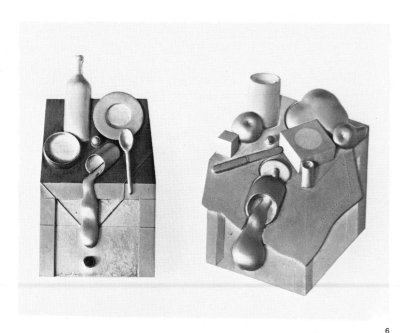

I was very excited when I read that. It made me fully realize about art and function. That is to say, that art has no function and that here was a writer discarding the function of communication in writing — a function which you would think essential to the art of writing. And yet she discarded it and, in so doing, was free to explore writing for its own sake. I'm not saying that art does not communicate anything. Of course it does. Any human gesture can be understood by any other human being, but it's the difference between the outside and the inside that I'm talking about. Whether you let the outside guide your work, or whether you can allow the work itself to lead you on. This is the crucial difference . . . Art, that is real creative art, is like original research. It has no function. If you ascribe a function to it, it ceases to be art. That is to say when you do your art for someone or something, or in order to sell it you destroy it and yourself in relation to it. Art has nothing to do with what anyone wants you to do or wants it to be. Nothing to do with selling it and nothing to do with anything except you and itself. The work generates itself, and new ideas and progress and learning come out of doing the work in a particular way. And so art is a process of exploration for the artist, and not a description of what is already known.

Cornelia Rating, from Germany, is another jeweller with strong views on this subject. The following extract taken from an article in the magazine *Goldschmiede Zeitung* in February 1972 further develops the argument for considering jewelry as an art:

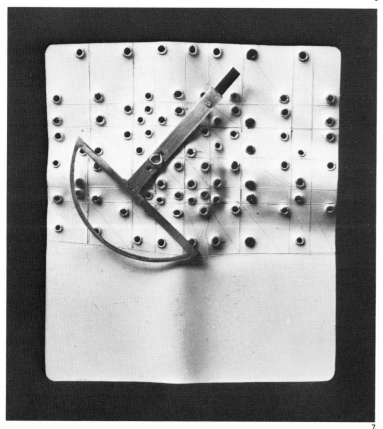

People's motivations in availing themselves of the medium of art are probably to be attributed, to some extent, to a natural desire of self-expression or communication. The artist will first create an object for himself with which he will then identify himself. He is thus fashioning a product that carries with it the personal message of its maker and is at the same time supposed to be generally understood by others . . . It is the function of the artist that he should engage his intellect on the themes and topics of the world around him, then to translate his findings, in a more or less coded form, into aesthetic information . . . He will thus create new realities on the basis of what was realistically experienced . . . Taking a look at exhibitions today, we find that jewelry is gaining in size and plasticity, expanding even to take on the form of a self-contained 'miniature object'. Frequently, what we see is really a reproduction of well-known artistic styles and schools. Thus, we encounter the artistic idioms, say, of constructivism, pop art, op art, concept art. Only the materials are different, while the artistic forms have been assimilated by such jewelry. Such assimilation of forms will drain away the meaning from the underlying artistic idea, and this is a typical symptom of fashionable rather than artistic approaches . . . Someone really ought to try and disengage jewelry from its involvement with non-functional application. Its intrinsic function is that of considering, emphasizing, and implying the

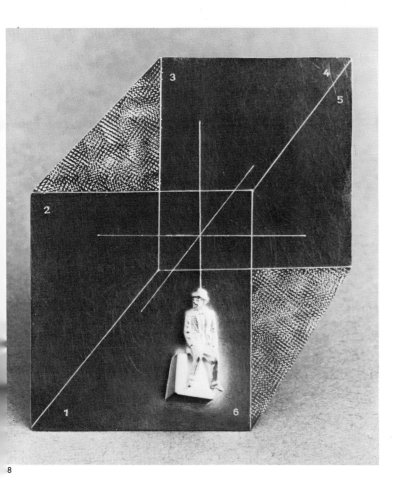

8

6] Hermann Jünger
Brooches
Gold, silver
3·5 cm (1¾ in)
1973
Photo: Ingrid Amslinger

7] Anton Cepka
Brooch
Silver
5·5 cm (2⅛ in)
1970
Photo: Pavel Janek

8] Hubertus von Skal
Brooch
Gold
6 cm (2⅜ in)
1972
Photo: Philipp Schönborn

shapes of the human body and of supplementing and harmonizing with the wearer's attire . . .

Many other critics question the validity of jewelry as a form of modern art. In her excellent book *A History of Jewelry* (first published in 1953) Joan Evans traces the development of jewelry from the twelfth century to the late nineteenth century. Miss Evans concludes by questioning the future and status of jewelry:

It is not easy to see the future for the art of jewelry; it may even be considered that as an art it has not a future. For all the centuries of recorded time it has existed as an art in which style and fashion were set by the taste of an aristocracy; bourgeois jewelry, peasant jewelry and jewelry in less precious materials, such as we now call costume jewelry, all imitated court fashions. This source of inspiration has come to an end.

By 1953, the date when Miss Evans drew her conclusions, the art of the jeweller was indeed thin on the ground, particularly in Britain. But in Italy, Holland, Germany and Scandinavia work of quality was being produced. As society changes, so does its culture, and jewelry, like other forms of art, has come a long way since the courts of Europe flourished. In questioning the jeweller's significance as an artist, efforts must be related to a contemporary situation. Many critics appear to ignore this principle. Primarily the jeweller's art is a communicative one. Many contemporary jewellers use the word 'communication' in their writings and conversation, when describing what they see as their function, each one bringing an entirely different meaning to the word. Essentially, this is a recent development.

The rebellion against commercialization leads the jeweller into a realm that he has not known before. The endless possibilities are now open and unexplored, providing an intriguing new freedom. Many young jewellers extend their reaction against traditionalism to produce work that questions the validity of jewelry, not as an art, but as a vehicle for social reform. As jewelry has been exploited for its ability to draw distinctions, it now can be used as an instrument against hierarchical dogma.

Many of the major pieces illustrated on these pages are works of art. They are not miniature sculpture, but jewelry. They have been, more often than not, created by jewellers, not sculptors or painters, but jewellers. These jewellers, at least, are artists.

9

9] Reinhold Reiling
Brooch
Gold, diamonds
7·5 cm (3 in)
1969
Photo: Egon Augenstein

2

New Beginnings 1945-60

10] Alexander Calder
Necklaces and brooches
Silver and brass
c. 1938
Collection: Mrs F. H. Mayor and Mrs Sybil Mesens
Photo: Peter Parkinson

11] Alexander Calder
Bracelet
Silver
1950
Photo: Hessisches Landesmuseum, Darmstadt

In time of war there is very little time for the creative mind and jewelry, more than any other art form, suffered during World War II. The strides taken in the 1920s and 1930s were abruptly halted. 1945 marks a dividing line for the art historian, for it was not only the end of a crisis, but with it came an end to a way of life we will never know again. World War II had changed the very structure of society and its attitudes, both cultural and sociological, were due to be revolutionized.

It was about this time that the visual arts in general took a new direction. Many artists had left Europe and settled in America, and Europe generally was left battered and exhausted. The artistic life of the USA had been enriched by the wave of immigrants from countries threatened by the German invasion. It is not surprising then to find that in the 1950s and 1960s America, and especially New York, became the capital and cultural centre for the visual arts. However, this is not so much the case with jewelry, for the origins of contemporary work are to be found in Europe, where the roots of the present renaissance are firmly planted. As well as the ancient traditions of the art of jewelry being found in Europe, in the USA in the twenties and thirties it was a rarity to find someone creating exceptional work, or a school or college that taught the subject on an advanced level.

Artists established in other media

There is no 'father figure' of modern jewelry, comparable in status to Cézanne or Rodin in painting and sculpture. Some claim this prerogative belongs to René Lalique, but unlike Rodin or Cézanne, Lalique's contribution was largely concerned with one specific movement that had little bearing on developments that were to occur later in the century, while Cézanne's and Rodin's influences can be seen even today. But one name does crop up with regularity and, although the USA was not in other ways the starting point, we should first look at the work of an American, Alexander Calder.

Calder was born in Philadelphia in 1898 and trained as an engineer. In 1922 he attended evening classes in New York to learn to draw. Then in 1926 he went to Paris and set up a miniature circus, composed of acrobats, dancers and clowns, which revolved on a small ring. At about this time he did a series of experiments with mobile toys and comic animals which were exhibited at the Salon des Humoristes.

Calder is regarded as an innovator in mobiles. As early as 1931 he began producing moving constructions, equipped with motors. Shortly afterwards he discarded these mechanical aids and created his first mobiles, which were set in motion by currents of air. It was perhaps this preoccupation with movement that led him to create jewelry in the thirties, surely the most mobile of arts for jewelry, when worn, is constantly on the move.

Calder's jewels were in themselves mainly static. They had a simplicity and honesty that was to influence many students who were interested in his work at that time. Unlike many sculptor-jewellers he made his own jewelry, and nothing is farmed out to craftsmen. Every mark on the metal matters to Calder.

Calder had been far more prolific in jewelry than his contemporaries, and his use of wire and the manner in which he formed his work was not dissimilar to primitive jewelry. His methods at that time required very little technical skill and so could be a model for many others. As a result forms that were then created by Calder were to be found in many jewellers' work during the years that followed, not only in America but also in Europe.

Other painters and sculptors at that time showed some interest in jewelry but to a far lesser extent. For example, Pablo Picasso modelled a number of medallions using his now famous bull's heads as inspiration. These were created when he was in Vallauris in France, in 1946, and were cast in gold. They show the artist's flamboyant style during those years. Some years later in 1952 he was to make a unique necklace again in gold 'following a visit to a dentist where he was fascinated by the possibilities of gold and dental machinery'. The French painter André Derain also modelled a number of pendants and brooches for his wife in 1945. Derain was one of the first artists to discover the zest and imagery of Negro art, and some of his jewelry was to reflect that interest in its direct and often virile approach to the subject.

Another French artist, Henri Laurens, made a series of jewels in modelled plaster that were eventually cast in gold. Reminiscent of his sculpture, these were made in 1951, three years before his sudden death in Paris. But it was Calder who was to attract the greatest interest and have the greatest influence during those years. Neither Picasso, Derain, Laurens, nor Ernst, who also made some pieces, contributed a great deal to the development of creative jewelry. In most cases their output was very small, and often only made as gifts for friends or relatives. Consequently the pieces were rarely, if ever, seen on exhibition until some time after this period.

One painter who did receive a great response to his contribution to jewelry was Salvador Dali. At the Milan Triennale in 1954, Dali caused a sensation when he presented his surrealist jewelry. The Spaniard's work, now in the possession of the Owen Cheatham Foundation, is world-famous. His use of precious stones and abundance of materials is staggering, but it is the incredible creations that remain in the memory. Dali says that his jewels are not intended to 'rest soullessly in steel vaults': 'Without an audience, without the presence of spectators, these jewels would not fulfil the function for which they came into being. The viewer then is the ultimate artist. His sight, heart, mind — fusing with and grasping with greater or

12

12] André Derain
Pendant and brooch
Bronze
Modelled 1945, cast 1959
Collection: Au Point des Arts Galerie, Paris
Photo: Worshipful Company of Goldsmiths

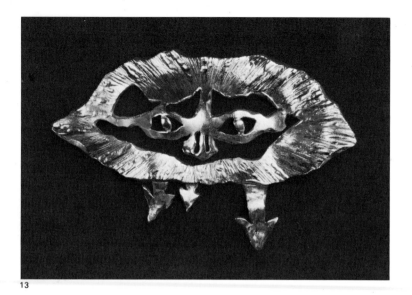

13

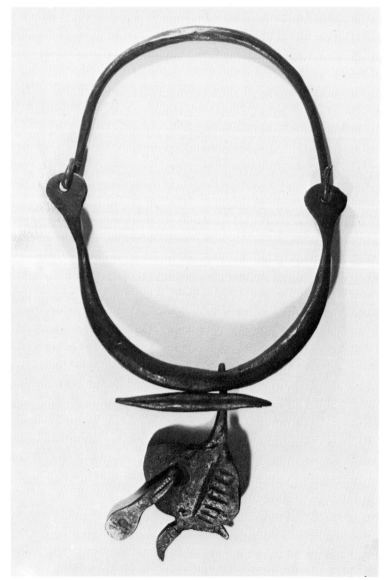

14

lesser understanding the intent of the creator — gives them life' (*Dali, A Study in his Art in Jewels*, New York Graphic, New York).

This collection of jewelry never ceases to amaze its audience. In a reshowing of some of the work at the Whitechapel Art Gallery in London, in 1971, it became apparent from the comments that they still have this power and attraction nearly twenty years after their creation. More artists were to follow Dali's example, though without the same reception. The French sculptor Jean Arp who had designed some jewelry in the thirties produced some work relating directly to his sculpture at that time in 'open form in which mass and space define and balance each other'. Afro, in collaboration with Mario Masenza, tried to produce this modern Italian artist's work in a commercial manner, but with questionable results. In some cases it is hard to trace the mark of the artist's work when his ideas have been translated into jewelry. The same cannot be said of Jean Lurçat's work. As well as being a tapestry-weaver and prolific painter, in 1959, like Max Ernst and many others, he collaborated with François Hugo in designing jewelry. Lurçat's surrealist jewelry is largely dominated by the motif of the sun. Unlike many of his contemporaries in the arts, his designs translate directly and harmoniously into jewelry. A small, but important, collection of his work is in the collection of The Worshipful Company of Goldsmiths in London.

In 1960, Lucio Fontana, the Argentinian-born sculptor, exhibited a small collection of his work, together with the Pomodoro brothers, in the exhibition of Italian artists' jewels in Dallas. (Fontana's parents had returned to Italy when he was six years old.) This artist's fundamental principle is liberty. His use of metal, stone, ceramic, precious or common materials, or the rent in a canvas, attracted him for purely experimental value, and his jewelry in the late fifties and sixties adheres to his general technique. Bracelets depict his personal style with slashes and pierced holes in the open surface of the metal, reminiscent of his earlier canvases. The American sculptor Zev, now living in Rome, first started making jewelry in Paris in the early fifties, mostly from forged iron. Since then he has continued to produce pieces in a number of different materials. He writes: 'My work in jewelry is an extension of sculpture and carries through my same attitude and regard for the magical. And somehow, in the very essence of jewelry the magic is more concentrated, making every piece a sort of talisman . . .' Zev's sculpture and jewelry is surrealistic, and often contains childlike dream images. This is particularly true of the later work he created in gold, as with one exceptional necklace that he created in 1968, which took two years to complete, and contained two pounds of gold, 157 diamonds and twenty-seven carved emeralds. It is now in a private collection in New York.

It is a common mistake to assume that an artist who is a painter or sculptor can necessarily create a work of art in jewelry. The medium is a difficult one and requires an attitude of mind, combined with

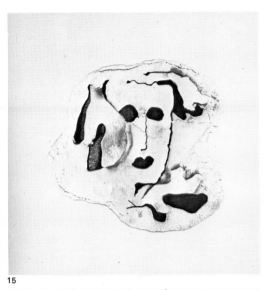

15

16

technical skills that are not to be acquired overnight. There is no guarantee that an established artist can immediately turn his hand to jewelry. As we have seen, there have been exceptions, and no one would doubt the validity of the experiments that have been carried out by artists working in other media. Nonetheless, the belief that for jewelry to be taken seriously it must be executed by an 'artist' in the accepted sense of the word, is still held by many people. Some of the finest works of art in jewelry have been created by artists who either do not work in any other medium or, if they do, are essentially concerned with jewelry, and not the reverse.

Germany, Switzerland and Austria

Jewelry has not followed all the styles and movements that have come about in art during this century, but it has absorbed most of them. In most cases they have been introduced into jewelry some time after their development in painting or sculpture. True to tradition, the jeweller has applied ideas handed down to him. However, after 1970, as travel and the exchange of ideas have become more rapid, the reaction to new styles has become much quicker.

The Bauhaus had as great an impact on jewelry, as it did on all the visual arts. Ideas conceived at that time are still valid, and in the late forties and fifties it became a great source of inspiration for many jewellers. Germany consequently gave birth to many creative jewellers who were to have considerable influence throughout the art. However, creative jewelry in the forties and fifties followed no one particular direction, and no one school or movement. It was diverse, comprehending various styles and periods in the history of art. Although the Bauhaus was the strongest single influence, particularly in Europe, it did not embrace all creative jewellers. Amongst those who reacted strongly against its teaching was Herbert Zeitner, born in Coburg in 1900.

His work in 1920 sometimes reflected the essence of the Bauhaus school, but it is for his later expressionistic style that he is best known. Principally devoting his energy to being an artist in jewelry, which is never easy and must have been almost impossible at that time, Zeitner continued through the years producing pieces of quality. The work illustrated here dates from the late forties and fifties. It has a quality akin to that of the work of the French painter, Marie Laurencin, or Marc Chagall. Perhaps the Russian's work is more comparable, for Zeitner's women, although gentle, do not always reflect the pathetic, but are often cheerful creatures. These portraits only represent a tiny part of this prolific artist's work; like many in this book, he is both sculptor and jeweller. In most cases the human form dominates and it is in his work as a jeweller that he excels. His contribution to this subject in Germany's development is considerable and shows the degree of self-expression that can be achieved within the small dimensions of a jewel.

13] Jean Lurçat
Brooch
Gold
c. 1960
Photo: Worshipful Company of Goldsmiths

14] Zev
Necklace
Iron
c. 1955
Collection: Gertrude M. Harris, San Francisco

15–16] Herbert Zeitner
Brooches
Silver
5 cm (2 in)
1948–50
Photo: Ingrid Günther

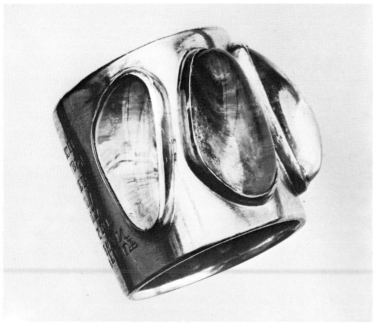

17

18

Completely different in style was Ebbe Weiss-Weingart, born in 1923.
At the start of her career, like many jewellers, she studied painting
and sculpture, and was a student of the Academy of Fine Arts in
Nuremberg. But the political situation forced her to find other means
of expression: 'You must realize that I started my studies when the
German culture was organized by the Nazis, whose dictatorial and
narrow policy drove me away from painting and sculpture. I needed
to find a way of expressing myself that was free from such
restrictions. Consequently, I became a goldsmith, but the sculptural
feeling and thinking is deeply rooted in my senses.'

Her first pieces were based on simple forms again in the Bauhaus
tradition, without 'any ornaments or showy accomplishments', and
were exhibited in the Milan Triennale in 1951. Considering the
period, these works were advanced, and may have foretold the
general mood that was developing in Scandinavia. By 1957 her work
had taken on a more formal appearance when she created a series of
bronze reliefs, plaques and jewelry that bore a strong resemblance to
the jewelry modelled two years later by Max Ernst, which were
executed in gold by François Hugo. Like Zeitner, she did not confine
her activity to jewelry, but also created a collection of studies in
bronze with strong figurative elements on a larger scale.

In the late fifties her jewelry changed quite dramatically, bearing no
resemblance to her previous work in this medium. Bracelets, rings and
brooches were entirely given over to textured surfaces. In this work
the texturing has become the brooch, as can be seen from the
illustration. It is as if the artist had taken parts from a much larger
construction, and one's eye is taken outwards into an imaginary form
of unknown dimension.

Ebbe Weiss-Weingart continues to produce stimulating work. By the
mid-sixties her pieces had taken on yet another quality, essentially
erotic. Continuing her interest in surface textures the work has
developed more form and sensuality (see fig. 131).

As one might expect from a people renowned for their proficiency in
working on a minute scale with watches and clocks, the Swiss have
numbered some of the world's most creative jewellers.

Max Fröhlich began his studies in 1925 at the School of Applied Art
in Geneva. He maintains that the traditions of the Bauhaus grew out
of a general situation in Central Europe at that time, dominant not
only in Germany but in Switzerland and Austria, and points out that
Zurich had been a centre for non-figurative art since the early thirties
(Mondrian being a classic example). He said of his early experience
as a student in Zurich: 'Imagine, in 1926–8 we were not allowed as
students of the metal department to produce life-model drawings or
modelling with any ornamental elements. *"Form ohne Ornament"*
(form without ornament) was the order of the day. The title of the

17] Ebbe Weiss-Weingart
Ring
Gold, silver, rock crystals, engraved
2·5 cm (1 in)
1947
Photo: Dr Weingart

18] Ebbe Weiss-Weingart
Brooch
Gold
8 cm (3¼ in)
1958
Photo: Dr Weingart

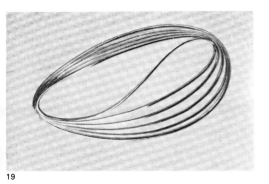

famous exhibition at that time.' Fröhlich does not take dogma too seriously, and admits that he too has produced a 'good proportion of the expressive stuff', but not forgetting to retain his sense of humour.

In 1945 he became head of the metal department at the Kunstgewerbeschule where he had studied as a student. He chose to neglect his own work so as to concentrate on helping his students, often against the trends set by accepted opinion. He feels that such restrictions are the best way to develop a personal style – 'something to kick against'. Even with this revolutionary spirit, his jewelry in the forties was primarily concerned with making simple statements. As with Calder, his love of metal is very apparent. Also as with him, stones rarely appear in his work. Pieces made in the early forties shared the American's involvement with metal in wire form. However, Fröhlich's work is far more precise and formal, and bears no connection with primitive jewelry, as we have seen happens in Calder's work.

Not all of Fröhlich's work at this time used wire. In some pieces he showed an interest in 'solid form' which create optical effects that he was to develop considerably in the late sixties, as can be seen with his suite of silver pendants at that time. This aspect of his work can be traced back to 1941, with a silver brooch made that year, and later in the following decade with more rounded forms. Perhaps one of the interesting aspects of this artist's work is the strong line of thought that follows through up to the present day. His work always manifests a keen perception of the changing world that surrounds him.

The method of fusing two metals together is a relatively recent departure in jewelry, the usual technique being solder. One of the first jewellers to exploit the possibilities of such a method was the Austrian Sepp Schmölzer, born in 1919. His work during the forties and fifties followed the styles of many of his contemporaries, but in the late fifties he brought a more fluid and romantic approach to the subject, and won acclaim with numerous exhibitions throughout Europe and outside the continent.

Holland

Although the Dutch contributed a considerable amount to the advancement of creative jewelry during the first half of this century with ideas planted deeply in 'the modern movement', in the period covered by this chapter new ideas, although visible, had yet to fully emerge. Holland's main contribution to jewelry came in the following decade when there occurred what might be termed a revolutionary force in that country.

However, pioneering work was done in Holland in the fifties, notably by Archibald Dumbar and Chris Steenbergen. At that time their work was not dissimilar. Dumbar disclaims any direct influences on his work during this period, and states that his work has now 'moved from Romanticism to the most sober, clean forms': 'Technical

19–20] Max Fröhlich
Pendant and brooch
Gold and brass
1940–2
Photo: P. Senn

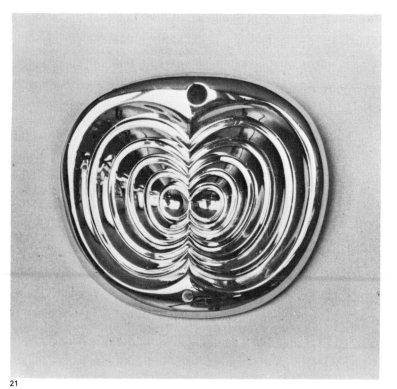

21

22

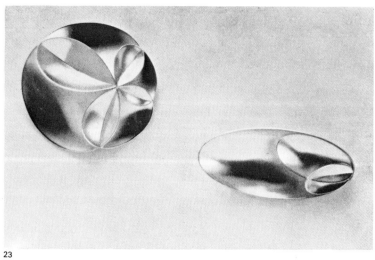

23

24

21] Max Fröhlich
Brooch
Gold
1941
Photo: Ernst Koehli

22] Sepp Schmölzer
Pendant (detail)
Gold, pearls
c. 1960–2

23] Max Fröhlich
Brooches
Silver
1952–3
Photo: P. Senn

24] Max Fröhlich
Pendant
Silver, enamelled spheres
1955
Photo: P. Senn

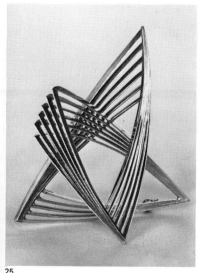

25

26

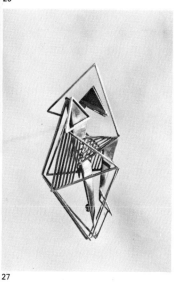

27

perfection and wearability are important to me, combined with beauty based on harmonious relationships between form and colour.' Unlike his contemporary, he then sometimes worked in a figurative style, as can be seen in the brooch made in 1955, 'New York'. But like Steenbergen, his jewelry primarily reflected sculptural ideas. Steenbergen, on the other hand, says it is possible to see Bauhaus influences on his work during the period 1940–50. His principal concern lay with sculptural ideas, and he considers Henry Moore and the Russian, Pevsner, to be influences at that time. During the sixties Steenbergen was to adopt a rather more mathematical approach.

Italy

The Italian Anton Frühauf, born in 1914, eschews distinction between the arts, like many other Italian artists. Starting his career as a portrait painter, he later became a goldsmith working in a stylized manner. Man, animals and Greek mythology were reduced to simplified forms within the jewelry he created. With little material at his disposal he sub-divided the surfaces, like that of a picture, and these figures, at times almost abstract in composition, became delicate ornaments retaining a close link with the past, but achieving results that were utterly contemporary. These fine pieces were made between 1955–6. Some of his later work bears a similarity to that of Ebbe Weiss-Weingart in Germany, who created a series of bronze reliefs at about the same time, but often Frühauf's work related directly to Greek mythology, and again, like the German, some brooches appear to be remnants of larger constructions. In the sixties his work became less figurative, when he began to use gold in a more rigorous style, reminiscent of the 'welded' sculpture of Ibram Lassaw. However, Frühauf's most creative period to date was that drawing upon Greek culture, when he simplified the graphic terms but retained the qualities of that age.

Mario Pinton, another Italian, shared Frühauf's delicate handling of materials. He studied under Marino Marini, who taught at the art school in the Villa Reale in Monza from 1929 to 1940, dates which art historians consider to be of great importance in the sculptor's development. Pinton shares his teacher's ability to transpose nature into purely plastic terms. Gentle and refined, the human body is sometimes the opposite in mood to his more usual domestic scenes of human activity. These scenes are not always obvious; in much work they are allowed to almost disappear leaving just an abstraction of his thoughts. Like his former teacher, he shares a love of the animal kingdom. But unlike Marini, whose superb horses appear rigid and immobile, Pinton's creatures move at speed, as depicted in his 'Bull' and 'Horse' brooches. These works are illustrated and discussed by Graham Hughes in *Modern Jewellery*.

25] Archibald Dumbar
Brooch, 'Perpetuum Mobile'
White gold and silver
6·5 cm (2½ in)
1956
Collection: Her Majesty, Queen Juliana
Photo: Cor van Weele

26] Archibald Dumbar
Brooch, 'New York'
Silver, copper and gold
9 cm (3½ in)
1955

27] Chris Steenbergen
Brooch
Gold, silver
7·8 cm (3 in)
1952
Photo: Cor van Weele

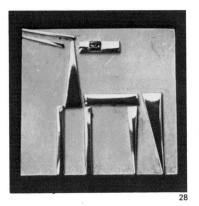

28   29

30

Essentially feminine in his approach to jewelry, this artist rejects the heavy handling of gold and treats the ancient metal with respect, making the wearer and spectator conscious of its nobility. His jewelry is rather unjustly neglected.

In 1954, Arnaldo Pomodoro and his brother, Gio, joined Giorgio Perfetti in Italy and started the 3P Group. They eventually split up, but their influence on jewelry was great, and it is now widely accepted that the Pomodoro brothers were among the first artists to exercise such influence. This can be seen even today; many students are often affected by their ideas, sometimes directly, and often when they are not even aware of these artists' existence. Like Calder, the Pomodoro brothers were primarily sculptors, but, unlike him, they are renowned for their artistry in jewelry. When they presented a collection of work at the Twenty-Eighth Venice Biennale, Marco Valsecchi wrote in the preface to the catalogue: 'These delicate ornaments quite probably contain the first ideas, the first indications, of a revival of sculpture.' Later, the brothers moved nearer to sculpture in the strict sense of the word.

Later differences appeared in their work and eventually they worked in quite different directions, but it is possible to assess their work in the fifties collectively. More often than not they exhibited their work together under the title of the 'Pomodoro brothers', and so individual characteristics were at that time difficult to define. In the fifties both introduced crystals into their work, particularly Arnaldo. Quartz and other crystallized stones were used in conjunction with precious stones, such as diamonds and rubies. Gold was the dominating metal either giving an organic structure to the work, or fused together in rectangular bars. This particular style was to become a recurring theme in much English jewelry about a decade or so later. About this time they experimented in cuttlefish casting — again, this method was to be adopted by many jewellers later.

In the late fifties Arnaldo and Gio created jewelry that was considerably more sculptural in the accepted sense of the word. This work was less organic and was a pointer to future developments in their sculpture: this particularly applied to Arnaldo. Spheres, sometimes pitted to reveal roughened textures within, contrasted with the outer surfaces of smoothly polished metal. By 1963 Arnaldo had developed this idea considerably. But the bracelet illustrated here, dated 1958, shows not only these beginnings, but the artist's interest in mechanical structures that were to become a major part of his considerable output.

In many ways Gio's work is more difficult to define, because during this period it took on great diversity. Unlike his brother, he was to retain interest in the use of colour and the formation of stones and corals and during the early sixties his work was relatively formal in its content.

28–29] Anton Frühauf
Brooches
Gold
3·2 cm (1¼ in)
1956

30] Mario Pinton
Centaur pin, pendant, brooch
Gold
c. 1959–60
Photo: Worshipful Company of Goldsmiths

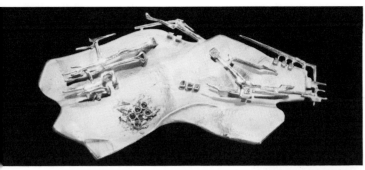

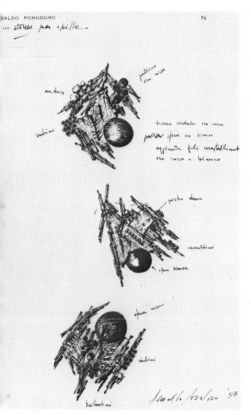

33

Unlike the other painters and sculptors who produced jewelry — excepting Calder — the Pomodoro brothers were both prolific and widely exhibited.

Scandinavia

A deep-rooted misconception exists that modern jewelry stems exclusively from Scandinavian countries. Undoubtedly the Scandinavian tradition of fine design has stuck in the public's mind. During the forties and fifties Scandinavia took the lead in exploiting the design market and, as far as jewelry is concerned, certainly made a lasting impression. However, as we have seen, notable talents exist outside of Northern countries. Moreover, jewelry in Scandinavia is very much a commercial product, with some notable exceptions.

The name of Georg Jensen is the most prominent of the Scandinavian jewellers. Born at Lyngby, near Copenhagen, Denmark, in 1866, and dying in 1935, he was a great innovator of creative silver and jewelry. At the turn of the century his work epitomized the Art Nouveau movement and at this time he worked quite alone, apart from one apprentice. By the late 1920s he had become a businessman, employing more than 250 people on his staff. Over the years the company has employed many talented and creative designers. Harald Nielsen joined Jensen in 1909, and later became the firm's artistic director. Both Jorgen and Soren Jensen, sons of the founder, have contributed to the firm's reputation. But probably the most outstanding members of the company were to be Nanna and Jørgen Ditzel, Bent Gabrielsen Pedersen, and the sculptor Henning Koppel. They produced advanced designs considered courageous during the 1950s.

In Sweden, Sigurd Persson had by the mid-fifties already achieved a reputation for his individual approach to the subject. According to Stig Johansson in an article in *Die Kunst* in 1974, 'Sigurd Persson has many purposes with his art. One is, quite simply to teach us to see, feel, discover nature again, understand the tremendous play of power developed in the moment of birth, of creation.' This concern with the power of creation can be found in his jewelry from as early as 1950. In talking about a brooch made that year, Persson says: 'In my thoughts in those days, as today, there was the wonder of growing. We have two sons, born 1945 and 1946. When I designed this brooch they had begun to reach the age in which one could observe their growth into human beings. It filled me with a lasting impression. You can see in the brooch a growing from one point, a seed. The picture of an embryonic development so as to say. Now, when I try to explain my ideas then, I can see that I am still concerned with the same problem. The apple below shows the "will to live" in nature over all.'

Persson, was primarily a designer at that time, and this brooch (see fig. 41) is very much the result of a design problem. His jewelry was

34

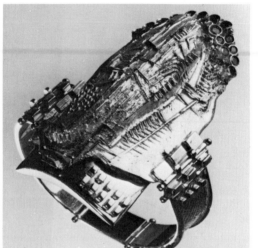

36

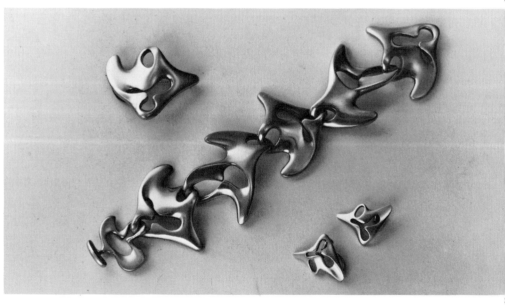

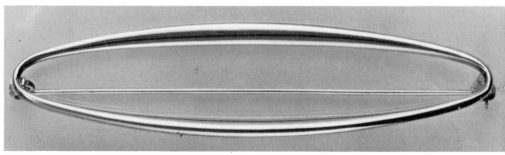

37

40

41

34] Arnaldo Pomodoro
Brooch
Red and white gold
. cm (2⅜ in)
1958
Photo: Sala Dino

35] Arnaldo Pomodoro
Bracelet
Gold
1958
Gem Montabello, Milan

36] Gio Pomodoro
Bracelet
Yellow and white gold, rubies
1958
Gem Montabello, Milan

37] Nanna Ditzel
Pendant
Silver
1957
Georg Jensen & Co
Photo: Junior, Guldsmedefagets Fallesråd

38] Henning Koppel
Bracelet, brooch and earrings
Silver
1947
Georg Jensen & Co
Photo: Guldsmedefagets Fallesråd

39] Bent Knudsen
Brooch
Silver
1956
get & Co
Photo: Eric Hansen

40] Nanna and Jørgen Ditzel
Bracelet
Silver
1955
Georg Jensen & Co
Photo: Georg Jensen & Co

41] Sigurd Persson
Brooch
Silver, red enamel
7 cm (2¾ in)
1950
Photo: Sune Sundahl

later to develop considerably into a much subtler expression, as can be seen by the ring illustrated in fig. 42 made five years later in 1955.

Persson's activities have brought him acclaim, and within the Scandinavian countries he is regarded with considerable respect and has almost become a legend. His work has been exhibited throughout the world, and its influence on others should not be underestimated. Apart from jewelry, he expresses his ideas in other directions such as sculpture and silver and various areas of industrial design. In the early sixties his jewelry was to be infinitely more refined, and his recent work still retains his interest in growth and the power that lies behind its creation. His influence as a teacher can be seen in the work of his former students wherever they are spread throughout the world.

Of all the creative jewelry artists in Scandinavian countries in the fifties, two notable talents emerged: Bertel Gardberg from Finland, and Torun Bülow Hübe, who is Swedish. Their work at this time was in advance of most jewellers, and reflected the very essence of what we now consider to be 'modern', and as such helped considerably to promote the subject, not only in Scandinavia, but throughout the world.

Bertel Gardberg was born in Helsinki in 1917, and entered the goldsmiths' school there. With numerous honours and awards in Italy and Germany, this artist, like the Swede, shares a major part of the reputation that we now associate with these northern countries. Torun Bülow Hübe, having worked in Sweden and France, now lives in Germany and has joined the ranks of Georg Jensen. Her work is now in the collection of the National Museum, Stockholm.

Persson and his contemporaries were to continue producing work that became more expressive and truly creative as the sixties unwound. Regretfully it cannot be claimed that the Scandinavian countries have kept abreast of what is currently happening, but whether there will be a re-awakening remains to be seen.

Britain and the United States

Creative jewelry in Britain during these years was practically non-existent. As in America there were numerous amateurs, but professional artists devoting their energy to the subject and working with advanced ideas were very few indeed. Peter Lyon, then primarily a sculptor, made a few pieces of interest, while Alan Davie, the English painter, produced many examples, initially in copper, brass and silver, to supplement his income. Robert Adams, the British sculptor, created some pieces in 1958, as did Anthea Alley. These were primarily intended as gifts, but two years later Miss Alley exhibited a collection of jewelry at the ICA, as did Alan Davie. Later she held an exhibition of her welded sculpture and jewelry at the Molton Gallery. Kenneth Armitage, Michael Ayrton, Lynn Chadwick and Bernard Meadows have all produced a little jewelry at one time or another, but Alan

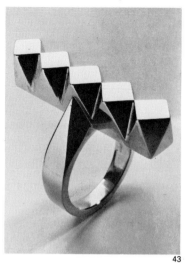

42

43

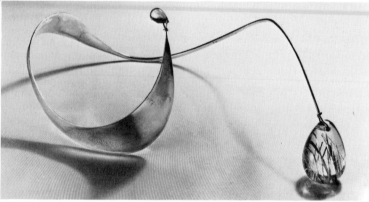

44

45

Davie was Britain's most prolific and creative contributor to jewelry during those years. Both his painting and jewelry show considerable preoccupation with the sculpture of the South Seas. Later, he was to join the jewelry department of the Central School of Art in London, where his colleagues were Richard Hamilton and Mary Kessell, bringing a fresh impetus to the traditional methods of teaching. E. R. Nele and Gerda Flöckinger (see p. 53) were students at this college during those years, and were influenced by him.

E. R. Nele and Gerda Flöckinger (see p. 53)

Another important figure who was to lecture at the Central School was the late Naum Slutzky. Born in the Ukraine in 1898, he studied fine arts and later engineering at the Vienna Polytechnic. He worked in the Wiener Werkstätte, and from there was appointed master to the department of product design in the Bauhaus in Germany from 1922 to 1933. That year he emigrated to England where he became tutor of the metalwork and engineering department at Dartington Hall in Totnes, Devon. From 1946 to 1950 he became a tutor at the Central School in London and later established and equipped the product design section of the School of Industrial Design at the Royal College of Art. He was then appointed Head of the School of Industrial Design at the College of Art and Crafts in Birmingham.

Like much work that stems from the Bauhaus, the concepts were extremely advanced. Slutzky's jewelry in the twenties and thirties was no less progressive. At that time he was creating kinetic work that bears comparison with Friedrich Becker's experiments in the late fifties and sixties and, like several contemporary jewellers, he then explored the idea of mixing gold and silver with less traditional metals. Sadly he was not a prolific artist and so few examples remain of his work, though the Museum für Kunst und Gewerbe in Hamburg has a small collection of his pieces.

Towards the end of the fifties there was a new wave of interest in organic forms. Crystals were used, often in conjunction with precious stones. John Donald, Andrew Grima and later David Thomas, Ernest Blyth and Frances Beck were the chief exponents of such work in this country. Since then they have developed their own personal ideas, but this lies largely outside the scope of this book. The Irish jeweller Breon O'Casey, son of the author and playwright, first studied art at the Anglo-French Art Centre, and later in 1956 was assistant to Dame Barbara Hepworth in Cornwall. His jewelry during the late fifties was primarily related to Celtic work. Since 1963 he and Brian Illsley have joined forces in forming a small company in St Ives that continues to produce jewelry of quality relating to this and other cultures.

Creative jewellers in America during this period heavily outnumbered their contemporaries in England. At the Second National Exhibition of Contemporary Jewelry held at the Walker Art Center in Minneapolis in 1948 over thirty contributors exhibited their work, including Ward Bennett, Harry Bertoia, Margaret de Patta, Claire von Falkenstein,

42] Sigurd Persson
Ring
White gold, diamond
3·5 cm (1½ in)
1955
Photo: Sune Sundahl

43 Sigurd Persson
Ring
Silver and white gold
3 cm (1¼ in)
1960
Photo: Sune Sundahl

44] Torun Bülow Hübe
Neckpiece
Silver, rutilated rock crystals
1959
Photo: Worshipful Company of
Goldsmiths

45] John Donald
Brooch
Gold and pyrite
6·5 cm (2½ in)
1959

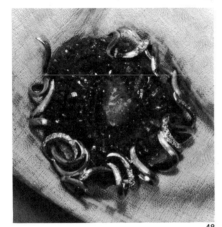

46] Alan Davie
Rattle
Silver
13 cm (5¼ in)
. 1949
Collection: Mr and Mrs W. G. Howell
Photo: A. & C. Cooper

47] Gerda Flöckinger
Pendant (detail)
Silver, enamel
. 1959
Photo: Worshipful Company of Goldsmiths

48] Andrew Grima
Brooch
Crystalized agate, gold, diamonds
. 1961–2
The Duke of Edinburgh's Prize for Elegant
    Design, 1966
Photo: Worshipful Company of Goldsmiths

Fred Farr, Adda Husted-Anderson, Sam Kramer, Paul Lobel, Philip Morton and Bob Winston.

In the June issue of *Craft Horizons* in 1966 John Prip and Ronald Pearson looked back over the forties and fifties in American jewelry. Their discussion made clear some of the differences between European and American jewelry:

John Prip: When I first came here in 1948 from Denmark, I was surprised and impressed by much of the work that was being done because I had never heard about it. When I first saw the work of Margaret de Patta and Sam Kramer — 'Mushroom Sam' — and Paul Lobel, and especially when I first saw the work of Bob Winston, it impressed me very much. Phil Morton was actively engaged in making jewelry then, and it was very interesting. It was different — a fresh approach . . .

Ronald Pearson: I think it is good to bring in the fact that what has happened here in the past twenty-five years has been without the benefit of any kind of tradition. People did not have a chance to train, as you did, as an apprentice. They had to learn whatever way they could.

John Prip: Most of the people who were interested here were trained as sculptors, or painters, or had designed or done things in other areas. They were ingenious, imaginative people who, I guess, simply decided they wanted to make jewelry. The fact that they really didn't know how was not enough to stop them. They learned as they went along and did extremely well, many of them. I think the US craftsmen who were working then really influenced what was being done over there — in Denmark, Sweden, Germany, and Holland.

Ronald Pearson: That's really a vital point, because usually the attitude is the complete reverse — that we're entirely the product of European influences. Well, what is the difference? Let's take someone like Margaret de Patta or Lobel or Winston or Kramer. How did they differ in what they started out to do from what an individual would have done in Denmark?

John Prip: Well, they simply did not have the years of trade-like conditioning. They approached it in a very free way. They were pursuing other goals, you might say. They were not tied down. Not that this will lead to grand, great things in all instances. Very often having some traditional background gives added strength. It can work either way. I remember the Walker Art Center had a number of jewelry shows — the first one that came to my attention was somewhere around 1949. They showed the work of twenty-five, maybe fifty American jewellers. I don't know how many were doing it full time, professionally, but there was a lot of work that was really good.

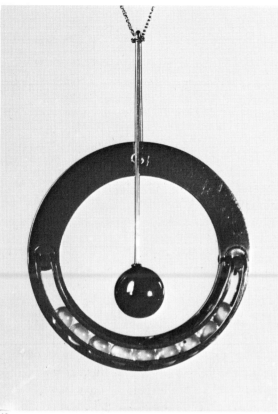

49

50

49] Naum Slutsky
Pendant
Gold, glass, chrome, silver, etc.
Mobile
c. 1929–32
Collection: Museum für Kunst und Gewerbe, Hamburg

50] Naum Slutsky
Bracelet
Steel
c. 1929–32
Collection: Museum für Kunst und Gewerbe, Hamburg

Ronald Pearson: What about the conditions in those early years – the early part of this twenty-five year period. What was the available schooling? There were only perhaps one, two, three schools that actually taught craftsmen in a fairly serious manner. What were the markets like – the conditions under which a person worked and developed – and how do they differ from today?

John Prip: As far as schools are concerned, the School for American Craftsmen was at that time rather new. There were places like Cranbrook and the California School of Arts and Crafts. The Philadelphia Museum School was doing something, and the Boston Museum School. But as far as what actually came out of these places – forget it! They might as well not have existed. It seemed, up to a certain point anyway, that the jewellers were not coming out of schools. They were people who decided they wanted to do this. You yourself were very much this way, although you did go to school for a while. You set yourself a goal – a way of life – and you were willing to go after it.

Ronald Pearson: One of the things that was noticeable when I went to the School for American Craftsmen in 1947 was that servicemen were returning, and some of them had been dis-illusioned with a mass type of society. They wanted to lead a more meaningful life, and the craft field offered some potential of this. Of course, at that time, it was strictly shop with very little else. You came, and you learned how to do it and to get some kind of a stimulation – it was really a first stepping stone. It wasn't intended to do everything for you. This was up to the individual . . .

Both these men were pioneers. America had no tradition of jewelry, and consequently was more open to new ideas without the inhibiting traditions that existed in Europe at that time. But as indicated, the activity was largely the domain of the gifted amateur and, although spirited, lacked the professional qualities that were to be found in Europe.

One of the most significant talents in America during this period was Margaret de Patta. Born in Washington, she started producing jewelry as early as 1935 and continued to do so until her death in 1964. She initially trained as a painter and sculptor at the San Diego Academy of Fine Arts and the California School of Fine Arts in San Francisco. She learnt the technique of jewelry from Hairinian, an Armenian metalsmith in San Francisco, but her philosophy of art was closely bound to the Bauhaus tradition. For a while she worked with Moholy-Nagy at the Institute of Chicago. Some years ago she described the possibilities she saw for jewellers:

We craftsmen engaged in producing objects for use, find ourselves historically bound to search out fundamental forms rather than to decorate form. A mere simplification of traditional form is not

1

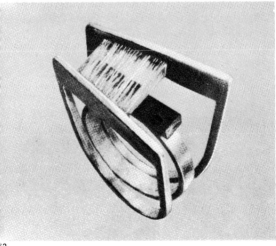

2

sufficient. New form emerges when a functional analysis is coupled with new materials, new techniques, or new human concepts. We live in a world of exciting new structural forms. We should be aware of the implications of such things as the Maillart bridges, the geodesic dome and the pre-stressed contours that are supplanting the right angle aesthetic in architecture. We have discoveries just as revolutionary to make in our own field.

Perhaps the most important contribution made to jewelry by Margaret de Patta was her use of light through transparent stones, and she was the originator of certain stone cuts that widened the visual scope and transparency of gems. Her work was entirely original and owed little to other artists' work.

Another important influence in American jewelry is the work of John Paul Miller. He was born in Huntington in Pennsylvania in 1918. His work in the fifties must have been a revelation to those who saw it. Like his contemporaries in Europe, he was concerned with the making of simple statements. In the cleanness of its forms his work is comparable to that of Steenbergen and Dunbar in Holland, but during the years that followed the forms grew far more complex. He was to become one of America's foremost goldsmiths and has achieved a reputation for the use of granulation — at its height of perfection in the Etruscan culture. Few jewellers have been able to master this difficult method of embellishing the surface of gold with tiny spheres and Miller is now considered the principal exponent of this method today. Many of his pieces depict marine life.

Alexander Calder had considerable influence on several jewellers in America, including Ward Bennett and Harry Bertoia. Both of them used Calder's methods of hammered silver, though, at their best, they, like Fred Farr, brought their own individuality to jewelry. Another influence during this period was Claire von Falkenstein. She is a sculptor, painter, and graphic artist, who first started making jewelry in 1945 in San Francisco, and who then left the USA for Paris where she has concentrated on jewelry as a means of experimentation for sculpture. She had exhibited her work more than most jewellers at that time — in Berlin in 1952, the ICA in London the following year, and later in Milan, Rome and the New York Museum of Modern Art.

By the time the Fourth National Exhibition was mounted in 1959 at the Walker Art Center, the standard of work in America had advanced considerably. The illustrated *Design Quarterly* published that year by the Center shows how far the creative jeweller in America had developed. Irena Brynner was by this time creating some interesting pieces that reflected the influence of Margaret de Patta. Miss de Patta headed the Metal Arts Guild in San Francisco in 1950, one of whose members was Miss Brynner. Others contributing to the Walker Art Center show in 1959 included Alma Eikerman, Mary Kretsinger, Elsa Freund and Ruth and Svetozar Radakovich, together

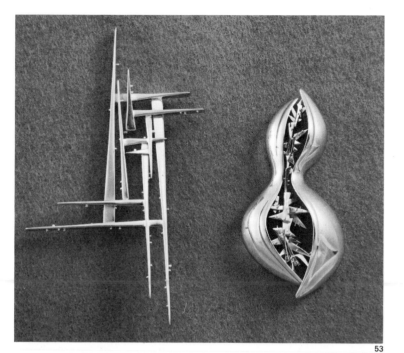

53

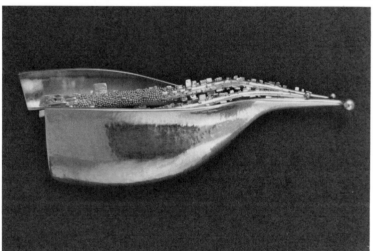

54

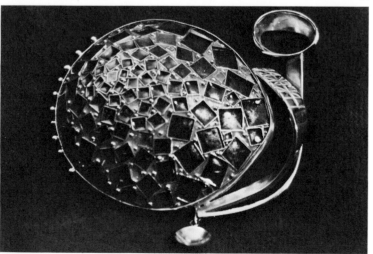

55

with some advanced work by Ray Hein, Michael Jerry, Dane Purdo, and Alice Zimmerman.

Mary Kretsinger is renowned for her experimental approach to enamel; her work at this exhibition gave some indication as to how she was to develop her personal style, while the work of Ruth and Svetozar Radakovich could not be more opposed to the enamellist's being primarily concerned with sculptural forms in jewelry which, considering the date, were of an advanced nature.

Sam Kramer's work is surrealistic, as is shown in the pendant in gold and silver, made in 1958, illustrated in fig. 57. Using traditional materials he incorporated in this piece a yellow and black taxi-dermist's eye set in an ivory mount, predicting the obsessive images of the found object that were later to dominate much American work. It gives the first indication of how American jewelry was to develop a style all its own.

Friedrich Becker and Hermann Jünger

Two modern German jewellers, Friedrich Becker and Hermann Jünger, exemplify well the changes in jewelry in the late fifties. Both figures of international reputation and influence, they started in the mid-fifties and had developed their own distinctive styles by the end of the decade.

Becker first studied aeronautical engineering, but after the war followed an apprenticeship as goldsmith and silversmith under Professor Karl Schollmayer. In 1952 he opened his studio in Düsseldorf, where he still lives and works.

In the introduction to the catalogue of Becker's exhibition at the Goldsmiths' Hall in 1966, Hans George Lenzen, director of the Werkunstschule in Düsseldorf, described the achievement of Becker's jewelry:

> Friedrich Becker . . . approaches the problem for the most part via a series of technological experiments, whose closest parallel is with the processes of modern architecture. They spring from the consideration of fundamental problems and could serve just as well as the basis of a preparatory course for architects. Becker's objective is the functionally and technically satisfactory combination of simple elements. By this means he attempts to achieve the greatest variety with the greatest economy of form.

This 'economy of form' can be seen in his work from the first pieces he created. Much of his early work shows clear evidence of the influence of the Bauhaus, and is comparable with the work of Fritz Schwerdt, who created austere pieces in the thirties. But Becker is continually experimenting. His first mobile pieces were created in 1963 with brooches, but many of the rings made in 1957 were set

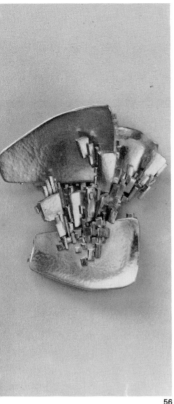

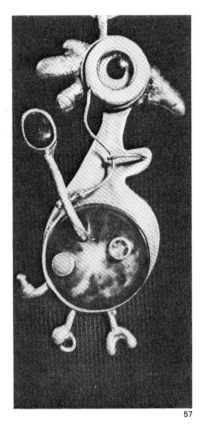

3] John Paul Miller
Brooches
Gold
952

4] John Paul Miller
Brooch, 'Seed'
Gold
·5 cm (2½ in)
956

5] Mary Kretsinger
Brooch, 'Pomegranate'
Gold, cloissonné enamel
·5 cm (2¼ in)
959

6] John Paul Miller
Pendant-brooch
Gold
·2 cm (2½ in)
956

7] Sam Kramer
Pendant
Gold, silver, ivory, garnet, green tourmaline, red
coral and taxidermist's eye
·. 1958
Photo: *Design Quarterly* 59

with stones that in fact could be removed from the shank. His first purely kinetic work was in the year 1966. Prior to that his pieces were 'variable', and needed the participation of the wearer who could rearrange their design at will. Many of Becker's pieces are difficult to photograph, as they rely on movement. The brooch illustrated, when worn moves with such ease and at a speed that is surprising when one considers its size. Unlike many creative jewellers Becker uses precious stones, but unlike traditional jewellers Becker makes them work for him. For example, one of his brooches has thirty-two diamonds which move at speed when worn — needless to say much depends on the energy of the wearer! But they can follow one after the other with such rapidity that they become one large circular ray of light. In 1968 Becker developed this idea with a more complex piece that had ninety-six diamonds on the outer circle and forty-eight sapphires on the inner mobile circle. The plate on the original brooch has been removed so one can see the interplay of the bars that extend from the centre to the outer rim that holds the stones. It is marvellous to watch in motion (see fig. 243).

Becker is still experimenting and producing kinetic jewelry. His interest in mobility is often extended into other media, such as film and objects. But he remains primarily an artist in jewelry. His work has never been better. Like a true artist he still develops and learns.

Hermann Jünger was born in Hanau in 1928. From 1947 to 1949 he was a student at the Academy there and by 1957 was making jewelry of importance that owed little to past accomplishments. His work has been unique right from the start. During the later half of the fifties he made pieces that were delicate and refined, reminiscent of Klee's drawings and the German painter Julius Bissier, whose influence Jünger recognizes in his letters. These delicate pieces were made with gently hammered units of gold suspended by thin gold wire.
Jünger wrote of them: 'My aim is to make jewelry in which balance plays an important role. This balance is formed from the shape, line colour and surface of every piece. These pieces put together form the unit which has its order and balance in itself. This means that every part is important and necessary to the order of the entire piece. You cannot take away anything without destroying this balance.'

This balance that Jünger talks of is to be found in much of his early work, and indeed is still there in his recent work to some degree. In some cases he places tiny figurative motifs into these early pieces, a bird or flower, or even a door, sometimes a numeral, adding to the humorous undertone to be found in many of his pieces. They appear to be there as some kind of private joke that he shares with the owner, not obvious, but subtle and personal. He is very much an artist given to understatement. Each part of his work is underplayed and never overloaded with art for the sake of the word.

58   59

As we will discover, Hermann Jünger was to be a great influence in creative jewelry in the sixties. The way in which he handles metal an colour can be seen in much of contemporary work today. In the late sixties he was to create a small but important collection of enamel brooches, two of which are now in the collection of the Schmuck-museum, Pforzheim. They show quite clearly the very refined qualities attributed to this artist's work, and the manner in which he uses colour points the way for the younger artists who were to follow in the seventies. Elements of sculpture and painting have been brought into these pieces, and there are points of comparison with the 'painted sculpture' that Picasso created at the same time (fig. 136).

With the exception of Calder, Dali, Davie, Pomodoro, Persson, de Patta, Kramer and possibly Fontana, much of the work discussed in this chapter went largely unnoticed at the time it was created. Even the experiments carried out by Derain, Picasso, Ernst, and others were restricted to a private world during those years preventing them from being known to the public at large.

With few exceptions, the jewellers were not exposed then to a receptive audience. This was particularly true as far as post-war Europe was concerned. Official support during the forties and fifties was strictly limited to the traditional Arts, i.e. drama, music, ballet, painting and sculpture. For example, in England the Arts Council restricted their activities to these media, consequently the jeweller and any artists working in other media were neglected. The Festival of Britain in 1951 underlined this lack of support, for as far as jewelry was concerned it was devoid of creative work. We will see that as the following decade came to a close this was to be partially rectified.

In America this was not the case, for in the forties and fifties large national exhibitions were given devoted to the subject. Consequently the public became more aware of such work and the artists them-selves became known to each other, whereas in Europe most artists worked in isolation and were not aware of the other's activities.

Perhaps because Calder and his contemporaries were artists in the accepted sense they found recognition easier to come by. The art critic or gallery director would look closely at jewelry created by painters and sculptors, for being 'artists' they would naturally be work of art, and worthy of attention. So who then was to assess the work of the creative jeweller? In most cases they had to wait until the following decade before recognition was granted them.

58] Friedrich Becker
Ring
Gold, rutilated quartz
1957
Collection: Goldsmiths' Hall, London

59] Friedrich Becker
Ring
Gold, rose quartz and heamatite
Removable stones
1962
Collection: Goldsmiths' Hall, London

60–63] Friedrich Becker
Brooch
Variable; in different combinations
White gold, diamonds
1963

60

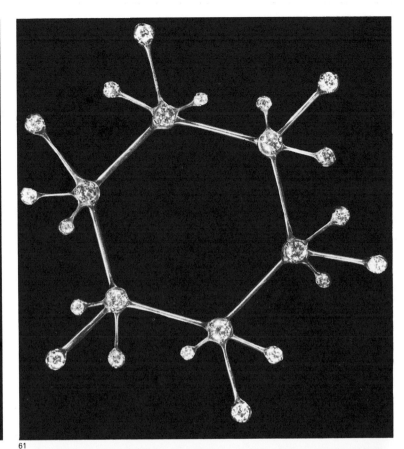

61

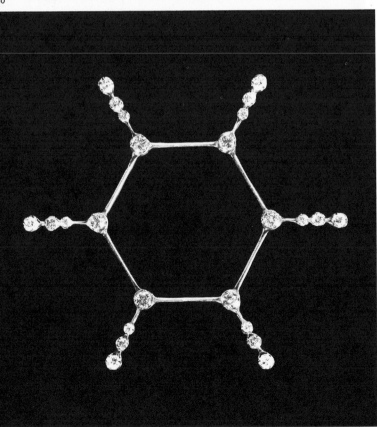

62

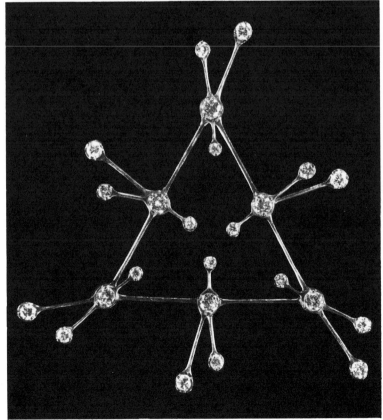

63

41

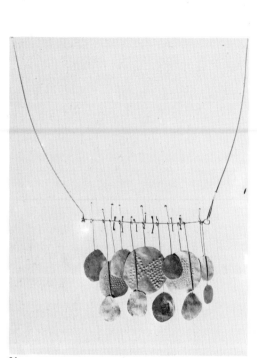

64

65

64] Hermann Jünger
Necklace
Gold
1958

65] Hermann Jünger
Pendant
Gold, cornelians, enamel
1957

3

Fresh Impetus 1960-70

During the fifties and sixties modern art in general attracted substantial publicity. With this and significantly greater official support more and more people were brought into contact with art than had been previously. Modern art, essentially rebellious in spirit, attracted young people, who may or may not have understood the experiments being made, but they could identify with the views expressed by some artists at that time.

Britain in particular saw the growth of many more art schools, which began to take a closer interest in fields of art other than the accepted forms and found talents that were to bring to jewelry a new impetus it had not known before. These schools provided an alternative to the universities, and contributed to a new cultural impetus, whereas in America this is less evident, as art schools and universities are often linked. In his absorbing book *Movements in Art Since 1945*, Edward Lucie Smith, the English critic writes:

> While it is difficult to prove that the various experiments in art education which have been made in Britain over the past twenty years have produced better artists, the impact upon popular culture has been undeniable. To take one specialised but important example, the Beatles had close connections with Liverpool College of Art, and practically every major pop group in Britain since the rise of the Beatles has had some link with an art school. Many of the musicians began to play when they were art students. Popular music took over the modern art life-style; and where the musicians led, the fans followed.

This popular culture manifested itself early in the work of British artists such as Richard Hamilton and Eduardo Paolozzi, whose exhibition 'This is Tomorrow' at the Whitechapel Art Gallery in 1956, drew spectators into an environment full of wit, gimmickry and glamour — qualities that were to be worshipped by the pop artists in the following decade. But while Pop Art itself did not percolate into the mind of the jeweller in the early sixties, a fresh impetus inspired jewelry as much as other arts.

The First International Exhibition of Modern Jewelry

A major event that took place in London in 1961 gives a picture of jewelry at the start of the decade. That year the Worshipful Company of Goldsmiths launched the first International Exhibition of Modern Jewelry at the Goldsmiths' Hall. This eventful exhibition spanned the period from 1890 to 1961, taking in the various styles and periods of jewelry over those seventy years. It was a mammoth undertaking, wit almost a thousand pieces on display, and, although not entirely devoted to creative work, was undoubtedly a landmark in the development of the subject both in England and elsewhere.

In the contemporary section there was a predominance of work by 'fine artists'. Some of them had in fact made their first pieces of

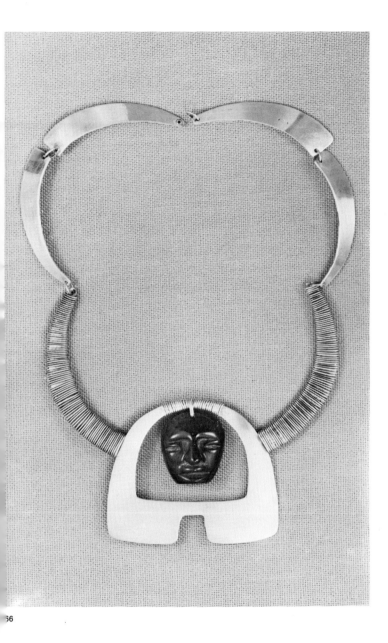

6] Nilda Nunez del Prado
Necklace, 'Totem'
Silver and carved stone
1961
Photo: Worshipful Company of Goldsmiths

jewelry only a year prior to the event, presumably for this exhibition. Quite possibly this was a conscious effort to raise jewelry on to a higher plane, to have the work of jewellers considered more seriously because they shared their exhibition with artists working in accepted art forms, who now, if only fleetingly, paid homage to their poor relations in jewelry.

This exhibition showed that there was no particular trend or movement in jewelry at this time. It also proved that there was a considerable interest in creative jewelry in many parts of the world, with artists exhibiting from all the major West European countries and the United States and Australia. The exhibition included work by those jewellers already well established, such as Sigurd Persson, Archibald Dumbar, John Paul Miller, Gio and Arnaldo Pomodoro, Mario Pinton, Friedrich Becker, Ebbe Weiss-Weingart and Mary Kretsinger, as well as others starting their professional careers, like Stanley Lechtzin, Gerda Flöckinger, Bruno Martinazzi, Anita Coudenhove-Kallergis and Nilda Nunez del Prado.

Gerda Flöckinger's collection at this exhibition could be thought of as rather typical of that period, inasmuch as she created enamelled pieces in simple forms with abstract compositions in relief. Later she developed her work considerably when she began to fuse metals, bringing a more fluid and poetic approach.

Bruno Martinazzi is both sculptor and jeweller. His work at the Halls exhibition in 1961 gave no indication of the developments that were to come later; indeed, his work at that time was rather conventional. Within a few short years, however, he was to produce jewelry of major importance.

Anita Coudenhove-Kallergis, from Greece, first started creating jewelry when she was in Paris in 1932. Since then she has lived in Vienna, Sydney and in 1938 emigrated to Greece. She was born in Vienna in 1898. Her work at this exhibition explored some ideas that were to be developed ten years or so later, particularly in England At the time she used unconventional materials — bronze, bone, glass, iron, pebbles, etc. — very often augmented into one piece.

Nilda Nunez del Prado's work was just as radical. Born in La Paz in 1918 into a family of artists, her career has been a varied one. Studying painting, sculpture and jewelry in Bolivia, she travelled extensively throughout America and Peru, where she studied folk art, and, later, danced with Martha Graham in New York. Primarily thought of as a sculptor, she first produced jewelry in 1946, with exhibitions in New York, Pennsylvania and Mexico. A close study of her work reveals present-day developments that apply particularly to some English artists involved in carving and mystical manifestations.

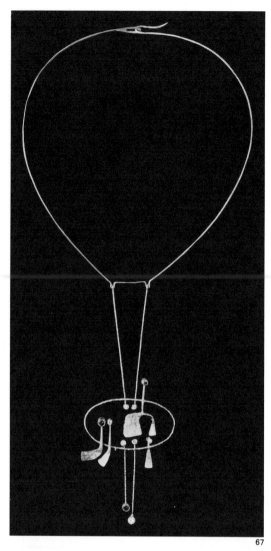

67]. Reinhold Reiling
Pendant
Gold, diamonds, sapphires
1962

68] Reinhold Reiling
Bracelet
Gold, diamonds, sapphires
1969

Germany: The Pforzheim College

A career devoted to creative jewelry is never easy, and the financial reward is limited. As with other artists, the jeweller is often employed as teacher or lecturer in art school and colleges, and many of the jewellers appearing in this book spend much of their time teaching. This is not an ideal situation as the artist needs time to create work of any real significance. Often the time and energy spent in passing on knowledge to students leaves them with only small reserves for their own creativity. However, as all teachers know, the satisfaction of stimulating interest and developing talent can be extremely rewarding and close contact with young people can often have a beneficial effect on the teacher, making him aware of new ideas that are taking place in younger minds.

One college in particular has shown the benefits of interplay between teachers and students, the college in Pforzheim. This has probably produced more creative jewellers than any equivalent anywhere else in the world. The enthusiasm and energy in the late fifties of Karl Schollmayer in large part created a fine art approach to jewelry. His teaching methods were perhaps unorthodox, but his personality was such that he was able to 'get inside' his students and draw out their individuality as creative artists. His lectures on Art History were based on his personal concept but, more important, his genius lay in being able to translate this complex subject into terms that would draw the most enthusiastic response from his students. Professor Schollmayer's book, *Neuer Schmuck*, will undoubtedly be a major contribution to the subject.

Only one real criticism can be made of the college. In recent years it has become possible to recognize in a jeweller's work the Pforzheim 'school of thought'. If there is to be a truly individual creative approach this mass thought within a college can ultimately be stultifying.

Reinhold Reiling is a jeweller of not only national but international importance. He started his career as an engraver, but soon found that his interest in the object he was working on became more important to him than his contribution to it as a craftsman. His interests lay and still do in sculptural ideals. Being born in Pforzheim, the heart of the jewelry industry in Germany, he was to become one of this country's most prolific jewellers. His work in the late fifties and early sixties was two-sided, some of his work showing an almost conservative approach, and the rest being more radically creative. Perhaps his strongest period has been from 1966 onwards, when the work became less 'precious' and figurative elements began to appear. This he has taken to extreme limits with photo-etching. Often family photographs are etched into the silver and gold. In other pieces the gold is scored with tiny scratches, showing his original interest as an engraver. The engraving is free and full of movement, but at the same time subject to Reiling's incredible control.

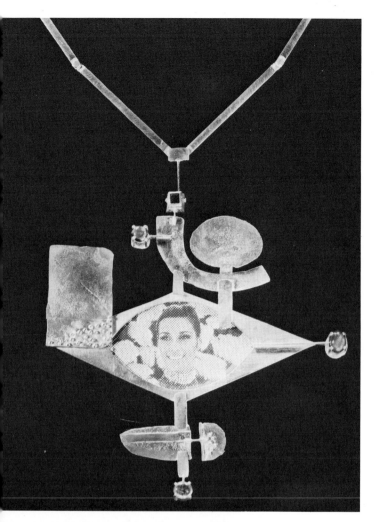

Klaus Ullrich is a brilliant craftsman in metal. His work in the first part of this decade followed the more traditional style prevailing in Germany at that time, but later he was to adopt a more challenging manner.

Both these men have passed on their knowledge to innumerable students. As the school in Pforzheim is attended by students from all over the world, their influence has spread far and wide.

Gold

The Belgian artist Emile Souply is primarily a sculptor but, unlike many of his fellow artists, his jewelry is directly opposed to his sculptural ideals.

Souply's jewelry in the early sixties reflected the teachings of the Bauhaus and earlier. Forms are vigorous, and nothing is elaborated or decorated, in a more severe reaction against traditional jewelry than the work of Persson, or his contemporaries in Scandinavia. There was no comparable work in Belgium at this time, and that most akin to Souply's is to be found in developments that were to take place later, particularly in Holland.

Later Souply returned to making jewelry, but in a more formal manner, the formality being not only in his choice of materials but in the principles lying behind the work. For the first time he used gold, and often baroque pearls. Jewelry exhibited in 1970 but dated five years earlier owed nothing to contemporary work, either in sculpture or jewelry and had a baroque appearance. Souply explained the change: 'I like to change my menus both gastronomic and intellectual. It appears to be a kind of ''cycle'' rhythm in my work which makes me do alternatively rigorous things, and then ''baroque'' ones.'

In making these pieces Souply was using the metal for the first time: 'I always try to respect the real nature of the material I use; its own personality inspiring its own language.' The truth to material is of course a familiar principle lying behind much artistic work. However, despite Souply's undoubted talent, his gold pieces at this time are uninteresting, many of the ideas having already been seen in work by Ebbe Weiss-Weingart nearly ten years prior to this. Since 1970 he has again changed his 'menu'; this time from 'à la carte'. His recent work, for example the 'Mercedes', is alive and full of humour (fig. 170).

Emile Souply's tentative approach to gold is typical of many artists. Gold can be worked like no other metal, with endless possibilities for design, but is often treated with a respect attended by conservatism. Dr J. Bronowski provides a clue to the jeweller's timidity in dealing with gold when he describes its basic appeal to men. In *The Ascent of Man* he talks of how gold became 'the universal prize in all countries, in all cultures, in all ages . . .' He explains in some detail

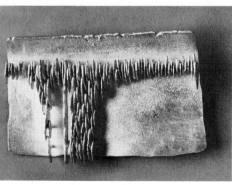

] Reinhold Reiling
ndant
old, photo-etching, tourmaline, sapphire, diamond
67

] Klaus Ullrich
ooch
old, diamond
5 cm (2¼ in)
63

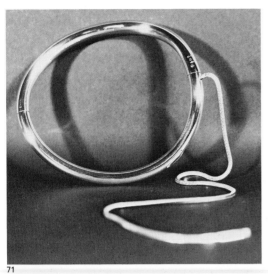

gold's unique qualities and the governing force behind man's worship of the material:

The ability of gold to resist what was called decay (what we would call chemical attack) was singular, and therefore both valuable and diagnostic. It also carried a powerful symbolism, which is explicit even in the earliest formulae. The first written reference we have to alchemy is just over two thousand years old, and comes from China. It tells how to make gold and to use it to prolong life. That is an extraordinary conjunction to us. To us gold is precious because it is scarce; but to the alchemists, all over the world, gold was precious because it was incorruptible. No acid or alkali known to those times would attack it. That indeed is how the emperor's goldsmiths assayed, or, as they would have said, parted it, by acid treatment that was less laborious than cupbellation.

When life was thought to be (and for most people was) solitary, poor, nasty, brutish, and short, to the alchemists gold represented the one eternal spark in the human body. Their search to make gold and to find the elixir of life are one and the same endeavour. Gold is the symbol of immortality — but I ought not to say symbol, because in the thought of the alchemists gold was the expression, the embodiment of incorruptibility, in the physical and in the living world together.

So when the alchemists tried to transmute base metals into gold, the transformation that they sought in the fire was from the corruptible to the incorruptible; they were trying to extract the quality of permanence from the everyday. And this was the same as the search for eternal youth: every medicine to fight old age contained gold, metallic gold, as an essential ingredient, and the alchemists urged their patrons to drink from gold cups to prolong life.

Gold is still treated with profoundest respect, so it is not surprising to find that experiments in jewelry are often conducted in other metals or synthetic materials that do not command such authority, nor cost as much. Consequently, jewelry created in gold tends to be of a conventional nature, though not always.

Some artists, however, reject the use of gold for political reasons as most of it is mined in South Africa, or prefer the use of other materials in their work, finding the restrictions too great an influence on what they want to say.

71] Emile Souply
Neckpiece
Silver
1962
Private collection
Photo: Yves Auquier

72] Emile Souply
Bracelet
Silver
1961
Private collection
Photo: Yves Auquier

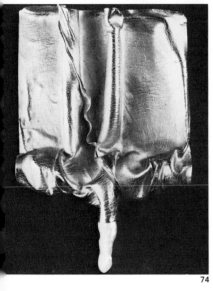

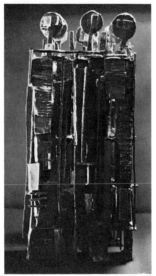

73

74

75

Italy

One Italian artist, whose work has already been mentioned, now challenges both of these two theories. Bruno Martinazzi is both sculptor and jeweller. When making jewelry he mainly uses gold. Unlike Souply, Martinazzi's jewelry and sculpture relate closely to one another. He was born in Turin in 1923, later entered the chemical industry, at the same time attending the Liberal Academy of Art in Turin. In 1951 he abandoned chemistry and began an apprenticeship in the workshop of Mussa, and in 1953 he entered the State School of Art in Florence.

From the beginning his work was chiefly concerned with the human form. One sculpture depicts a close group of war-like figures lined up like soldiers in a tight and immobile cube. His jewelry was much more open and fluid, but retained strong human elements in a rather romantic fashion. These early pieces manifest an interest in the rounded shapes of the female body.

By the late fifties and early sixties his jewelry was to change dramatically. The human form almost disappeared, the work taking on an almost traditional aspect. He appears to have become obsessed with texture, and precious stones appeared in many pieces that have little to do with his past achievements. However, by 1965 he had renewed his interest in the human figure, this time less elaborate, and again returned to a tight grouping of figures.

In the late sixties Martinazzi was to enter a most critical period of his development to date. He created a series of sculptures in aluminium and bronze that again return to the group element. These appear as if they are inflated, like the 'Giant Icebag' by Claes Oldenburg in 1971. These powerful creations are almost menacing in their impact.
At about the same time, his jewelry was again to use the body, but this time by isolating parts of the human anatomy. Here he challenges our awareness of ourselves, demanding that we look again and reappraise the body's beauty when translated into jewelry terms. Often these sensual pieces are charged with erotic undertones.
His sculpture and jewelry now complement each other, as can be seen by his stone carvings. These monumental pieces directly relate to his jewelry, without the jewelry becoming just reduced sculpture. Each piece has its own 'being' and life of its own fully holding our attention and stimulating our imagination in their isolation. A clenched fist, a foot, or one single finger has infinitely more power, and is far more stimulating than his more complex works of the early sixties.
It is not merely the isolation of one part of the body that is interesting, but the meaning they have when taken out of context. For example, with his sculpture, the stone carvings are often produced on a large scale, giving the hand or single finger monumental importance and, placed outside in the open countryside, they can relate to the spectator in a manner that makes him aware of the space that the sculpture occupies, and of his own body or parts of it in relation to

76

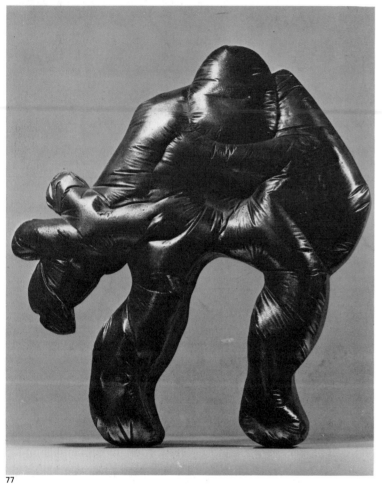

77

this situation. Likewise in his jewelry, the wearing of a finger, or a bottom, as a brooch draws attention to the physical presence of the object. The very placing of jewelry depicting parts of the anatomy or the human body is a participatory factor inherent in the piece.

As with Calder and the Pomodoro brothers, Martinazzi is one of the very few sculptor-jewellers whose work has contributed seriously to both media, and without doubt he is one of the most important figurative artists in jewelry today. In recent years, his jewelry has turned to other forms other than the human body, as can be seen in the 'apple' brooch illustrated in fig. 81.

Italian jewelry during the 1960s had reached standards that could be compared with any country in the world, and some consider it was ahead of most other countries. The Pomodoro brothers were at the height of their inventiveness. Arnaldo had already created pieces that were less obsessed with texture and, by the mid-sixties his interest in engineering construction led to a more mathematical approach to the subject.

The early sixties saw his work become less organic, and more geometric elements appeared. By 1964 the work was to be concerned with mobility. Like the wheels on a train, his jewelry moved within given limits. In some cases the pieces had little contact with his past achievements, and were freer to explore undiscovered possibilities. In one pendant made in 1965 Pomodoro groups a number of circular units that were free to revolve within the frame of the piece. Here there are no decorative elements or textures whatsoever, and the work is almost severe in its impact. The following year he made one of his most important jewels — a single column hanging from a simple chain, created in white and yellow gold. It combines his early interest in texture with the simplicity of form of unmarked tubes. Within the pendant, and protruding from it, hangs a number of simple mobile rods. This important work is now in the collection of the Schmuckmuseum in Pforzheim.

His brother, Gio, was creating work then in quite a different manner, being concerned with the relationship between rectangular forms. These forms were held within circular frames of the jewelry, as in the pendants made by him at that time. In fact to see his most challenging work we have to look to recent years, when he has produced pieces that reflected more clearly his concern with colour, structural and sometimes architectural shapes. A ring produced by him at this time explored that constructional aspect. But perhaps his strongest work during those years was a pendant 'Open Foetus' that showed his concern with the grouping of spheres giving a clue to his interest in mechanical components. This pendant again reflects the artist's interest in colour and bulbous forms.

76] Bruno Martinazzi
Brooch
Gold
1954
Photo: Rambazzi

77] Bruno Martinazzi
Sculpture, 'Adatoide'
Aluminium
67 cm high (26½ in)
1969
Collection: the artist

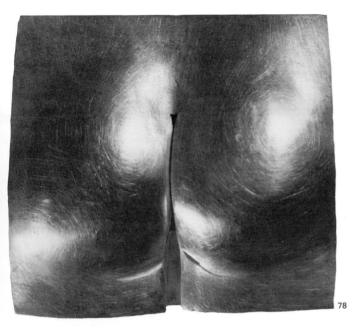

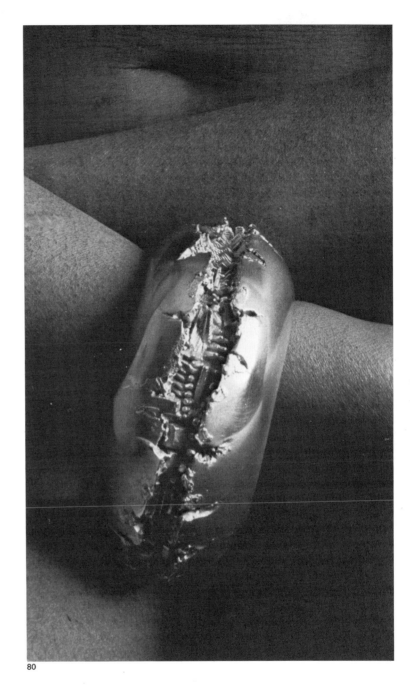

78

79   80

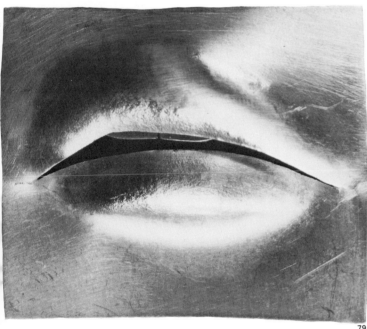

78–79] Bruno Martinazzi
Brooches from the series 'Economic Growth':
'Backside' and 'Mouth'
Gold
4 cm (1½ in)
1968–9
Private collection, Amsterdam
Photo: Pucci Giardina

80] Arnaldo Pomodoro
Bracelet
Gold
1963
Marlborough Gallery, Rome
Photo: Ugo Mulas

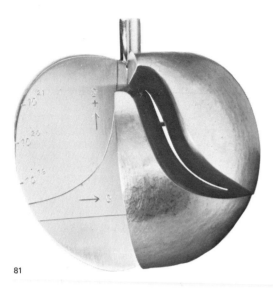

81

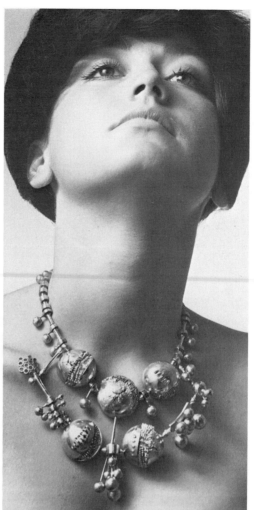

82

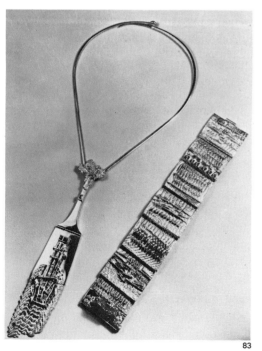

83

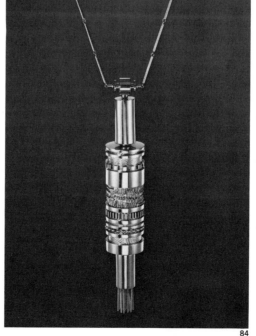

84

86

Britain

In Great Britain the 1960s saw a growing interest in creative jewelry. Undoubtedly the Goldsmiths' Hall exhibition had stirred the imagination of several people, and it was followed by an increase in the amount of work produced.

A major influence on the new informality in the work of British jewellers was Gerda Flöckinger. She was born in Innsbruck in 1927, emigrated to England in 1938, and studied jewelry under Alan Davie at the Central School of Art in London. The first exhibition of her work was in 1954.

Her work in the fities and early sixties was concerned with simple forms and enamelling, and embryonic images that were to develop later. In 1968 she held a one-man show which was in several ways a turning point in her career at the Crafts Centre of Great Britain. By this time her work had changed dramatically. She had begun to fuse metals in 1963 and by 1968 had developed the technique considerably. Many pieces in this exhibition had visual poetic tranquillity. Nothing is allowed to jar or interfere with the original thought. Gentle, feminine and full of colour, her work is jewelry through and through. Often carving the stones that were to be set into rings and necklaces, her work shows clearly the romance she has with jewelry. In recent work, colour is drawn from ancient alloys that have become even more precious with subtle tones that become more and more apparent as one 'journeys around her work'. This exhibition eventually led to the Victoria and Albert Museum offering her their first one-man show of work by a living jeweller, which took place in 1971.

Throughout her career, this artist has done more than any other to promote jewelry in Britain. Constantly defending the creative jeweller she has paved the way for artists who were to follow her, and who in consequence are treated with far more respect than in the past.

Another artist working in Britain who has won recognition for her work is Helga Zahn. She was born in Germany in 1936, but has lived in England for several years. From the outset she has questioned the accepted aesthetic values of jewelry. Her early work shows clean, uncluttered lines with a circle the dominating figure in many pieces. Stones, when used, are selected for colour and form, and unpolished pebbles were used for colour and tactile quality. She is both jeweller and painter, working with a firmly established correspondence between the two media. An example of this can be found in a series of silkscreen prints she produced in 1966–8. Here again the circle is an ever-recurring theme.

Movement has been an integral part of her work from an early date. The large discs used in several pieces revolving with the movement of the body when worn. In more recent work this has been accentuated.

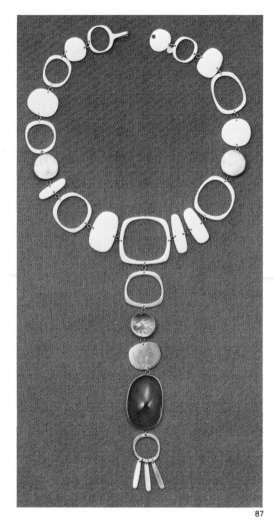

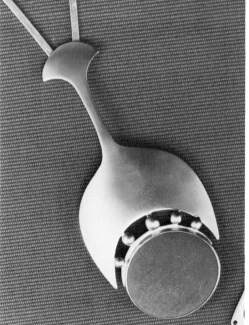

87] Gerda Flöckinger
Necklace
Gold, aquamarine, rose quartz
1963
Photo: Worshipful Company of Goldsmiths

88] Gerda Flöckinger
Rings
Silver, gold, pearls, garnet
1967–8
Photo: Julian Nieman

89] Helga Zahn
Rings
Silver
Limited edition of 10
4·5 cm (1¾ in)
1966
Part collection, National Museum of Wales,
  and the author
Photo: Cyril Wilson

90] Gerda Flöckinger
Ring
Silver, gold, coral cameo
3·5 cm (1½ in)
1970
Photo: Ray Carpenter

91] Helga Zahn
Pendant
Silver, brown pebble
12·5 cm (5 in)
1965
Photo: Worshipful Company of Goldsmiths

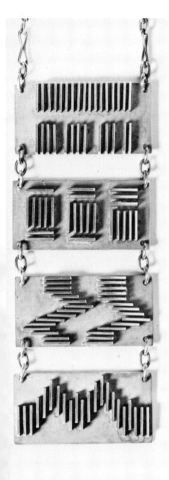
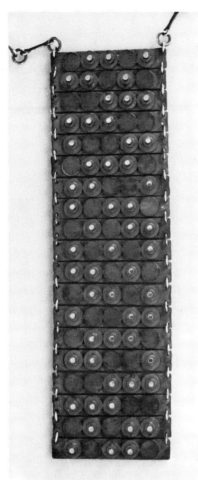

Colour is now used more strongly, and in one pendant made in 1973 silver cylindrical units are suspended between two green plastic wires, terminating in one amber bead. It is a subtle work which demonstrates her sense of scale and control of colour.

Her jewelry reflects her interest and knowledge of graphics. The scale is often large — it is not for the half-hearted, being bold and decisive. As with many artists whose work is of this calibre, people often question the wearability of such pieces.

This jewelry is not intended to be an accessory to the wardrobe, but to be worn carefully with complementary clothing. For example, she produced a series of rings in a limited edition in 1966, at the height of her most creative period. Although considered large in scale, the rings are perfectly in tune with the scale of the body and give visual weight to the hand.

The problem of the wearability of jewelry has been examined by several jewellers. In her book *Jewellery and Sculpture through Unit Construction* published in 1967, Patricia Meyerowitz wrote:

> This book is mainly concerned with the process of assembling small scale parts into finished objects which can be worn.
> The method of contemplating what these parts should be — their proportions and their relationship to each other — need not differ from that applied to sculpture, painting, or any other art, and what I would term creative jewelry, like these arts, has no function.
> The fact that the finished piece can be worn need not determine what form it should take, nor what the component parts should be, for this kind of jewelry is rewarding to make and to look at whether it is finally worn or not. One can, in fact, make a piece for its own sake, with the intrinsic idea as its only reason for being.

Patricia Meyerowitz's own jewelry is, in fact, immensely wearable. Sophisticated, with mathematical ingredients, her work is the result of intensive research and dedication to her beliefs.

Desmond Clen Murphy, and Peter Hauffé, used natural formed crystals as vehicles for their jewelry. Hauffé, however, was one of the first serious artists in this country to explore the possibility of movement in his work. Many of his pieces at this time were considerably more advanced in this respect than any other contemporary work in Britain.

An important element in British jewelry in the seventies was to be figurative work. Patricia Tormey and Rita Greer were precursors of this style during the sixties. Patricia Tormey's work is largely given to the human form, though her work concerns itself with the grouping of figures, often with a sense of the erotic. Rita Greer's jewelry is essentially romantic and plays on the fantasies of dreams and organic images.

92
93

[92–93] Patricia Meyerowitz
Pendants
Oxydized silver
14 cm (5½ in)
1965–6
Photo: Tony Stone

55

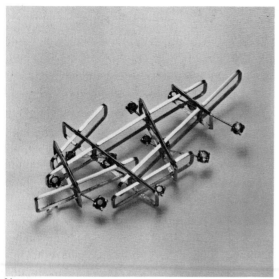

94

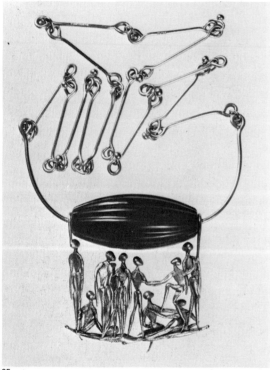

95

94] Peter Hauffé
Brooch; mobile
White gold, sapphires
9·5 cm (3¾ in)
c. 1966
Photo: Worshipful Company of Goldsmiths

95] Patricia Tormey
Pendant
Gold, cornelian
7·5 cm (3 in)
c. 1969
Collection: Edward Lucie-Smith, London

Holland

The term 'body sculpture' is now often used to describe work to which many people feel the word jewelry is not applicable, especially when the pieces are large or all-enveloping. This is not a good term, and is often unnecessary and misleading. Many of the pieces that could fit into this category are at best affected. But long before this type of work became fashionable two Dutch artists did a series of experiments into the possibilities of such constructions, which was based on an intellectual approach with much serious dedicated research and exploration.

Emmy van Leersum and Gijs Bakker were trained as goldsmiths in Holland. They became dissatisfied with the traditional approach of their contemporaries and decided to experiment. In 1966 they presented a collection of their work at the Galerie Swart in Amsterdam and the following year at the Stedelijk Museum. The same year the exhibition went to the Ewan Phillips Gallery, London. The pieces show the result of extensive research and mainly comprised a series of collars and bracelets made from aluminium. They chose this metal in place of the traditional materials of silver and gold, largely as a reaction to the ostentation of jewelry. Its lightweight properties enabled them to produce experimental forms. Since that time they have continued to produce work of importance and are now considered to be the leading innovators of contemporary design in jewelry in their country.

In 1969 an exhibition was mounted at the Van Abbemuseum in Eindhoven under the title Objects to Wear, comprising work by Leersum and Bakker, Nicolaas van Beek, Françoise van den Bosch, and Bernhard Lameris. The exhibition later toured the USA arranged by the Smithsonian Institute in Washington. These five artists who work quite separately share one fundamental principle. They minimize their forms, and use the body as a medium for their work rather than merely an object to be decorated.

Emmy van Leersum and her husband, Gijs Bakker, have continued since that exhibition to develop their ideas about Minimal Art. In their exhibition at Electrum Gallery in London in 1972, they presented their most recent work. The jewelry shown at this exhibition consisted of a collection of thirty or more bracelets in aluminium, closely related to one another in form. Together with these bracelets, the exhibition showed a collection of experimental clothing, which in ideas and production reflected a similar method of construction to that of the jewelry. The forms of the clothing came about by using a stretch material that incorporated the use of rings or hardening agents. By accentuating certain parts of the body, the artists' aim was to 'correct any imperfections which may exist in the human form'. The clothing gave the wearer great freedom of movement and produced a sensual experience when worn.

96] Emmy van Leersum
Neckpiece and bracelet
anodized aluminium
1967
Matthijs Schrofer

97] Gijs Bakker
shoulder piece
blue anodized aluminium
1967
Matthijs Schrofer

98]

100

101

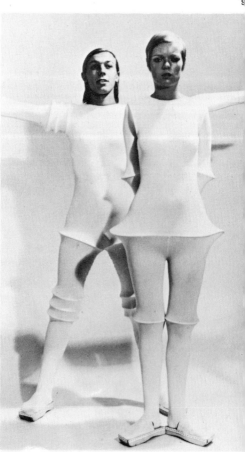

98] Gijs Bakker
Bracelet
Clear acrylic
Multiple
1967

99] Gijs Bakker
Bracelet
Aluminium
9·5 cm (3¾ in)
1969
Photo: Rien Baren

100–102] Emmy van Leersum and Gijs Bakker,
Experimental clothing
Stretch nylon with hardening agents
1970

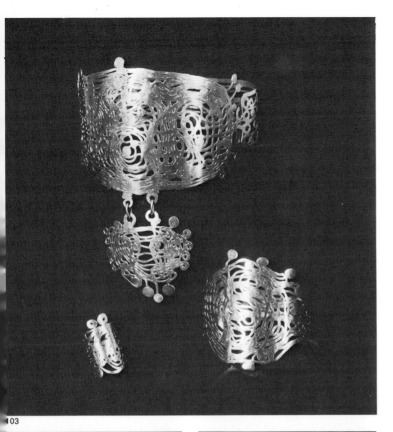

103

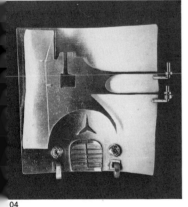

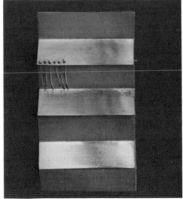

104 104   105

These two artists have had a considerable effect on other Dutch jewellers, as was shown by the exhibition Sieraad 1900–72 at the Zonnehof Museum at Amersfoort (see p. 181). In fact, so great has been their influence that many young people in Holland are now merely duplicating what Bakker and Leersum have already achieved, with the result that much contemporary work in Holland is repetitive.

Eastern Europe

Towards the end of the sixties it became clear that the renaissance in creative jewelry had spread to many parts of the world. In Czechoslovakia the exhibition Stříbrný Šperk Jablonec 68 showed artists' work from several parts of Europe, including the Socialist countries: Jerzy Zaremski from Poland, Florica Farcasu from Rumania, and Anton Cepka, Libuše Hlubučkovā, Darina Horvāthovā, Jaroslav Kodejš, Blanka Nepasickā, Eleonora Rejtharovā, Josef Symon, Helena Frantovā, and Paval Krbálek from Czechoslovakia. Most of these artists have been working along similar lines as their colleagues in the rest of Europe.

But this was no sudden surge of activity. As in the rest of Europe, the Socialist countries had had their pioneers, such as Florica Farcasu from Bucharest. Since her student days in the thirties her work has been exhibited widely throughout Europe, with numerous awards and distinctions. Essentially Romanian in spirit, her early work draws on folk art, and when describing her thoughts she refers to the elements of nature as motivating her ideas. Her work resembles that of Gerda Flöckinger but unlike this artist, Florica Farcasu's images are primarily two-dimensional. Both, however, have an interest in a sense of balance. With little doubt she loves her work and the materials she uses: 'I apply the goldsmith's technique to the noble wire, which I direct pursuing, through storms of ascendant circles and spirals, the mysterious way through constellations . . .'

Pavel Krbálek, born in Miroslav, Czechoslovakia in 1928, and who now lives in Lucern, has for many years created jewelry of great strength and individuality. Long sweeping curves dominate his necklaces, reminiscent of some current American work. His works often retain the marks of the goldsmith's hammer and reflect the surface of the metal.

One of the principal creative jewellers from Czechoslovakia, Alena Novákovā, also emphasizes the surface of her work. Born in 1929, she studied sculpture at the Academy of Applied Arts in Prague, but it was to be her work in jewelry that brought the greatest attention from critics and museum directors, and she has exhibited her work regularly. During the sixties she developed an individual style which owed little to other artists. With a minimal amount of 'energy' she draws attention to the surface texture of matt silver, bending the metal to exploit its reflecting properties in forms that are often

103]   Florica Farcasu
Necklace, bracelet and ring
Silver
c. 1968–9

104–105]   Alena Novákovā
Brooches
Matt silver, citrine
7·5 cm (3 in)
1967
Photo: Dvořák, Prague

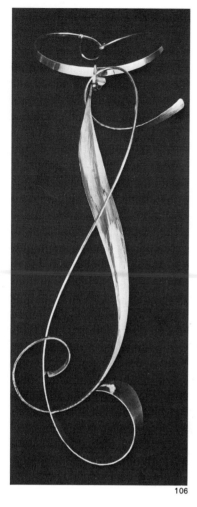

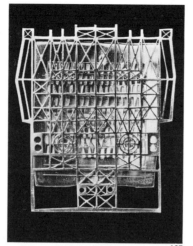

107

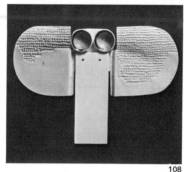

108

109

106

106] Pavel Krbálek
Pendant
Silver
c. 1972
Photo: J. G. Perret

107] Anton Cepka
Brooch
Silver
8·5 cm (3½ in)
1967
Photo: Pavel Janek

108] Anton Cepka
Brooch
Silver, glass, acrylic
11 cm (4⅜ in)
1973
Photo: Pavel Janek

109] Anton Cepka
Mobile sculpture
Aluminium and steel
70 cm high (27½ in)
1968
Photo: Pavel Janek

geometric. Her sense of scale and proportion is very apparent in these pieces when she places focal points to which the eye is drawn. In some pieces her work takes on an almost figurative style, abstracting visual images from a technological world.

The influence of Nováková's talent is to be seen in younger artists' work in Czechoslovakia, such as Anton Cepka. However, Cepka's approach in the late sixties was entirely his own, and is now considered to be one of his country's most outstanding talents in creative jewelry. He was born in 1936 in Western Slovakia, studying at the School of Arts and Crafts in the capital, Bratislava, and continued his studies at the College of Applied Arts in Prague. He is both sculptor and jeweller and both media reflect his interest in the modern world: 'Everything both old and new holds the magic of the era. The technical world today with its scientific mission, precise calculations and inventions can be considered in aesthetic terms. Computors, radar antennae, television screens, jet planes, space technology are all a great influence on man. These are the stimuli for my work; I am trying to make jewelry that is a reflection of this world.'

Not surprisingly for a country renowned for its glass, several artists in Czechoslovakia are now using glass as a means of expressing their ideas. It is to be found in sculpture, furniture, and in the jewelry of Jaroslav Kodejš and Lubuše Hlubučkovà.

Kodejš's first experiments came about in the latter half of the sixties. From 1967–8 his work appeared to be rather indistinctive, with necklaces taking on the bulbous and irregular qualities that can be achieved with this material. But in 1969 his work was to forego this style and take a new direction. He incorporated both silver and glass into forms that exploited the properties of both these materials. With the opposing basic shapes of the circle and the square, Kodejš achieved results that married both these elements successfully.

While Kodejš is concerned with opposing forms in glass and silver, his contemporary Libuše Hlubučkovà appears to be involved with the relationship between these materials. The results could not be more dissimilar. Hlubučkovà brought out the transparent qualities of this material. In 1969 she was working on necklaces hung with rounded irregular drops of glass, pure and clear. Later, the work was to become more simplified. These later pieces at first appear almost regimental, but on closer inspection a balance of irregularity has been achieved. In 1971 the work was again to be simplified – honest and direct, the statements are positive and consistent.

The diversity of contemporary jewelry in Czechoslovakia during the sixties can be seen by comparing the work of these artists to that of Blanka Nepasickà. Her work provides a complete contrast not only in

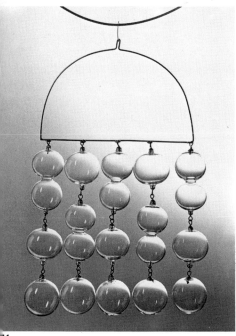

the materials she uses, but in the entire concept of the subject. Perhaps the only comparison between her work and that of others in that country is her love of silver, and her ability to manipulate this alloy is shown in much of her work. In 1968 her concern lay with the surface qualities of the metal that she brought into play against rigid horizontal bars. In the early part of the seventies her work was to take on more organic form, but she retained her interest in the textures of her work. The formality of her former work then disappeared and in bracelets made in the early seventies a much more rigorous spirit erupted, almost brutal in their impact. They seem to have been in battle, but emerged triumphant.

The Czechoslovakian-born Josef Symon now lives in Vienna. Although also a sculptor, his reputation rests largely on his jewelry. It often combines silver and gold, swerving and moving like waves of water, ebbing and flowing. Essentially romantic in his approach, he has produced some of the most poetic and lyrical pieces of jewelry of this period.

Other Eastern European countries have not produced artists nearly as progressive in their thinking, with the exception of Jugoslavian-born Georg Seibert. He now lives in Berlin and studied in Pforzheim. Unlike others who strive to conceal the solder and points where metals meet, but, like many sculptors who use welding methods, Seibert brings out these embellishments into the open. In an emphasis upon the means of construction this idea of exploiting what could be termed imperfections is taken further in some necklaces where the fastening is not concealed but made an obvious and integral part of the design.

Germany, Switzerland and Austria

As the sixties developed, Germany became a power-house of activity, with many jewellers producing fine work. The colleges in Munich and Hanau, and in particular Pforzheim, had produced a number of students who were to enliven the scene considerably, and at this time artists already mentioned, notably Becker and Jünger, were producing work of high quality.

In the Hanau Academy, Eberhard Burgel, a lecturer, had started a series of miniatures and brooches in 1966, which was completed and shown at the Galerie Orly in 1972. The following year they were part of an exhibition in London entitled Jewelry and the Human Form at the Electrum Gallery. Burgel's work during the sixties took an almost surrealistic approach. Brooches form small relief panels, depicting either solitary figures or groups. Thinly worked gold sheet, sometimes incorporating engraved ivory, is gently and sensually used as his canvas on which the fantasies of his private world are re-enacted. Like plays, his pieces have titles which are relevant to an understanding of them. Sometimes erotic, often humorous, Burgel's Samson and Delilah, Pan, Venus and Sesame, Charlie Chaplin and Marilyn Monroe portray a world of romantic images.

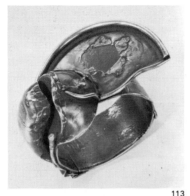

113

114

115

112] Josef Symon
Bracelet
Silver and gold
1972

113] Georg Seibert
Bracelet
Silver
1970
Collection: Schmuckmuseum, Pforzheim
Photo: Günter Meyer

114–115] Eberhard Burgel
Pendants, brooches
'Homage der Dürer', 'Venus'
Carved ivory and gold
10 cm (4 in)
1967/8
Photo: Uwe Bräunlich

In Switzerland, Othmar Zschaler continues to explore the possibilities of the close study of strata in the earth's structure, and injects these ideas into his jewelry, each piece showing this obsession with the governing forces of movement in rock formation. The early work of Helfried Kodré from Austria also tends to reflect these elements, though possibly from a different source. His recent work has less organic and more constructional elements. This harder line is in direct opposition to his wife's work, Liza Defner, where the forms of nature are a strong influence on her jewelry.

Kurt Neukomm, a Swiss born in 1938, has been recognized by several awards. Recently he has used large mounts for his jewelry that allow the spectator to either wear the brooch or enjoy the piece framed in slate as a wall construction. This artist is a brilliant technician and craftsman, but perhaps for the creative jeweller today his work is rather too precious.

Klaus Neubauer, in Germany, like Kurt Neukomm, used wall mounts as an integral part of the jewelry. He believes that 'by wearing one part of the object an intensive contact between the wearer and the wall relief becomes apparent'. Neubauer's forms often resemble those by Jean Arp, but unlike this artist's jewelry these are often three-dimensional. Later Neubauer's work was to extend from the surface of the structure spreading itself out into organic formulations.

Australia and New Zealand

Australia at present suffers, as do South Africa and New Zealand, in the emigration of its artists to Europe and America. In some cases, they return bringing with them the stimulus they found abroad, but often London, Paris or New York embraces their talent and they remain. Some artists, like Wolf Wennrich, who was born in Germany and educated there but has lived in Australia since the fifties, travel the other way. As a creative jeweller Wennrich shares with a handful of others in stimulating a new approach to the subject in that country. However, Emanuel Raft is more typical.

Raft came to London in 1966 from Australia where he had a considerable reputation as a jeweller, painter and sculptor. His work in the sixties was chiefly made from silver set with rough uncut opals. These vigorous pieces owe something to the Pomodoro brothers, but he was to soon forego this method of working and evolve a more individual style. His work became more geometric, reflecting some contemporary trends in sculpture from the younger school of artists in England. In many pieces he incorporated mobile units. Colour was introduced into his work through the use of oxidized silvers and titanium, sometimes combined with enamel or stones of strong exciting hues.

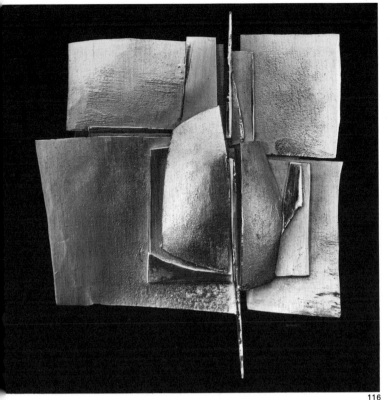

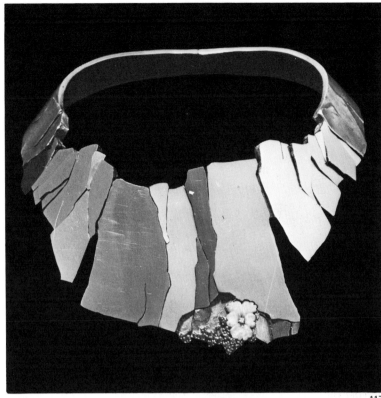

116

117

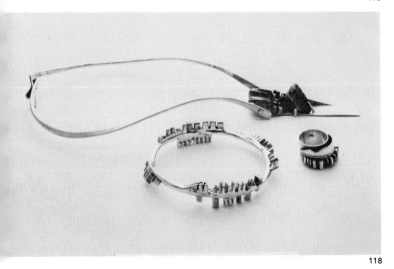

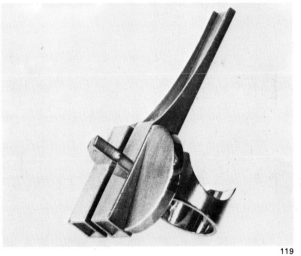

118

119

116] Othmar Zschaler
Brooch
Silver
1968

117] Helfried Kodré
Necklace
Silver, gold, rubies, carved crystal
1970

118] Emanuel Raft
Pendant, bracelet and ring
Silver, uncut opal
1967
Photo: *Design*, Design Council

119] Emanuel Raft
Ring
Silver
5 cm (2 in)
1970
Collection: Goldsmiths' Hall, London
Photo: Angela Turner

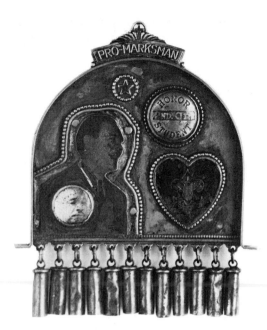

120

121

Rod Edwards also made the journey to England in the late fifties and established a studio in London. His work was bold and unconventional by English standards during this period, and he is considered by many of his colleagues to be one of the most proficient technicians today.

New Zealand is lucky in having attracted artists who have taken with them characteristics bred in their home country, but much of the work is derivative — although it is possible to find originality in younger people's work. For example, Jens Hansen was born in Denmark and is clearly still influenced by the school of thought there but tries to apply his own personal concept to the subject. The Swiss-born Kobi Bosshard is another, while the London-born Tanya Ashken well exemplifies how one can achieve a fresh approach in a new country.

At the early age of thirteen she was granted her own hallmark, being the youngest person ever to be given this privilege. In 1957, Miss Ashken attended the Central School of Art in London, and in 1960 married the New Zealand painter John Drawbridge. After a five-year stay in Paris, where she studied sculpture, both she and her husband moved to Wellington. Her sculpture resembles Brancusi's, while her jewelry is similar in its use of the reflective properties of metal to that of the Australian Rod Edwards.

The United States
America has enjoyed a renaissance just as active as in Europe, although, with a few exceptions, the work has been less progressive. As did William Morris and C. R. Ashbee in England, the American jeweller turns to the past for his inspiration, often producing work that is Art Nouveau in style, with fabricated and forged twists and curves. Nature is fully explored, resulting in organic fantasies. Another movement that has emerged in jewelry in America is 'assemblage', prompted largely by an exhibition mounted in 1961 at the Museum of Modern Art in New York under the title The Art of Assemblage. As mentioned in the previous chapter Sam Kramer's jewelry had predicted this trend.

One of the chief exponents of assemblage in jewelry in America is Fred Woell. Primarily his work is made up of a collection of 'found objects' assembled as in other media. His work is often witty, making comments on his anti-jewelry beliefs.

> I like satire. I try to intensify the bizarre and sacrosanct absurdity by using commonplace materials which have little or no intrinsic value . . . I like to think that an object gets its value from what you make of it, and not of what it is made . . . I try to make an object look both new and old at the same time. By that I mean I like to keep the freshness of the fingerprint of the artist, while allowing the work to possess a quality of age and a life of its own.

This attempt to produce something that looks old is repeated in some of the work of Bob Ebendorf, and several other American jewellers.

Much of modern American jewelry has faced a crisis of development. In *Contemporary Jewellery: A Craftsman's Handbook* Philip Morton reports: 'In 1964 the St. Paul Gallery exhibition raised the question of whether contemporary jewellery had reached a plateau of expression. The jury of that show found the majority of entries "repetitious or imitative, or contrived with the obvious effect to be different".'

However, there are several other creative jewellers in the USA, notably Stanley Lechtzin, Arline Fisch, Domingo de la Cueva, and Olaf Skoogfors, who have exhibited regularly in America since the fifties.

Stanley Lechtzin, one of the best-known American goldsmiths, was one of the first American artists to experiment with electroforming, having started in about 1964. Since his first exhibition in the Museum of Contemporary Crafts in New York in 1958, he has held numerous shows throughout America and Europe. He has said of his work:

> I attempt to create personal values using materials and processes which today are used in a mechanical and anonymous manner by industry. The control which I exercise over the metal as it grows in the electrolytic solution is a source of stimulation. This process is analogous to numerous growth processes observed in nature, and this has considerable meaning for me. It brings to mind crystal growth, the growth of coral under the sea, and the multiplication of simple organisms as observed under the microscope. In this, I experience a relationship between technology and nature.

Arline Fisch draws upon other cultures for her inspiration, and has done intensive research into the ornaments of pre-Columbian, Egyptian and medieval work. She is primarily interested in organic forms, which often carry her work into body ornaments, and in recent years she has extended her interest into American Indian cultures, incorporating leather and feathers into her work. As a result her work has become gradually ritualistic, which she says 'seems to fit logically with my own needs for more humanistic and imagistic forms as well as for larger scale effects which are still comfortable to and compatible with the human form. It also somehow is an appropriate direction for the times — or so it seems to me at the moment.'

Like Fisch's work, that of Cuban born Domingo de la Cueva — often body sculpture — appears to grow from an almost surrealistic source. Roland Penrose has commented: 'The artist is not blinded by the richness and rarity of the materials he uses, but is able to instill into his designs analogies with natural phenomena, or echoes of sumptuous rituals of past civilisations.' Also like Fisch, he draws on the past for his inspiration.

123

124

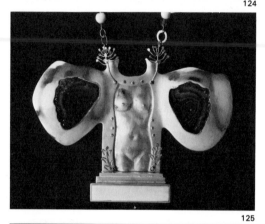

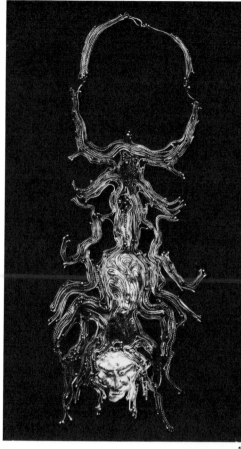

125

1

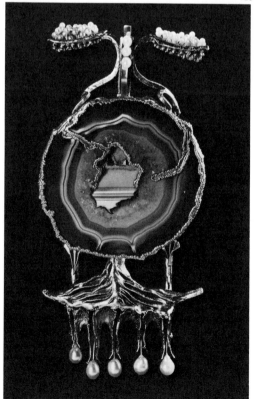

127

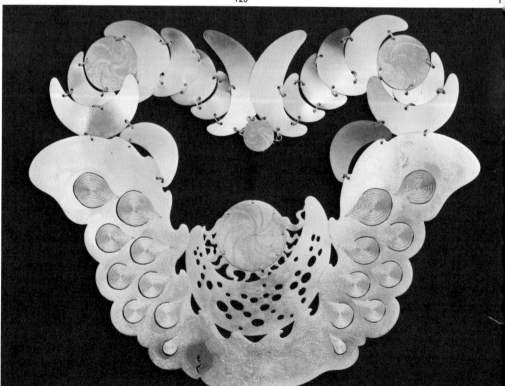

12

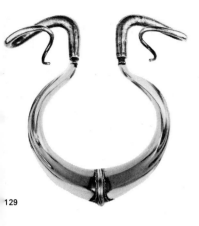

129

123] Bob Ebendorf
Brooch, 'Man and his Pet Bee'
Copper, brass, tin type and enamel
10 cm (4 in)
1971
Photo: T. N. Daniel

124] Arline Fisch
Pendant, 'The Devil Himself'
Silver
16·5 cm (6½ in)
c. 1970

125] Arline Fisch
Pendant
Silver, gold, crystals
1973
Günter Meyer

126] Marci Zelmanoff
Pendant
Bronze and silver
c. 1970–2
Photo: Peter Moore

127] Stanley Lechtzin
Brooch
Silver gilt, agate, Biwa pearls
c. 1969–70

128] Domingo de la Cueva
Breast plate, 'The Impossible (Marriage of Sun and Moon)'
Silver and gold
32 cm (12½ in)
1969
Photo: Ferruzzi

129] Stanley Lechtzin
Torque
Amber, polyester, silver gilt
c. 1972

Artists established in other media

Italy has seen a major experiment in the production of jewelry in a project run by Gian Montebello. In the catalogue to an exhibition presented by the Institute of Contemporary Art in Boston, under the title Jewelry as Sculpture as Jewelry, Loretta Yarlow, the curator, described how the project works:

In 1967, Gian Carlo Montebello initiated a unique workshop in Milan, the Gem Montebello Laboratory, to which artists of international reputation were invited to produce pieces of jewelry in collaboration with Montebello's small, and highly skilled staff . . . As it is not an unusual practice for the contemporary sculptor to submit plans and diagrams of his work to a welder in order to have a three-dimensional form made of his work, this practice is similar to the way the artist and staff work together at Montebello. A prototype is made for the artist to inspect, correct if necessary, and finally approve. The Montebello artisans create final versions, either in small limited editions or as unique pieces.

Since 1967 Montebello has attracted a number of artists to participate in this project. Not all these artists have been equally successful in translating their ideas into jewelry, but some outstanding work has been produced: Pol Bury's square braclets with moving spheres of gold; Del Pezzo's necklace in silver, gold and anodized coloured aluminium; the same materials used by Amalia Del Ponte in rings but in subtle colours; bracelets by Fontana; the famous 'Nana' theme interpreted into brooches by Niki de Saint Phalle; rings by Gastone Novelli; the Pomodoro brothers work at this time; and the set by Joe Tilson called 'Ziggurat'.

Many other artists have at one time or another produced either the design for jewelry or created the pieces themselves. Jean Cocteau produced a small collection executed by the goldsmith François Hugo in 1959. Merlin Evans and Elizabeth Frink made their first pieces in 1961 for the Worshipful Company of Goldsmiths, and a fine example of the artistry of Giorgio de Chirico is superbly captured in his brooch made in 1959, part of Signora Isabella de Chirico's collection in Rome.

Georges Braque produced a collection of 133 jewels in collaboration with Baron Henri-Michel de Lowenfeld, which was exhibited in Paris in 1963. Although they were superbly executed they seemed to lack the genius that went into his painting. In 1968 a collection of work by Wassily Kandinsky was made although Kandinsky did the drawings for most of these pieces between 1903 and 1904, the remainder between 1936 and 1939. The pieces were made in collaboration with Max Pollinger and Cornelia Rothel and were first exhibited at the Leonard Hatton Gallery in 1969 in New York and later at Galerie Anne Abeles in Cologne and Galerie Hans Goltz in Munich.

1

13

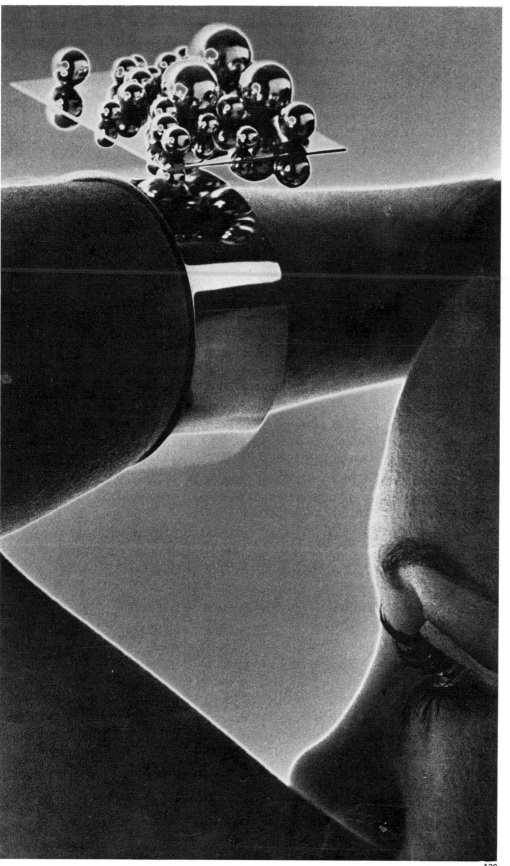

130

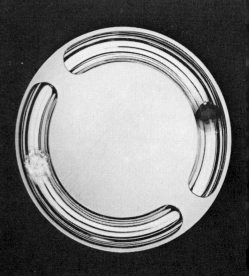

13

134

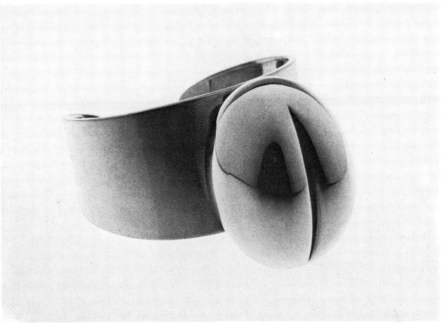

135

130] Pol Bury
Bracelet
Red gold, with moving spheres
Edition of 50
1968
Gem Montebello, Milan
Photo: Ugo Mulas

131] Ebbe Weiss-Weingart
Brooch
Gold
5 cm (2 in)
1965
Photo: Dr Weingart

132] Sigurd Persson
Bracelet
Gold, silver
9 cm (3½ in)
1963
Photo: Sune Sundahl

133] Friedrich Becker
Brooch
White gold, sapphire and diamond, kinetic
5·2 cm (2 in)
1968
Private collection

134] Niki de St Phalle
Cufflinks, 'Serpents'
Gold and enamel
Edition of 19
1971
Gem Montebello, Milan

135] Lucio Fontana
Bracelet
Red gold
Edition of 4
1968
Collection: Marchesa Albani, Italy

136] Hermann Jünger
Brooch
Silver and enamel
5 cm (2 in)
1969
Collection: Schmuckmuseum, Pforzheim

136

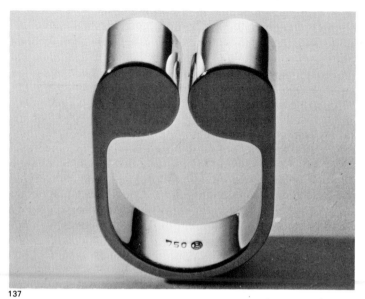

137

138

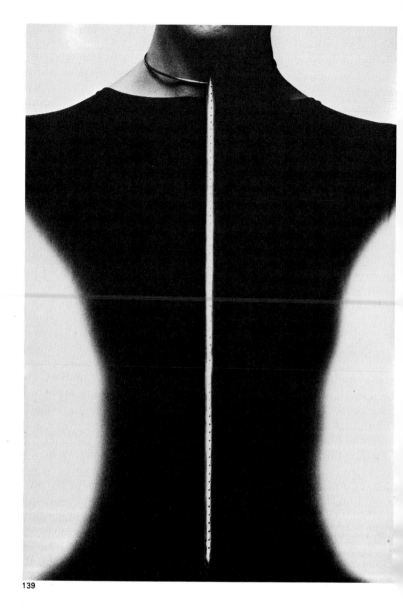

139

137–138] Friedrich Becker
Rings
Gold
1966
Collection: Goldsmiths' Hall, London

139] Lucio Fontana
Pendant, 'Anti Sofia'
Gold
Edition of 30
1967
Gem Montebello, Milan
Photo: Ugo Mulas

The sixties were prolific years for the creative jeweller throughout the western world. The awakening interest in this neglected art had by the end of the decade proved an activating force against the traditional and conventional approach to the subject. Several of the artists already mentioned in the chapter on the fifties, such as Persson, Becker and Jünger, were creating some of their best work to date. However, despite the experiments of some jewellers, most jewelry in the sixties lagged behind the innovations in painting and sculpture. Pop, Op, Kinetic, and Minimal art left little mark upon jewelry. But, in general, the following years up to the present have seen a far greater awareness of the possibilities that exist for the goldsmith and his art.

4

Reaction and Revolt 1970-75

140

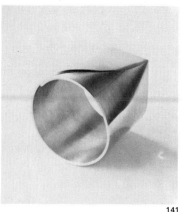

141

142

143

144

140] Robert Smit
Ring
White gold, acrylic
4·5 cm (1¾ in)
1970
Collection: Schmuckmuseum, Pforzheim
Photo: Günter Meyer

141–144] Emmy van Leersum & Gijs Bakker
Bracelets
Aluminium
7·6 cm (3 in)
1971

145] Robert Smit
Plate
1970
Photo: Günter Meyer

As far as creative jewelry is concerned, the first half of the 1970s will almost certainly be recorded as one of the most innovatory and imaginative periods in the history of the art. Following the pioneering work in Europe and America in the sixties, a new generation of artists emerged who were to question the significance of jewellers, and our awareness of their ideas and beliefs. They even questioned the achievements of the previous decade from which their own work developed.

Many young artists have taken a fresh look at the subject, re-evaluating and questioning its significance in a society that faced major world problems. Does jewelry have any place in such a problematic world? Can it contribute? Does it matter? Such questions are of concern to all artists, but to the jeweller perhaps of particular significance.

One of the principal concerns facing artists today is that of communication. The jeweller's art should be a communicative one; his art is entirely mobile, its being comes about and is about the human body. Jewelry is created and worn for much the same reasons as Gertrude Stein wrote – 'for herself and strangers'. Real creative jewelry should be capable of drawing people closer together. This type of jewelry is not worn as a status symbol, its intentions are not to draw attention to social position – indeed the contrary would apply – but rather to attempt to show the outside world the personality of the maker.

Tendenzen '70 – New Horizons

Jewelry in the 1970s has changed dramatically, for within this gentle art a revolution has taken place – a revolution not only in style or design, for the entire concept of the subject has been rethought, passing the middle aged and middle class in true rebellious spirit. The old idea that jewelry was made exclusively of precious alloys and gems has given way to experiments with new materials, often combining traditional materials with new ones.

This revolution has not taken place overnight, but started in the sixties. No one artist or event motivated this surge of new ideas, but the catalogue for the exhibition Schmuck '70 – Tendenzen (Jewelry '70 – Tendencies) lists a number of young artists, then unknown, who were to play an important role in this new concept of jewelry. The exhibition was the second in a series of bienalles organized and mounted by the Schmuckmuseum in Pforzheim, Germany, the only museum in the world devoted to the promotion of creative jewelry. The exhibition was intended as an international assessment of creativity in jewelry and over sixty-five artists were represented from all over Europe and the USA. Many of the contributors whose work has already been discussed were represented, but there were other artists whose work led into the new decade.

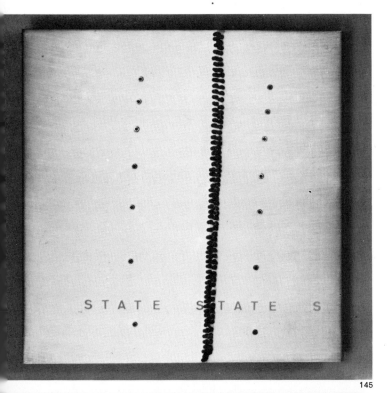

145

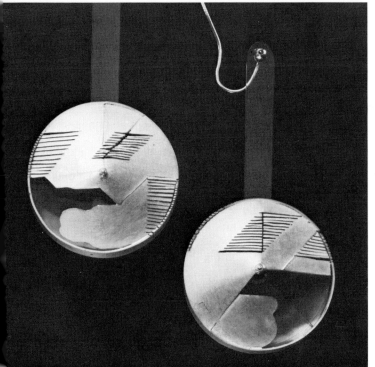

146

Three Dutchmen, Nicolaas van Beek, Onno Boekhoudt and Robert Smit produced some outstanding work for the exhibition. Unlike most Dutch jewellers the last two artists are not concerned with the simplification of form as advocated by Leersum and Bakker. Smit, since this exhibition, has moved even further into computer-programmed work, and has now made several large objects in the form of relief panels. His jewelry at this point was largely experimental, appealing to technological rather than romantic ideals. (Regrettably he no longer makes jewelry.)

Boekhoudt's work is subtly and finely drawn. Indeed, drawing is an important activity for this artist. Unlike most jewellers in Holland, Boekhoudt's work is not concerned with form. He uses basically the circle and square — two forms which he treats as a canvas on which finely drawn lines are placed precisely. He achieves a visual impression that relates to the Dutch minimal artists and in particular to the English constructivist, Malcolm Hughes, and in some instances to the slashed canvases of Fontana. Boekhoudt's work can also be compared to the Argentinian's experiments, although the Dutchman's 'cuts' can hardly be described as slashed. His pieces are not aggressive, but he uses space in the same way as Fontana.

Sergi Aguilar (see also p. 87) from Spain exhibited a number of pieces constructed with mathematical precision. His work then was given over to 'hard edge' sculptural jewelry, and could be compared to the 'new generation' of sculptors in Britain in the mid-sixties. The forms used by David Hall and Tony Smith, or even Anthony Caro, are often to be found in Aguilar's work during this period.

Ulrike Bahrs' exhibit combined steel and silver with a material new to jewelry, acrylic. The human form was dissected, sometimes almost unrecognizably so, and the colours were soft and delicate. Much of her work at that time related obliquely to Art Nouveau, but she was fully in control of its influence and did not allow it to dominate. Her pieces were subtle and refined, often with graphic tones and a quality of humour — in evidence in much contemporary work, especially in England. Perhaps the most important new talents who contributed to the 1970 Tendenzen exhibition were Hubertus von Skal, Claus Bury, and Gerd Rothmann.

Gerd Rothmann is also a great humourist, and humour infects much of his work. Colour plays a major part in his jewelry; the form is usually very simple and acts as a frame for the colour within. One set of four brooches at this exhibition displayed butterfly silhouettes against a brilliantly coloured striped background of acrylic and photographs (see fig. 2)

Also in 1970 Rothmann created a 'suite' of jewelry comprising four brooches and a bracelet in steel and acrylic placed in an opaque box. Each piece could be worn separately but when all were 'at home' in

their box the work took on an entirely new conception. This set is now in the collection of the Stedelijk Museum, Amsterdam.

At the same time he also became conscious of the fact that his jewelry was beyond the reach of most of the people interested in it. His use of inexpensive materials did not mean that they could be so at low prices, as the work involved in making jewelry from acrylic and steel is no less arduous or time-consuming than that made from traditional materials. To solve this problem he designed a series of multiples in unlimited editions which would therefore fall into most people's price bracket, and as a result, Rothmann's work has become widely available. The multiples took the form of a plate that could be adapted as bracelet or pendant, and often contained mobile units, such as numerals, discs or ball bearings. In some later editions Rothmann extended the idea of mobility by creating a form of bagatelle. Some of these were produced in a small limited edition. The idea of multiples and editions has appealed to many jewellers. Zahn in Britain produced such an edition in 1966, and Leersum and Bakker did much the same thing with an acrylic bracelet at about the same time (see fig. 98).

In 1972 Rothmann became intensely interested in the form of the artichoke. It appeared again and again in many of his pieces. A small gold brooch made about this time shows his ability to make the simplest statement with this form — again a reminder of the possibilities which can exist whilst working on a small scale.

Since 1973 Rothmann has foregone his intensive experiments with acrylic, and turned instead to the more traditional material of gold, combining it with steel. In a collection of brooch-objects he took the circle and egg as his dominating theme, handling both materials with great respect, and producing works of finely balanced scale and proportion. A little earlier he made a small collection of bracelets in oxidized steel and gold, which were masculine and rigid, in an almost military manner (see fig. 237).

Skal was born in Czechoslovakia but has lived in Germany for many years now. This artist has been creating exceptional pieces since the mid-sixties. His work is without parallel, and is undoubtedly amongst the best half dozen creative jewellers in the world. The details of his work are so refined, and yet not for a moment does he lose the over concept.

Like Martinazzi, Reiling and Eberhard Burgel, Skal shares a pre-occupation with the human form. Unlike these other artists, Skal is obsessed with one particular image, that of a tiny man. Neatly suited and wearing a trilby, he appears again and again, each time differently situated, sometimes seated, with large ears for wings, sometimes sporting a long penis several times his size. He appears again in contemplative mood sitting in an acrylic ear, or amongst a group of

147] Hubertus von Skal
Brooch
Acrylic, silver
7·7 cm (3 in)
1970
Collection: the author
Photo: Angela Turner

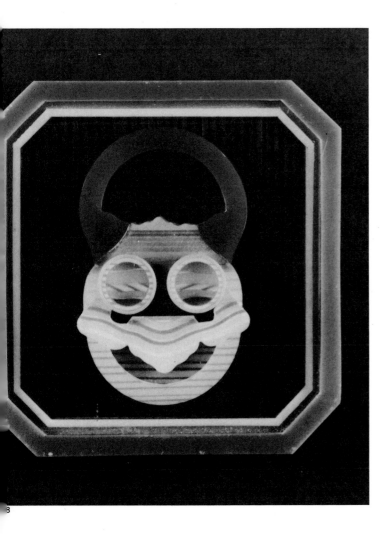

four or five friends. In one exquisite piece he is found astride a gold bicycle, mounted on a steel four-post plinth.

Skal has also produced a number of humorous pieces that depict an isolated penis, or with tiny legs that set it scampering off in pursuit of a mate. Other images in silver and gold such as moon-like faces, bees, the human profile, sometimes incorporate small colourful stones. Colour is an important factor in Skal's work — the goldsmith's alloy is treated like a painter's palette. Acrylic is also used, gently and delicately, and as a backcloth for the more conventional metal.

In 1972 Skal produced a piece with human heads mounted on pins, set into a steel tray. Each gold-headed pin can be removed, but when contained in their base the pieces have a life style like a Giacometti sculpture. An object made the following year dissociates itself from all human elements. With mechanical precision, this piece again takes the form of a tray, or plinth consisting of two gold, concave receptacles set into matt steel and raised by four short threaded pillars. The sheer formality of this work has a hypnotic quality which in turn becomes an almost sensual experience for the spectator.

Skal's contribution to contemporary jewelry, once overlooked, has now inspired a considerable following in Germany and, recently, in England.

One more artist shown at the exhibition demonstrates the fresh approach that was abroad at the start of this decade. At the time of this event Claus Bury was twenty-four years old. In 1969 he left Germany, where he had studied at Pforzheim, to live and work in London, and that year his jewelry was to change violently. He was at that time employed in the workshop of Andrew Grima, but in his spare time he experimented with a material far removed from the goldsmith's normal materials — acrylic. For a few years he was to devote his energy to this material.

He had received a goldsmith's traditional training, and now looked for new ideas outside that field. From the outset, Bury was interested in engineering components, but it was in the use of acrylic that he was to attract attention. His work was extremely intricately programmed, complex yet clearly defined, drawing the spectator inwards down an ever-receding tunnel of light and colour. In some cases his work in the late sixties made use of acrylic sheet, concealing components lying beneath the outer surface. They were perhaps large in scale, and many have been severely critical about this aspect of his work (fig. 292). Two years after Tendenzen '70, in 1972, he was to share the prize for the International Jewelry Competition at the Schmuck-museum, Pforzheim, with Martinazzi, Maierhofer and Waltrud Rees. Still only twenty-six, his winning brooch for this competition was a masterpiece. It was made from gold and acrylic, and must rate amongst

3] Claus Bury
ooch
rylic
:m (2¾ in.)
70

149] Wendy Ramshaw
Set of eleven rings
White gold, grey chalcedony and agate
Nickel-silver stand
7·6 cm (3 in)
1973
Collection: Worshipful Company of Goldsmiths
Photo: Bob Cramp

the major pieces of jewelry created during the twentieth century. It now in the collection of the Schmuckmuseum, Pforzheim (fig. 290)

After seeing the London exhibition Objects and Acrylic Jewelry at Electrum Gallery in 1972, Professor Goodden of the Royal College of Art in London invited Bury to attend the college as a visiting lecturer. The young German's methods of teaching were received with some trepidation by the students, with the one notable exception of Roger Morris, who was to gain much from Bury's approach. The exercise proved to be a rewarding one for Bury, however, and on his return to Hanau, Bury created another major piece — again a brooch, but this time made entirely from gold. The brooch itself relates to much of Bury's earlier work. Superbly constructed, it is part of a collage, consisting of pencil and crayon drawings of the piece, acrylic mount for the brooch and detachable pin, with explanatory notes on material method and time involved. The collage is framed, signed and dated 'Hanau January 1973'. Bury is concerned in the piece with communicating his ideas to the spectator. The fact that the pin is set apart from the brooch itself indicates the artist's determination to involve the spectator in the construction of this work. The drawings again reflect this thinking, and the explanatory notes take the idea to its limits. It is unlikely that this important piece would have come into being were it not for the artist's problematic visit to the RCA in London. This fine work was the forerunner of a series of such pieces consisting of collages, drawings and jewelry. At the 1973 Tendenzen he exhibited a 'book' extending this idea into three 'pages' of drawings relating to the brooch. Each page, framed and bound, gave information on the jewel itself, and the 'tunnel' so familiar in this artist's work was extended into and through these pages. The tunnel here enabled the spectator to 'enter' the book and through this eventually reach the brooch. His work is pervaded by a sense of orderliness, which in some of his 1973 pieces makes the work rather flat and lacking in the vitality of his best work. In 1973 Bury was to pay his first visit to America. Again his work was viewed with scepticism. On his return to Germany he was to change direction yet again. In the summer of 1974 he attempted further explanations. This time he was to produce a series of pieces that extended the explanatory method into precise cataloguing of his research into new material combinations. One of the principal innovators of acrylic jewelry, he now devotes his time to combining a multitude of materials and using them as a painter would oils.

By marrying silver, gold, copper, and other materials with chemicals achieves a new dialogue. Perhaps Claus Bury more than any other jeweller will bring us a new aesthetic that combines the ability of the goldsmith with the intellectual approach that has for centuries been failing in much creative work.

Bury's work in acrylic at the Tendenzen '70 contributed to a general concern with this new material. Acrylic work by him, Skal, Ulrike

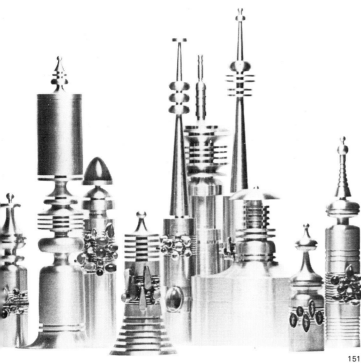

150

0] Wendy Ramshaw
t of five rings
ver, green cornelians, amethyst
5 cm (1¾ in)
71
oto: David Watkins

1] Wendy Ramshaw
ty' turned brass and nickel silver stands holding
vels
73
oto: David Watkins

Bahrs, Gerd Rothmann and Robert Smit, was the most original at the exhibition, although all five work in different directions.

Acrylic was then a relatively new material for jewelry. Although these artists exploited the material to its fullest, they were not the first to use this exciting medium. Ken Cory, an American, and Juli Guasch, in Spain, had experimented with acrylic in the sixties, and the forerunner of this material, bakelite, had been used extensively in the twenties and thirties. But more important than the choice of material was its use. Acrylic was not used merely as a substitute for gem stones or decorative effects but as a medium in its own right; an expression of each artist's individual and unique talent.

Developments in Britain

At the same time as the Tendenzen '70 exhibition in Germany, a much smaller event was taking place in London's tiny Pace Gallery — an exhibition of the work of Wendy Ramshaw. Trained in illustration and fabric design, Miss Ramshaw is a self-taught jeweller. From this, her first one-man exhibition, she has over the past years developed into one of Britain's foremost creative jewellers. She had, in fact, exhibited her work since the mid-sixties, but it was with this event that she began to create serious collector's pieces. Unlike many contributors to this book, Wendy Ramshaw chooses to use the traditional materials of silver, gold and enamel, though her methods are in no way traditional. They are very much products of the machine age, her instrument often being the lathe. Her work at this time was, and still is, concerned mainly with relationships. For example, she is renowned for being the chief innovator of the ring set: groups of rings individual in themselves but conceived as one unit. These units can be interchanged one with another in an endless range of subtle and sometimes dramatic arrangements. This, as we have seen, has been done by Becker with his brooches but, unlike Becker's work, Wendy Ramshaw's rings exist when apart from one another. Many of her ring sets incorporate mirrors, enamel and stones in subtle colour relationships which are displayed to their best advantage on the wearer.

As with much of the work we have been looking at, her jewelry can be enjoyed when not worn. In fact she has done much to draw attention to this aspect of creative jewelry in general. Her stands and mounts for these pieces are very much an integral part of the work. Early pieces were mounted on simple acrylic rods, but later these became more elaborate incorporating enamels and worked in brass and German silver.

Each piece from her studio is undoubtedly jewelry — this cannot be said of all creative jewellers. Some claim, rather harshly, that this prolific artist tends to be repetitive, but like many serious artists, she works slowly, developing and exploring new ideas. Unfairly, a new collection is expected each 'season', treating jewelry as part of the

154

fashion world. Truly creative jewellers cannot be expected to fulfil such demands. One hardly expects the painter or sculptor to change his style so regularly. However, her exhibition in the Goldsmiths' Hall in London in 1973 displayed new developments. The mounts for her rings had become considerably more elaborate, and colour dominated the exhibition. At about this time she began to experiment with sandblasting. Necklaces and brooches were made using this technique, with patterns reminiscent of Paul Klee's drawings. Some work further explained her preoccupation with the relationship of forms which was becoming increasingly complex, as in one brooch made of layers of gold like a forest of tiny forms.

With the few exceptions of work discussed in the previous chapter, creative jewelry in Britain generally lagged behind the rest of Europe up to the seventies. Then, within a relatively short space of time several interesting artists emerged producing work capable of comparison with the best anywhere. In June 1971, when the Electrum Gallery opened in London, it exhibited the work of several new jewellers of merit then living and working in Britain, most notably Charlotte de Syllas, Catherine Mannheim and David Watkins.

Charlotte de Syllas's work is difficult to define, chiefly because the influences upon her appear to come from a number of early cultures. That is not to say that her work is diverse, for each piece somehow relates to another, although she may employ a number of different skills and techniques. She is dedicated to her art, and will often devote up to two or three years to making a single piece. Time as such is of little consequence, and her techniques are acquired slowly like a medieval craftsman. Working only to commission, Charlotte de Syllas's work is rarely seen on exhibition. She sees her work as 'a way of being able to see the world better, a by-product, a form of mediation'. Often the boxes for her jewelry are quite beautiful, and are of great importance to her. For one ring, the box takes the form a pair of clasped hands carved in partridge wood (fig. 4)

Catherine Mannheim forms part of a group of figurative artists working in Britain, which also includes Rita Greer, Patricia Tormey, Geli Lukin Johnston, Barbara Cartlidge, Claire Murray and Gunilla Treen. Catherine Mannheim was born in South Africa, and studied jewelry under Friedrich Becker in Germany. In 1966 she set up her studio in London. At this period her work was somewhat diverse with little continuity, but in the early 1970s she developed a very personal style. Her work often combines gold and silver, and many pieces have an oriental feeling, reminiscent of Japanese prints and manuscripts. She tends to focus on exteriors, the geometric shapes of houses contrasting with the organic forms of trees and clouds. Her recent work appears to be strongly influenced by the work of the English painter Ivor Abrahams (fig. 1).

152] David Watkins
Ring
Gold, amethyst, tourmaline, agates
1972

153] Barbara Cartlidge
Bracelet
Silver, gold; mobile
1973
Electrum Gallery, London
Photo: Cyril Wilson

154] Catherine Mannheim
Brooch
Silver, titanium, gold
5 cm (2 in)
1973
Collection: John Jesse, London
Photo: Angela Turner

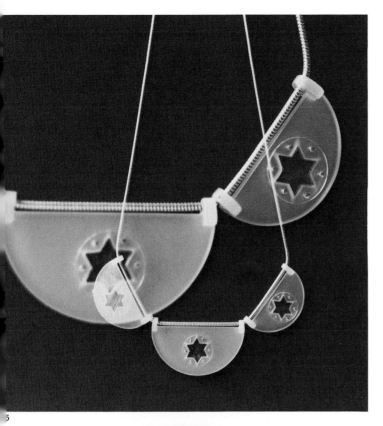

5] Gunilla Treen
cklace
rylic, silver and moss agate
73
oto: Ray Carpenter

6] Gunilla Treen
ooch
rylic and titanium; mobile
73
oto: Angela Turner

Wendy Ramshaw's husband, David Watkins, is both a sculptor and a jeweller. He was born in Wolverhampton in 1940 and studied sculpture at Reading University until 1963. Apart from his work as a sculptor, Watkins has been involved in various areas of popular music as a professional musician, record producer and composer. His interest in the entertainment world led him to work on special effects as model maker for Stanley Kubrik's film *2001*. In the early seventies his jewelry was concerned with space — in the terrestrial rather than astronomical sense — with white enamel surfaces interposed with clearly defined domed silver units. Since then Watkin's jewelry has advanced considerably. At the present time, he is more concerned with colour and form. Materials used are often acrylic, turned on the lathe, and dyed. Computer programmed drawings are sometimes used, as one would use any other tool, resulting in bracelets and necklaces that are quite exceptional.

In 1973 he and his wife held a joint exhibition at the Goldsmiths' Hall, London. As can be seen, their work is quite distinct from one another. At his best, Watkins's work allows the material full expression. His torques and bracelets are among the best acrylic work produced in England at the moment. A one-man exhibition at the Arnolfini Gallery in Bristol and the Crafts Advisory Committee's Waterloo Place Gallery in London in 1975 further confirmed his status as a major jeweller.

In an article in the *Guardian* in 1973 concerned with whether women equal men in intellectual and artistic creativity, Eva Figes argued with John Grigg that 'agreeable surprises await you, gentlemen, in all the arts'. Well, as far as jewelry is concerned, it has already happened. Historically jewelry-making has been a male preserve, but not any more, especially in Britain.

The British figurative artist, Gunilla Treen, is a case in point. She exhibited in the exhibition Figurative Jewelry in 1973. At that time many of her pieces were devoted to figurative themes, but evolved later into more abstract forms. In most cases there is an element of mobility in her work. One set of brooches in acrylic contain mobile units within each piece. The interesting thing about this set is that although each brooch was conceived quite separately, and it was her intention to split them up, when seen all together they form a composite whole and interrelate almost like a jigsaw.

For a time Miss Treen was engaged on a Design Research Fellowship with the Worshipful Company of Goldsmiths, and her constant search for new materials and techniques produced this fresh approach to the subject. Sometimes she will use a combination of materials, such as titanium, steel, acrylic, gold, silver and ivory, all in the one piece. Her inventive spirit allied to a delicate and feminine approach has brought a subtle freshness to creative jewelry in England.

157]

Susanna Heron was born in 1949, the daughter of the English paint[er] Patrick Heron. She started making jewelry in the mid-sixties under Breon O'Casey, but it was not until she left the Central School of A[rt] and Design in London in 1971 that she developed her own individu[al] style. An exhibition the following year showed her to be concerned with the use of coloured resins, from which she emerged a master [of] this difficult medium.

Her work fell into two categories: firstly, abstracted forms that some times related in style to hard edge painting, then, later, figurative elements began to appear. In both cases resin is fully exploited for i[ts] translucent qualities. The figurative style is used to record elements in nature and an early set of four earrings depicting the seasons of t[he] year partly illustrate this aspect of her work.

Susanna Heron, and her husband David Ward, who is also a painte[r] spend much of the year in Cornwall, and marine life figures in much of her recent work. Trawlers, fish and seabirds are beautifully record[ed] A set of hairpins made in 1972 fully illustrate her ability as a draugh[ts] man and by looking at her drawings one can see the importance sh[e] places on this activity. For her first London exhibition that year she created an important necklace. With a circle as the starting-point, a bouquet of flowers hangs within its silver circumference. Her work was, and still is, primarily concerned with colour, and relates more directly to painting than to sculpture.

In her most recent work the resins have undergone certain changes. The colours now merge into one another, creating a further sense o[f] movement, while the outer edges of the pieces take on the figurativ[e] outline. This technique is to be found in work made after 1973.

Not all the bouquets go to the ladies in Britain however. David Poston, David Courts and Colin Churchill, ex-students of Gerda Flöckinger, formed an experimental jewelry department at Hornsey College of Art in the sixties. There is a strong relationship between [a]ll these artists' work and that of their former teacher, but the strength [of] Gerda Flöckinger's teaching is such that while undoubtedly influenc[ed] by her teaching and work, they have been allowed to develop their own aesthetic. These three young jewellers, Poston in particular, share Gerda Flöckinger's rebellious spirit.

Poston has radical political beliefs, and he led a famous sit-in at Hornsey College of Art in 1968. They show in much of his work. Though, like many jewellers, he shares a love of gold, he chooses n[ot] to use it in his jewelry because of its associations with South Africa and apartheid. The tactile quality of jewelry is of considerable importance to him. The pieces he creates are often sensual and erot[ic] and, like another pupil of Gerda Flöckinger's, Charlotte de Syllas, he is happy when carving away at something. Poston's most exciting work sometimes results from the use of rather mundane materials

157] Susanna Heron
Necklace
Silver, resins
32 cm (12½ in)
1972
Private collection, London
Photo: Cyril Wilson

158] Susanna Heron
Necklace, 'Bird pulling worm'
Silver and resin, white and purple
1972
Collection: Stedelijk Museum, Amsterdam
Photo: Tim Street-Porter

159] Susanna Heron
Hairpins
Silver, resin
18 cm (7 in)
1972
Electrum Gallery, London
Photo: Cyril Wilson

such as cotton and string, with the occasional secretive bead slipped into the piece for the owner to discover. In fact, his jewelry has much similarity, perhaps unconsciously, with the weavings of Sheila Hicks. Other jewellers follow similar lines, such as Rita Schumauer and Louise Todd from America, and Sonja Hahn-Ekberg from Sweden, but Poston's work is by far the most refined and subtle.

Four ex-students of the Royal College of Art in London, Eric Spiller, Cameron Duff, Rosamund Conway and Roger Morris, further illustrate the diversity of style in British contemporary jewelry. Each of them are non-figurative and highly individualistic artists. Spiller 'constructs' his pieces — they often contain mobile parts in acrylic, steel or brass. Miss Conway uses mixed media of ivory, silver, ebony and tortoise-shell while Duff uses the traditional materials of silver and gold. Sometimes links with Art Deco appear, but his work is entirely contemporary in spirit.

Roger Morris, while still a student of the Central School of Art, worked in silver and gold with slices of agate. Since entering the Royal College of Art, and through his contact with Claus Bury, his work has changed considerably. Acrylic is now his principal medium. Morris has produced some of the most subtle acrylic jewelry made in this country and his work, like that of Susanna Heron, is essentially English in feeling — quiet and restrained, and given to understatement.

Several British jewellers have shown great interest in carving, including Caroline Broadhead and Susan Vadadi, as well as some of those mentioned above. Others have taken up the idea of movement. Brian Glassar and Jeremy Ross have produced kinetic work, while David Taylor's work relies upon the wearer's movements to effect change in his pieces. But although there are certain recurring pre-occupations in British jewelry, there is no homogeneity of style. Work such as that discussed rubs shoulders with the wrapped objects of Czech-born Karel Bartosik, who has produced rings and cufflinks 'packaged' in silver and gold, complete with gold string and labels.

Pop Art

Of all the various styles and movements in painting during the past decade or so, none can claim as great an influence on contemporary jewelry as Pop Art. Its influence can be seen in one form or another in much of the work illustrated here, but more on the European than the American, although the principal artists of the movement are American.

In Britain Pop's main exponents are Mike Milligan and John Plenderleith. Most of Plenderleith's work is Pop-inspired, in particular his shiny and glittering 'Toothbrush and Paste'. He has made rings in the form of a cup and saucer, a television set, with inserted screen revealing a stripper in action, aeroplanes, cars, an acrylic egg in a silver

158

159

160

160] Colin Churchill
Pendant
Silver, engraved
6·5 cm (2½ in)
1973

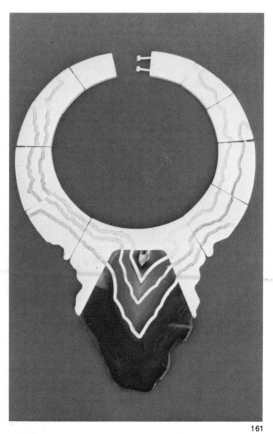

161

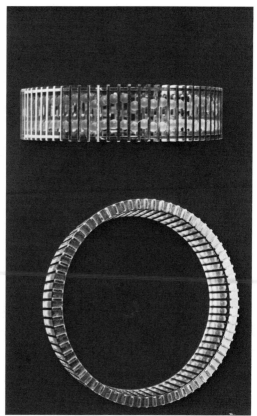

162

1

164

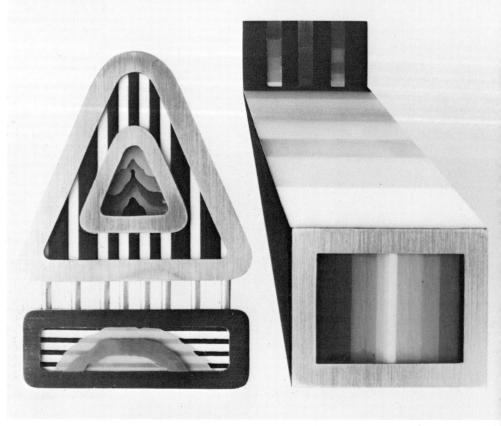

1

161] Roger Morris
Necklace
Silver, agate
25 cm (10 in)
1973

162] Eric Spiller
Bracelets
Rhodium-plated brass,
   glass ball bearings
Mobile
8·5 cm (3⅜ in)
1972
Photo: Eric Smith

163] Roger Morris
Brooch
Acrylic, steel, gold
5 cm (2 in)
1973
Private collection, London
Photo: Ray Carpenter

164] Brian Glassar
Bracelet
Silver, resin; mobile
9·5 cm (3¾ in)
1972
Electrum Gallery, London
Photo: Angela Turner

165] Roger Morris
Brooches
Acrylic, steel, gold
1973
Electrum Gallery, London

166] Susan Vadadi
Pendant, 'Gas Mask'
Oxidized silver, gold, carved ivory, moonstones
23 cm (9 in)
1972
Collection: John Jesse, London
Photo: Ray Carpenter

167] John Plenderleith
Two wedding rings, 'Plug and Socket'
Silver
1972
Private collection

168] David Poston
Necklace
Ivory, string silver and lapis lazuli
12 cm (5 in)
1973
Photo: Ray Carpenter

166

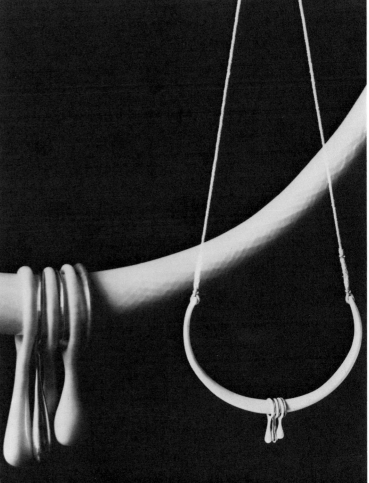

167

168

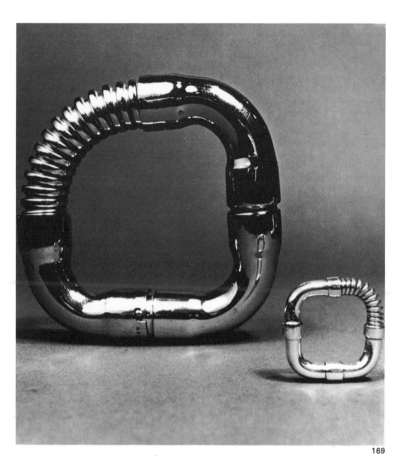

169

1

171

1

173

169] Marion Herbst
Bracelet and ring
Chromium-plated copper
18 cm/3 cm (7⅛/1¼ in)
1971
Galerie Sierraad, Amsterdam
Photo: Hans Hoogland

170] Emile Souply
Pendant, 'Mercedes'
Acrylic and gold
13 cm (5 in)
1973
Photo: Emile Souply

171] Marion Herbst
Brooch
Silver, acrylic
7·5 cm (3 in)
1972

172] Marion Herbst
Sculpture
Polyester resin, acrylic, aluminium
2·70 m × 1·30 m × 60 cm (8 ft 10 in × 4 ft 3 in × 2 ft)
1972
Photo: Hans Hoogland

173] Melanie Oudemans
Bracelet
Aluminium, acrylic
1972
Galerie Sierraad, Amsterdam

frying pan — all these perfectly scaled to the hand. Unlike many other jewellers inspired by the Pop cult Plenderleith has learned one of the most difficult and fundamental rules that apply to any art — when to stop.

Mike Milligan is rather more fashion-orientated, but no less a product of the movement. His 'Fairy' pendant is in its way also a homage to Art Nouveau, and in particular to its master, Lalique. Both these artists are now concerned with the commercial aspect of jewelry, and have not sufficient time to devote their energies to creating such important pieces. Nonetheless, their ideals are more often than not carried into this realm, and the fashion world reaps the benefit of their talents.

Holland

The Pop Cult penetrated European jewelry in a less obvious manner than in England, as can be seen from the recent work of Emile Souply in Belgium, and Karel Niehorster and Marion Herbst in Holland. The latter is deeply concerned with communicating her ideas and the fact that the vast majority of people do not understand what she is trying to say in her work has prompted her to use everyday objects and materials in the hope that her message will thus become more accessible to the public. Shower tubing, covered in chromium plated copper, has been used to form imaginative bracelets; imitation diamonds in paste are scattered inside a sardine tin. With the help of her friends and her sculptor husband, Berend Peter, she has also made two short films. The first records the making of 'The Big Ring' — a project in which one of her rings was enlarged until it stood twelve feet high.

The Dutch have been at the forefront of the art of jewelry since the 1940s. The advanced work of Emmy van Leersum and Gijs Bakker in the sixties brought about a change of direction in creative work in that country, becoming increasingly intellectual in its content. In the 1970s they took their exploration of new techniques to extreme limits with invisible jewelry. Emmy van Leersum used the transparent qualities of clear acrylic in bracelets that related closely to her earlier work, while her husband, Gijs Bakker, began in the early seventies to use the perishable material of wood. In 1973 he produced 'shadow' jewelry. By placing a thin wire band tightly around the arm, the bulging flesh became the 'jewelry' which in turn disappeared when the wire was removed leaving an imprint on the body. Since 1966, both he and his wife have tried to draw our attention to the human body. Their jewelry was never intended to decorate, but rather to emphasize the anatomy of the wearer through its relation to the jewelry (figs. 374–8).

There are now so many artists in Holland that follow Leersum and Bakker that it is impossible to record all their activities here, but we shall look briefly at some of the notable contributors associated with the Galerie Sierraad in Amsterdam, which was opened by Hans

174

175

Appenzeller and Lous Martin in 1969. Here Appenzeller talks of their attitude to the subject:

The work of many Dutch jewelry designers is based on some general principles which are both formal and ideal. The form of the piece is of primary importance: the form may be developed more or less independently from the body or may be based on a close relationship with it. Generally a solution is sought which combines a satisfactory form with the best advantage of wearing the object, without violating the essential qualities of the form.

The designs are characterized by their simplicity; they are based on geometric principles or are made with reference to the part of the body on which they will be worn. Clarity of form and construction are always stressed.

The material used for a certain design is chosen for its specific properties. Besides traditional materials such as gold and silver more unusual materials are applied, such as stainless steel, perspex, aluminium, German silver, iron, wood, furs and rubber.

Precious metals are used only if inherent to a particular design. As a result of all this, the designers are able to produce their jewelry in larger editions, which is the policy of most of the designers exhibiting in Galerie Sierraad. Most jewelry is made in limited editions of a maximum of twenty pieces (when more are made the state subsidy expires).

Within these general principles, the gallery's contributors have achieved great diversity of style. Bruno Ninaber's jewelry explores the tensions that can be brought about between different materials. Jan Templeman uses a variety of materials including ivory, which he might combine with silver, often using the dotted line as a form of focal point. In some ways Templeman's work could be considered the most decorative of this group. In recent work these lines have been combined with smears of gold, reminiscent of paint strokes. Melanie Oudemans has produced a series of individual parts of bracelets and necklaces that can be rearranged when connected either together or in layers. The same basic element is available in different lengths. The four different elements of her necklaces can be rearranged into two single-layered or one double-layered bracelet. Dick Wessels is primarily concerned with the colour and transparent qualities of acrylic. Colour, when used is treated simply, in bands rather like 'hard edge' painting. While his work when concerned with the transparent quality of this material relates to Op Art, more recent work follows the more American approach of 'found' objects.

Frans van Nieuwenborg exploits the elasticity of rubber in geometric forms, and uses chromium and aluminium in many pieces. Harriet Mastboom combines acrylic and silver in bracelets that again exploit

174] Françoise van den Bosch
Bracelet
Aluminium
1971
Galerie Sierraad, Amsterdam
Photo: Robert Schlingemann

175] Lous Martin
Bracelets
Chromium-plated copper
1971
Galerie Sierraad, Amsterdam
Photo: Gijsbert Hanekroot

176] Hans Appenzeller
Bracelet
Aluminium, rubber
1972
Galerie Sierraad, Amsterdam

177] Hans Appenzeller
Bracelet
Rubber, aluminium
1972
Galerie Sierraad, Amsterdam

the translucency of acrylic.

The directors of the gallery are also jewellers. Lous Martin produces chromium-plated jewelry primarily based on the form of a tube. By cutting away sections, he draws our attention to the inner parts of the metal, often by opposing basic forms such as the square and circle. His co-director, Hans Appenzeller, has in recent years completed a series of bracelets whose forms derive from the basic problem of holding the bracelet onto the wrist.

I started from the basic facts; the form of the part of the body on which the piece is to be worn and a tube as an abstraction of this form, which had to be combined. A tube which is worn on the arm without means of opening has to be big enough to be put over the hand. This creates a discrepancy between the tube and the arm. To eliminate this I have added an element to the form. However, I have always tried to make this element an essential part of the form which gripped around the tube and also held the bracelet to the arm. In this way it adapts the unalterable size of the tube to the size of the arm. The elasticity of the rubber enables the tube to be put over the hand.

Holland, as we have seen, is to a large extent dominated by jewellers who explore and research the possibilities of simplified forms — a refreshing parallel to those Dutch artists, sculptors and painters who explore minimal and conceptual art.

Spain

In complete contrast to the simplified forms of Dutch jewelry, much of the work to come out of Spain in recent years relies upon complex relationships and tensions. Joaquim Capdevila's recent work with volume and the painted surface of metal combines tension between metals and the use of the wavy line in opposition to angular structures.

Montserrat Guardiola at her best illustrates the voluptuous spirit that can be achieved with silver. Polished surfaces are made to contrast with silver touched by frost. In some cases her pieces look as if they have been segmented from a larger structure. Another Spanish jeweller of interest is Juli Guasch, who was one of the first to seriously explore the use of acrylic in jewelry. He is a prolific artist, and since those early experiments has in recent years turned his attention to scale and proportion within sculptural jewelry. The work of Sergi Aguilar has been mentioned briefly; he is an artist who has successfully combined the roles of sculptor and jeweller, as Martinazzi has done. His sculpture has similarities with the two English artists, Phillip King and William Tucker. His jewelry, however, is very much his own and his metal constructs are among the most interesting work created in jewelry today. Plates of metal are hinged or bolted together with precision. The outer edge cut sometimes with

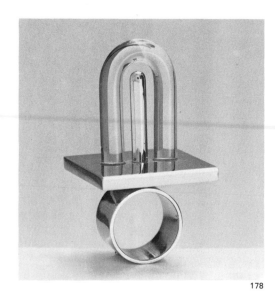

178

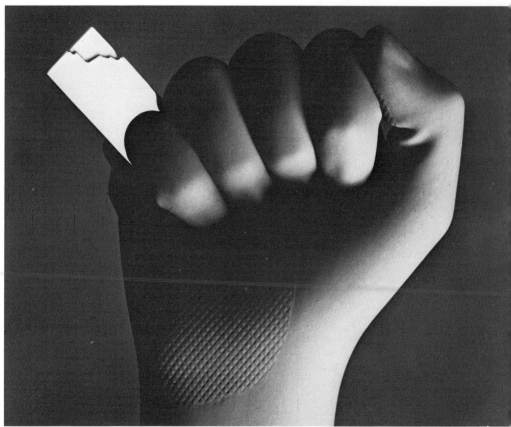

17

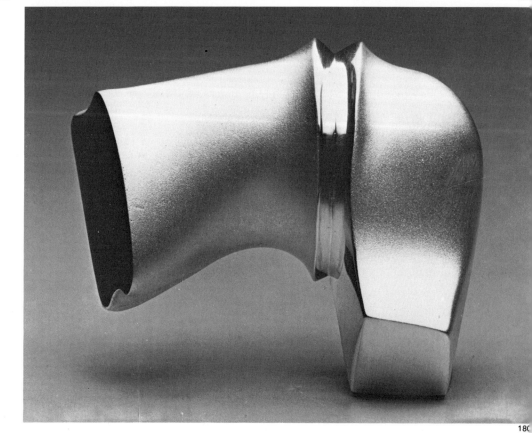

18(

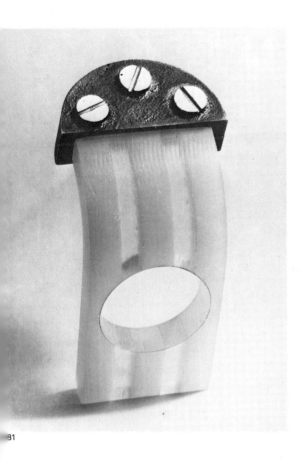

irregular lines contrasts with the overall geometric form of the pieces. These plates can be opened up thus extending the brooch. In probably his most subtle piece to date, 'Cop', Aguilar gives the feeling of the weight and strength of a blow. One moment is captured in this piece — the split second in which a rod hits a bar, bending it under the impact (fig. 294).

In 1972 Aguilar, Capdevila, Guardiola and Guasch, all from Barcelona, created a collection of jewelry from a study of six basic forms, each artist arriving at his or her own conclusions. This collective experiment resulted in 'an exciting game testing the results of the different variations obtained from a single shape, when interpreted by four distinctive personal standpoints'. This idea is not in itself new, for such experiments are common practice in teaching students, but it was an exceptional experiment for four such mature artists to undertake.

Austria and Switzerland

Advanced creative jewelry in Austria and Switzerland is not as prolific as in Germany, but nevertheless both countries have produced some figures of stature.

On first impression the work of the Austrians Waltrud Viehböck and Peter Skubic appears to be dissimilar, but closer inspection reveals that they are both interested in the relationship that exists between chosen units or forms in opposition to one another. For example, in a ring by Skubic made in 1970 two towers of metal rise from the shank, one holds a domed black coral the other a pearl. Three years later, he used the same basic ingredients with entirely different results. The brooch made of white and yellow gold depicts what looks like the foot of a bedstead. Again two circular units dominate the piece. Viehböck, on the other hand, offers another interpretation of this relationship. A bracelet made in 1973 depicts two large tubes placed across the plain armband and incorporating mobile units. A necklace made the same year uses a similar idea.

One major talent working in Austria at the moment whose work has already been mentioned but deserves closer attention is Fritz Maierhofer. Born in Vienna in 1941 he trained initially as a watchmaker and then studied jewelry. He came to London and worked in the workshop of Andrew Grima, where he met Claus Bury.

Both artists at that time found they shared a mutual interest in exploring ideas outside the field of jewelry. This relationship was further developed when they both discovered a liking for acrylic. Bury had been working with this material since 1969 and so Maierhofer's interest in the younger man's work became a driving force, stimulating ideas that had until then not been formed.

81

78] Juli Guasch
ring
silver, acrylic
1970
Collection: C.A.S.S.A. Gallery, Milan

79] Juli Guasch
ring
silver, ivory
1971
Collection: Museum of Modern Art, Madrid

80] Montserrat Guardiola
brooch
silver
cm (2¾ in)
1973

81] Fritz Maierhofer
ring
silver, acrylic
5 cm (1¾ in)
limited edition of 30
1971

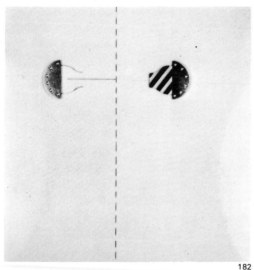

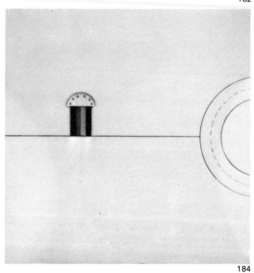
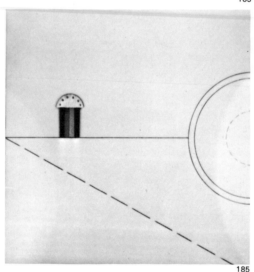
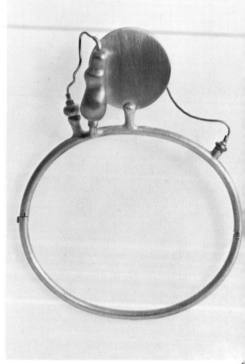

182

183

184

185

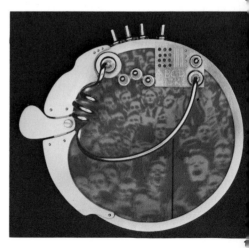

182–185] Fritz Maierhofer
Brooches
Silver, acrylic
9 cm (3½ in)
Limited edition of 30
1972

186] Otto Künzli
Brooch
Silver, gold
5·5 cm (2¼ in)
1973

187] Otto Künzli
Bracelet
Silver, gold
9·5 cm (3¾ in)
1973

188] Piet Van den Boom
Brooch
Silver, photo linen
6 cm (2⅜ in)
1973

189

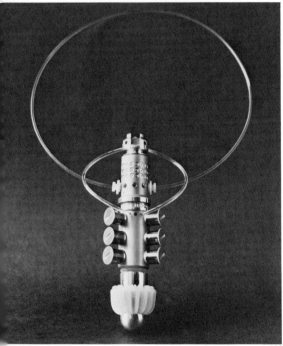

190

In 1970 his work was often given over entirely to acrylic, and, like Bury's, it had few traces of the goldsmith's traditional materials. This can be seen in the circular brooch made up of variable mobile elements — a principle used by Becker in his hexagonal and circular pieces in 1962–3, but with totally different results.

A year later he created the first mounts or frames for his work. These usually took the form of plaques which held the jewelry. His concern with these was to produce pieces which could be detached from wall ornaments, leaving related pieces behind and creating a spacial relationship between the wearer and the jeweller.

Maierhofer combines the traditional materials of gold and silver with acrylic in pieces that draw attention to their construction — a revolutionary act when one considers that goldsmiths tend to be secretive about their techniques and hide all signs of soldering and labour in the end product. His rings, bracelets, pendants, and brooches are made from laminated acrylic sandwiched between silver or gold. The screws, often an integral part of the construction, were given maximum space and used as focal points. Like his contemporaries, Bury and Rothmann, Maierhofer's work is very colourful. He also has produced some excellent multiples or editions, as with a series of rings made in silver and acrylic in 1971, followed by a similar edition of pendants and brooches. In 1972 he shared the prize at the International Jewelry Competition in the Schmuckmuseum, Pforzheim, with Bury, Martinazzi and Waltrud Rees.

Since 1973, like Bury and Rothmann, he has returned to the use of traditional alloys, but retains a closer interest in acrylic than do his friends. All of the early fundamental principles peculiar to this artist's work have been retained; colour, confrontation, tension and clarity.

Otto Künzli is amongst the leading Swiss jewellers. Born in Zurich in 1948 he studied at the School of Art and Craft in his home town, and continued his studies at the Academy of Art in Munich under Professor Hermann Jünger. Like many young artists he has not yet established a clear style. Bracelets and rings often depict visual connecting elements, such as may be found in electronic or radio apparatus, while his brooches refer to a more figurative, geometric formality as in elliptical pieces illustrating elements such as rain and clouds. But like his teacher's, Künzli's work is refined and subtle.

The Swiss Pierre Degen now lives in London, and his recent work is concerned with technology. Radio and computer parts are assembled in a manner both inventive and spirited. In 1972 he produced a collection of 'throw-away' jewelry. The work was intended to attract the interest of the general public and to show that jewelry can be both creative, fun and inexpensive. This series was produced in limited numbers from acrylic foil. The following year Degen was awarded a prize in the De Beers International Award 1973.

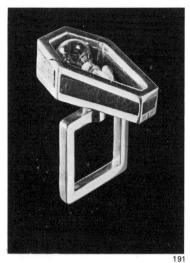

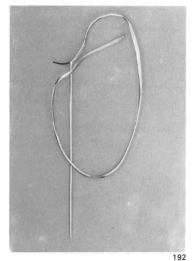

191

192

193

194

Reto Keppler of Zurich can be compared to the Dutchman Ruudt Peters. Both artists are extremely prolific, and are in some ways rath 'obvious' jewellers. They share an interest in death and decay, as wi Keppler's coffin ring, 'The End', made from silver and wood with an electric light bulb depicting the corpse, and again with the ring 'Berlin Wall'. Peters has also produced a collection of objects and brooches with funereal associations, using graves and tombstones.

Italy

The creative jeweller in Italy is at the moment rather elusive. Exceptional jewelry artists such as Martinazzi, the Pomodoro brothe Pinton and Frühauf are all actively continuing their work but with th exception of Franca Grilli and Francesco Pavan younger talents hav not as yet shown themselves. Franca Grilli has created some poetic pieces somewhat similar to Calder's work, but with more delicacy a a greater feeling of weightlessness. A subtle use of space in this wo is its principal attribute. Francesco Pavan is concerned with similar ideas, but for quite different results, producing work related to constructional and optical elements.

Germany

There are now so many creative jewellers in Germany that it would impossible to include even a fair proportion here, so those whose work is most original, as well as those who produce the highest quality, have been selected.

Bernd Swegebrecht's voluptuous work relates to industrial landscap such as oil refineries, or possibly the world of science fiction. This artist is consistent in exploring these ideas within the limits of jewel but the validity of the work has been questioned as it could relate ir purely sculptural terms. Heinz Breuker's jewelry is also concerned with optical illusion and, like Gerd Rothmann, he produces multiple

Lutz Quambusch produces pieces of even greater complexity: 'I wa to form structures as complex as possible in a space as tight as possible – to create centres of high energy. I engineer mobile, multi-membered, unscrewable, cave bearing and multi-fingered objects – the extreme expression of well conceived, rational uselessness – the refinement of perfect absurdity.' With these beliefs the artist's work results in pieces just as explicit. Multi-fingered rings crawl across th hand like a rocky mountain range.

One of the most interesting young figurative jewellers in Germany is Norbert Mürrle. Born in Pforzheim in 1948 he studied there and in a relatively short space of time gained his master's degree at the colleg in Pforzheim. Much like Skal, Mürrle uses a recurring theme in much of his work. Cows are depicted entering or leaving a landscape, perfectly proportioned and precisely placed into brooches or rings. Like other contributors to this book he also works on a larger scale, and his proficiency as a painter further illustrates his diverse and

191] Reto Keppler
Ring, 'Coffin Ring'
Silver, wood, glass, gold
1973

192] Franca Grilli
Brooch
Gold
11·5 cm (4½ in)
1973
Photo: Giuliano Gameliel

193] Bernd Swegebrecht
Brooch
Silver, acrylic
9·5 cm (3¾ in)
1972
Photo: Johannes Schmidt

194] Heinz Breuker
Ring
Steel, acrylic
1971

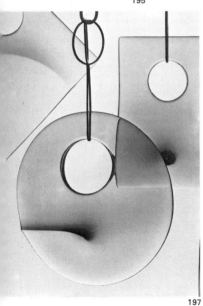

95] Cornelia Rating
rooch
ilver, acrylic
972
ollection: Schmuckmuseum, Pforzheim
hoto: Günter Meyer

96] Christoph Rose
racelet; intended for the blind
teel, silver
973

97] Svatopluk Kasaly
endants
lass
971
hoto: Jiří Erml

98] Laděna Víznerová
racelet
ilver, glass
972
hoto: Taras Kuscynskyj

many-faceted interests and talents.

A new approach to jewelry has been developed by Christoph Rose, through making jewelry for the blind. In the Tendenzen '73 exhibition in the Schmuckmuseum, Pforzheim, Rose exhibited a series of such pieces. The reaction was mixed. The obvious question arose as to whether it was possible for a jeweller who had the use of his sight to make jewelry for those without sight. This artist had for some time been very aware of the tactile quality of jewelry, and maintains that his own sense of touch is highly developed. He has started to do many things with his eyes closed.

> This blindness was under control, just by closing my eyes, I need not have the advice of a blind person, I could experience it myself. Blindness is a handicap in the world of those that see. If the ones who see, adjust, it is always an act. So it is clear to me that not the slightest regard had to be taken to people who can see these jewels. My wife and I performed a series of tests. She collected various objects, some of them I hadn't had in my hands for years. I had to identify them blindfolded. The stunning result was I identified them all with no mistake within seconds. We repeated that test several times with different objects so the conclusion was that we retain an excellent memory by touching, without training.

Similar tests were carried out with various materials that projected feelings of sympathy or aversion. While talking about Christoph Rose's experiments in Germany, the English jeweller David Poston remarked how Rose's work cast critical light on jewelry-making: 'We are all making things for blind people . . .' whether literally or not.

Eastern Europe
While no progressive jewelry has come out of the Soviet Union, other East European countries contrive to produce work to rank with the West. In Czechoslovakia Laděna Víznerová and Svatopluk Kasaly have produced exceptional pieces in glass. Laděna Víznerová's work has developed slowly. She is essentially concerned with the inner qualities that can be brought to play in this medium; air bubbles and organic fantasies figure largely in her poetic work. In early pieces in the sixties metals were inserted into the glass, but in more recent work, it is the glass itself that is the governing element. 'Glass being my great love, I could go on praising it for ever.'

While Víznerová appears to be primarily concerned with what is happening within the glass, her contemporary Svatopluk Kasaly is more interested in pure form and the reflecting power of this medium. Like Víznerová, he has been experimenting with glass since the sixties. He renounces the purely decorative use of jewelry, and would probably agree with Leersum's and Bakker's concept of the subject, as their work is similar in many respects. Nothing is elaborate or decorative, his ideas are clear and concise. Forms created in glass or

199

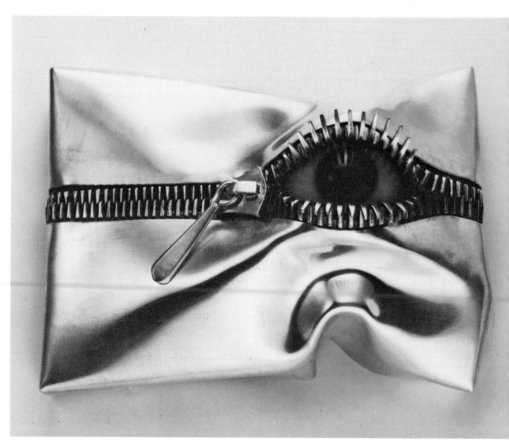

200

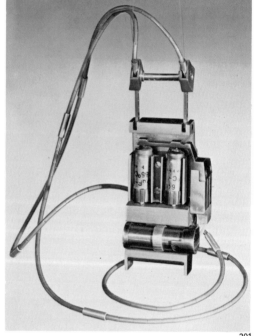

201

202

203

4

silver relate to the human form and are sensual and warm, exploiting the tactile quality of the materials. Kasaly's work is often rhythmic, as if the glass had been caught while still in its molten state, and, like a bubble, one almost expects it to disappear.

Scandinavia

The Scandinavian countries have been less active in this surge of creativity in this decade. Much of the work concerns itself with achievements that were made in Finland, Sweden, Denmark and Norway in the fifties and sixties. The influence of Persson, Jensen, Ditzel, Gardberg and their contemporaries is still to be felt in these countries. There are exceptions, such as Christian Gaudernack from Norway, who like many studied at Pforzheim, and the influence of the college can still be traced in some of his work. Poul Havgaard from Denmark in some ways follows the American attitude to the subject. Cast iron breast pendants and buckles combine with heavy leather in many of his pieces. He, like Bjørn Weckstrøm, creates designs for the firm Lapponia Jewelry in Helsinki, often in large editions. Weckstrøm has produced some good design for this firm and through it reached a wide audience, much the same as Georg Jensen did in the 1950s. Flemming Hertz, another Dane, explores the idea of edible jewelry with rings that contain caramel and sugar, with throw-away acrylic bands, while Sonja Hahn-Ekberg's principal medium is thread.

These experiments result in work reminiscent of the radical spirit found in diploma shows, but sometimes the concepts are rather sparse. Gaudernack, however, is worthy of further consideration. Although much of his work reflects developments in Germany, he maintains an original approach and, with the possible exception of Per Arne Lundahl Terrs from Sweden, he is one of the few young progressive jewellers in Scandinavia.

France

As in Scandinavia, the advances made in early twentieth-century jewelry in France have not been carried on to the present day, largely owing to the lack of good jewelry departments in French colleges. There are, however, some jewellers of note, the most prominent being Joel Degen, Paloma Picasso, Bernard François and Henri Gargat.

Henri Gargat learned his basic technique as an apprentice in a jewelry firm in Lyon. His work now is primarily concerned with mobility. He has produced multiples, using aluminium and mercury in a ring that uses both these materials to advantage. 'La Bague Geminée', a double ring, to be worn on two fingers at once, is topped with a ballbearing in a groove that slides effortlessly back and forth. Joel Degen, a Frenchman now living in London, has for some time produced work of interest. His recent work involves the assembly of radio and computer parts, often resulting in some excellent jewelry. Paloma Picasso, daughter of the artist, produces highly individualistic

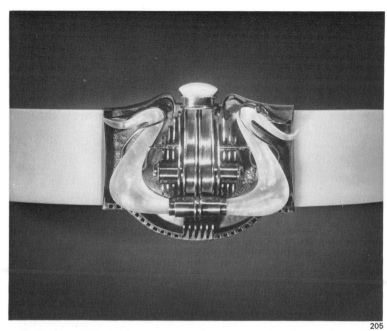

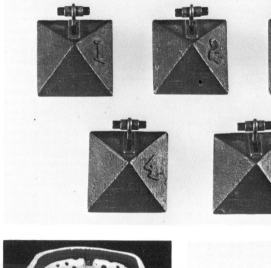

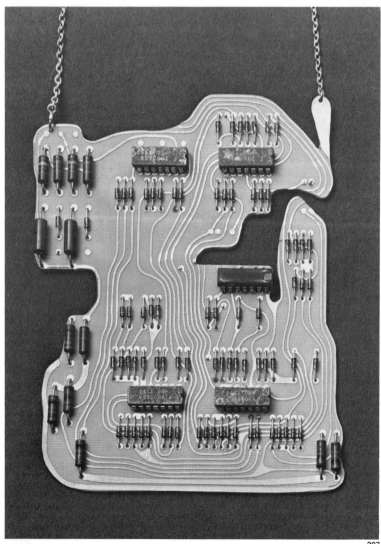

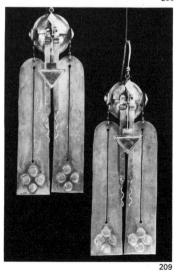

205

207

208

209

11

work which owes little to other recent developments: 'The design of my jewelry is usually based on naturalistic subject, and the actual forms are not at first sight apparent. I use the abstract shape of these natural forms regardless of their meaning.'

The United States

One of the major difficulties in studying the work of modern jewellers is that their styles frequently lack continuity — particularly in Canada and England, but less so in Europe. Ideas are often quickly recorded, without thorough exploration, then on to the next idea, consequently there is no relationship between one piece and another. If this applied to the work of individual artists, it applies even more to an overall view. The problem is particularly acute in the USA. Of the many hundred creative jewellers in the USA today it is only possible to give a brief assessment of the more notable achievements.

Fred Woell continues to produce jewelry, Lynda Watson environmental work, such as an aerial-view necklace. Lechtzin, Fisch, Paley, Prip, Ebendorf, and others, have all extended their experiments since the sixties. Carolin Kriegman makes large-scale body ornaments, Gerry Evans and Barbara Ellen Brodsky body ornaments made out of a mixture of different elements. Richard Barth experiments with electronic and computer parts. The list of different styles grows with almost each artist.

Noma Copley is one of the chief contemporary exponents of Pop Art in jewelry, where continuity can be seen. In an introduction to her exhibition at the David Stuart Galleries in Los Angeles in 1973, Marcia Tucker wrote: 'Her pieces are visual and physical transformations of function, material and scale: conceptually they relate to Dada and the Surrealist tradition . . . in this exhibition of "notions" the simplest utilitarian items become truly witty sculptures, worn so that they seem to function in reverse: a gold spool of thread encircles the finger; a zipper-ring parodies the zipper's real use, tiny buttons seem to hold the human earlobe together.'

Peter Blodgett and Ed Samuels have been influenced by European jewelry, Blodgett from a trip he made to Europe in 1973. Samuels makes mainly erotic pieces, which in recent years have shown a debt to Martinazzi, although this is now less so. Samuels is at his best when depicting miniature scenes of sexual pleasure on belt buckles or brooches.

No greater example of American diversity could be found than that between the traditional, cloisonné enamelled work of Robert Kulicke and Jean Stark and that of Barry Merritt and Mary Ann Scherr. Whereas Kulicke's and Stork's work is medieval in style, Mary Scherr is concerned with the functional possibilities of jewelry and has created belts and bracelets that contain crystals to detect air pollution and necklaces that monitor the wearer's heart beat. Working with an

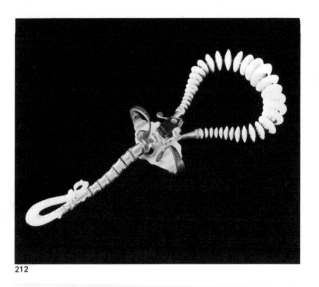

212

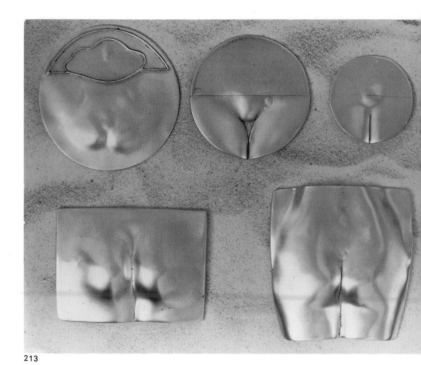

213

212] Albert Paley
Pendant
Silver, gold, bronze, cameo, pearls and resin
45 cm (17¾ in)
1972–3
Photo: Roger Smith

213] Ed Samuels
Erotic jewelry
Silver
1971

214] Richard Mawdsley
Pendant, 'The Pequod'
Silver, green agates
12·5 cm (4⅞ in)
1972–3

215] Ken Cory – Les le Pere
Brooches
Alphabet series
Gold, copper, enamel
5·5 cm (2¼ in)
1973
Photo: Larry Bullis

214

215

216

electronics specialist and chemistry professors, Miss Scherr has designed a silver box to wear as a pendant that warns of contaminated air, fully equipped with oxygen face mask. The device blinks whenever sulphur dioxide in the air reaches an irregular level: Barry Merritt, on the other hand, produced work around 1970 which was very closely related to Pop Art and was influenced by Fred Woell. Now Merritt's principal concern is with the torso itself, as opposed to ways of placing objects on specific parts of it. Three major pieces made in 1972–3, now collector's pieces, illustrate this new departure: 'Bullet Woman', 'Wonder Woman' and 'Deco Queen'. 'Bullet Woman' is perhaps reminiscent of the fantasies conjured up by Ian Fleming in his James Bond novels. Merritt envisages eventually covering the entire body, adding or taking away pure jewelry as the wearer sees fit. His work is both original and stimulating.

Another artist who has avoided the conventional is Ken Cory. Born in Washington in 1943 he studied at the California College of Art and Washington State University. Even as a student, his jewelry tended to react against traditional aspects of the subject, and in 1968 his work often contained materials that in themselves indicated this revolt. Leather and stone were used in a brooch that literally poked its tongue at us, leaving little doubt as to the artist's intentions. In the early seventies Cory continued his exploration of new materials and techniques, but now includes the traditional alloys. Trying to ignore the monetary value of materials, he sees no reason why a diamond should not be set in plastic. Unlike many, Cory is concerned with the functional problems of jewelry. His work is often relatively small in scale, and he considers weight and even safety to be important considerations when making any piece.

In 1973 Cory produced a collection of enamel brooches based on the alphabet, strongly influenced by Pop Art. At his best, Cory explores whatever material he uses to the full. His ideas are fresh, explicit and consistent.

Japan

Any new style or movement in art tends to spread itself eventually to the four corners of the earth. In painting, for example, a style that was contemporary in New York in the 1950s would have been taken on in Cuba, India, or Kenya, ten years after the wave had broken in Europe or the USA. This also happens in jewelry. For example, in the Triennale '73 International Jewelry Arts Exhibition in Tokyo European work could be seen to have had a great influence on the Japanese. It seems a great pity that the native Japanese jewellers did not draw on their own rich cultural background for inspiration. Japan has for hundreds of years been far more aware of good design than the western world, in ceramics, furniture and architecture. Jewelry to them is a relatively new experience, their rich and elaborate kimonos being sufficient adornment. Sadly Western influence has taken over, and the Japanese market is buzzing with activity in the commercial field. However,

217

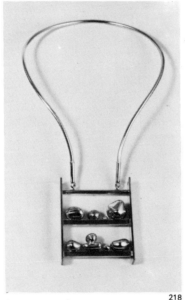

218

16] Yasuki Hiramatsu
Ring
White gold
·5 cm (2½ in)
. 1973

17] Yoko Urashima
Brooch
Silver
cm (3½ in)
1973

18] Hajime Kimata
Pendant
Silver
cm (2¾ in)
1973

19] Hirosh Iguchi
Brooch
Aluminium
cm (2¾ in)
1973

219

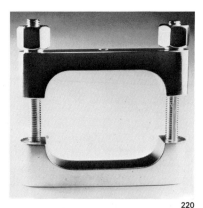

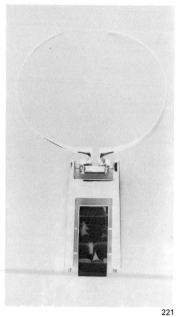

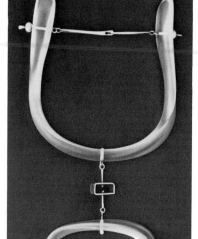

Yasuki Hiramatsu, Hajime Kimata, Yoko Urashima, Hiroshi Iguchi and Yasuhiko Hishida are five artists who create work that is entirely related to the world we live in, and yet retains Japanese cultural influences. To Western eyes it has that fine, pure and restrained feeling reminiscent of Japanese interiors.

Australia, South Africa and Canada

Australia continues to lose many fine jewellers, a 1970 emigrant being John Stokes who produced uncut crystals mounted in architectural formation. His achievements are quite remarkable, given the way crystals have been over-used by unimaginative jewellers.

In contrast, Rodney Matthews and Frank Bauer work with man-made materials — resin and acrylic. Rodney Matthews has made a series of pendants and rings with interchangeable resin panels. Bauer, who was born and trained in Germany but who now lives in Sydney, uses mundane objects as a basis for his ideas, chiefly acrylic and steel. Nuts, bolts and screws dominate his recent production. The tension and pressures brought about by these engineering components are an obvious challenge to him. Locking devices and the tension and elastic qualities of metal springs go into some of his pieces, sometimes reminiscent of Tinguely's sculptures.

A group of four artists emerged in Victoria in 1972, dedicated to elevating the status of jewelry in Australia; they were Norman Creighton, Marian Hosking, Rex Keogh, and their teacher Wolf Wennrich. What holds them together is a shared reaction against the mediocrity of mass-produced goods and a belief in the value of fellowship amongst artists.

Since that time the Group has exhibited widely in Australia, producing work in a variety of materials that include acrylic, steel and traditional alloys. Like Bury, Maierhofer and Rothmann, their work questions wearability and function.

Even South Africa, with its gold and diamonds, has seen experimental work in other materials. Günter Schmitz has been making jewelry since the mid-fifties when much of his work was rather typical of the period. Recently, however, he has made a series of acrylic pieces in the European style.

Dieter Dill studied at the College in Pforzheim. His work has all the qualities attributed to that famous school and displays the influence of Reiling and Ullrich. Dill finds himself in a lonely position in South Africa where his combination of traditional and unorthodox materials has little recognition, but says he is optimistic and looks to the future when he hopes the public will become less conservative.

Perhaps the most creative jeweller from South Africa is Eberhard Dechow. He has also studied in Pforzheim but since then has

220] Frank Bauer
Bracelet
Silver—adjustable
7·5 cm (3 in)
1973

221] Rod Matthews
Pendant; interchangeable panels
Silver, resin
1973

222] Frida Blumenberg
Necklace
Acrylic, gold, silver, Pre-Columbian beads
30 cm (11¾ in)
1973

223] Helge Larsen and Darani Lewers
Pendant
Silver, acrylic, postage stamp, leather
6 cm (2⅜ in)
1973

developed his own direction, owing little to any other artist. Working primarily in silver and acrylic his work in the late sixties was predominantly concerned with light. Acrylic is selected for its translucent quality and not colour. He places or rivets white or transparent sheet on to the surface of silver in forms which create their own colour.

Frida Blumenberg was born in South Africa in 1935. She has travelled extensively and lived in London for a while in the mid-sixties. Her work then was bold, firm and masculine, the forms decisive and sensual. Now living in America, she too has introduced acrylic into her work. The new material is used in much the same bold and primitive manner as she uses silver, but with the transparency of the medium adding a new dimension. Like Miss Blumenberg, Marion Menzies has this inner strength in her best work. Round and bulbous ambers are used with copper and brass which combined with silver and just the right amount of African influence is seen to make her work peculiar to that country.

Canadian jewelry, like that of Australia and South Africa, has to a large extent been neglected, as much Canadian work reflects what goes on in the USA. A notable exception, Harold O'Connor, does original work that owes little to other American artists. His real roots are German, as he studied under Professor Reinhold Reiling in Pforzheim. As with so many of Reiling's students his influence is very apparent, but during the past few years O'Connor's style has changed from the rather organic structures typical of so many products of the school of Pforzheim to much more simplified forms.

As we have seen, figurative jewelry has been a dominating style in the early seventies in England, and with little doubt, few have the ability to inject such warmth and sincerity into their work as the Canadian artist, Geli Lukin Johnston, who used to live in London. Often her work takes the form of room settings or interiors. Changes of scene can be brought about with interchangeable plaques slotted into the outside frame. For example, in one pendant depicting a room setting, a tiny painting hangs above the mantelshelf. The painting can be removed and another substituted, or the space can be left free, taking our eye into another dimension. Engraving is an important part of her work. Unlike many who use this technique Miss Johnston allows the medium to be free, not dominating the overall concept. Modestly she writes:

My work is very personal. Each piece has a particular meaning for me which, I hope, is conveyed to the eventual owner. The designs are derived from favourite objects, remembered experiences and observations. But it is also very important to me that I carry out all the construction of the finished piece. I would much rather do my own, technically imperfect engraving than send the piece to another engraver.

24] Frida Blumenberg
necklace
silver
1962
photo: de la Porte, Johannesburg

225] Dieter Dill
necklace
silver, acrylic
0 cm (7⅞ in)
1972

101

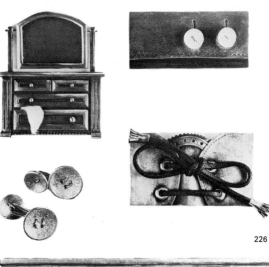

The technical imperfections she refers to are in fact where her strength lies. Were these pieces to be engraved with accuracy and perfection they would undoubtedly lose their soul.

South America

Amongst South American jewellers who have not just followed Nort American ideas, the Brazilian Haroldo Burle Marx has for some years established himself as one of Brazil's more interesting creative jewellers. Much of his work derives from architectural influences, often Aztec. Nelson Souza came to study at the Central School of A in London in 1973, as there is no equivalent in his native São Paulo. His work, often figurative and humorous in style reflects English jewelry at the time. In Venezuela the Polish-born Harry Abend, who worked with Kenneth Armitage, is both sculptor and jeweller. His jewelry and wall reliefs are complementary and are in many way reminiscent of the work of the English sculptor Mary Martin.

Argentina produced several interesting artists in the sixties but creative jewelry was slow to acquire any significant talents, the exceptions being Fontana, who has already been discussed, Alicia Penalba, and Rodolfo Azaro. Azaro came to England in 1969 with an award from the British Council Art Scholarship. While at Birmingham University he made a few pieces of jewelry for his own amusement, which later became a light-hearted exhibition at the Electrum Gallery, London, entitled Jewelry from the Silver Screen. The exhibition comprised a collection of jewelry made from Polyeste resins. Each piece depicted a character or personality from the world of the cinema: Tarzan, Jane, King Kong, the Keystone Cops, Dracula Frankenstein, Judy Garland. The year prior to Azaro's exhibition, the Galeria Peninsula in Madrid mounted an interesting exhibition of the Argentinian Ariel Scornik's jewelry. This artist, who was born in Buenos Aires in 1942, is mainly concerned with mobility in jewelry. Like Friedrich Becker's, his forms are kept to a minimum, drawing the eye to the mobile quality of any piece rather than its structure, and resulting in geometric severity.

Creative jewelry in the mid-seventies is varied, and full of contrasts. Never before has there been such an abundance of activity in the subject, with ideas and tendencies that often contradict one another. From the severity of the 'Dutch school' to the sometimes figurative and often humorous work to be found in Britain, from the sophisticate German tradition with their incredible control and sense of order, to the baroque motivating ideas advocated by so many Americans, there is a plethora of ideas that motivate increasing numbers of creative jewellers. Even in countries not known for their modern arts, contemporary jewelry is beginning to take hold. Countries like India, Persia and China, Greece and the Middle East may still be largely dominated by ancient cultural traditions, but even here the situation is changing rapidly.

226] Geli Lukin Johnston
Brooches and cufflinks
Silver, gold, ivory, leather
7·5 cm (3 in)
1973
Electrum Gallery, London
Photo: Angela Turner

227] Geli Lukin Johnston
Brooch, 'Welsh Dresser'
Silver, gold, ivory
5 cm (2 in)
1973
Private collection, London
Photo: Cyril Wilson

In the late sixties Nikos Nafpliotis from Athens came to London and studied under Rod Edwards. He produced some jewelry using natural stones set in rugged settings, which had the warmth and colours associated with Greece. He has since returned to Athens.

In Jerusalem Arie Ofir, head of the jewelry and silver-smithing department at the Bezalel Academy of Arts and Design, has in recent years attracted lecturers from Germany and elsewhere to bring to his students a more progressive stimuli. He has produced two promising students in Beny Bronstin and Esther Knobel.

Before closing the historical section of the book, it is worth looking at a problem that has been raised constantly in connection with contemporary work, the question of size. Should jewelry necessarily be confined to the scale of the body? Must it be limited to the boundaries of the human form? At what point does jewelry end, and sculpture begin? These are questions which concern several creative jewellers. Some react positively — others, like Rüdiger Lorenzen, leave the questions open. He considers that the question of whether a piece is to be worn is the owner's, not the artist's.

Lorenzen considers all his work as small-scale sculptures, and treats them accordingly. Like many jewellers, Lorenzen loves metal, particularly the warmth and 'depth' of silver. With incredible control and ingenuity, Lorenzen uses silver and gold as if they had just been discovered. The surfaces of brooches and rings are sometimes brushed, or coloured by oxidization with geometric precision and rigidity, and in some pieces, as with rings he made in 1972, there is a feeling of architectural stress and colour, reminding one of the work of Le Corbusier (fig. 286).

Most goldsmiths are strongly in favour of accepting the limitation of wearability and many argue that this restriction is in no way limiting. They believe that clear distinctions between jewelry and other activities are essential, while others feel restricted by the scale of the human frame and take their work further into realms that have until recently been the prerogative of other arts. Some pieces need the participation and discretion of the wearer. What one person would term 'unwearable' another might wear with ease and confidence. For example, some consider the more advanced work of Wendy Ramshaw to be unwearable or impractical — but there is not yet a single piece from her studio that could not be worn with ease, and excitement. But all of the jewelry we have been looking at needs to be worn with care and discretion and, like most works of art, should be treated with respect. The jewelry that is made to be worn all day long does not really need to be created by an artist.

A useful parallel is ceramics. When shopping for crockery, the first consideration is function and practical design. On the other hand, if one chose to buy a bowl for its aesthetic beauty, then the practical

228

229

228] Rodolfo Azaro
Pendant, 'Tarzan'
Polyester resin
20 cm (7⅞ in)
Edition of 50
1973
Collection: the author
Photo: Ray Carpenter

229] Rodolfo Azaro
Pendant, 'King Kong'
Polyester resin
20 cm (7⅞ in)
Edition of 50
1973
Photo: Ray Carpenter

aspect would be considerably less important. Of course the two often merge, as with the work of Bernard Leach or Shoji Hamada, but works of art would enjoy a respect that purely functional pots may not necessarily be accorded. As Lee Nordness asks in his introduction to the book *Objects USA*: 'Should non-functional objects alone be candidates for fine art? Can a chair ever be a work of art? Can a teapot? . . .' The most important criterion is that if wearability be the prime aim then clearly size, weight, and structure are important factors, and the jeweller must accept these limitations, learn to work within them, and *use* these governing factors in his work. Susanna Heron is a case in point.

The greater possibilities are open to the jewellers who are less concerned with function. It is now possible to see the emergence of a new art that will use the ability of the goldsmith and his traditions, to create new definitions of jewelry. Within this new art there are many avenues to be explored. Time will tell whether future critics can claim one title for all twentieth-century art, such as the Modern Movement embracing all the styles and concepts in one. But with so much activity in jewelry, especially during the present decade, I feel sure that this neglected art will be considered one of the most active and challenging media to have re-emerged during this century.

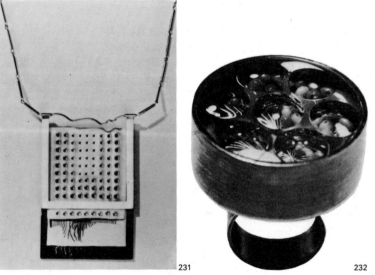

230] Georg Seibert
Object
'Die Drillspur der Nieten zum Orden Altar'
Steel, aluminium, silver, gold
30 × 30 cm (11¾ × 11¾ in)

231] Rudiger Lorenzen
Pendant (detail)
Silver, steel
1971

232] Ariel Scornik
Ring
Silver, coral, crystal
Optic and kinetic
Edition of 20
1969

5

Artists' Statements

Ulrike Bahrs – Germany

To me making jewelry means a direct confrontation with personal experience. It is in pictures – as opposed to mere abstractions – that inner experiences find their spontaneous expression and can be realized by overt consciousness.

These pictures are a symbolic expression for a reality which is partly subconscious. They serve as intermedia for basic psychological functions, such as feeling, thought, and intuition.

This symbolic perspective requires a special kind of awareness, namely the knowledge of the reality of pictures, of the senses and of their meaning.

I am fond of toying with gems and forms and colours. In lapis lazuli I recognize the shape of the sky, in unpolished ebony I realize the night. I like to play with the stories and thoughts which these gems and objects evoke in me, such as the fiery glass rubies

from Bali, about which I have been cheated so charmingly.

Thus thoughts arise and pictures take shape. They can be interpreted and are connected with thinking and feeling, being sometimes elevated into symbols. These are sketched and the drawing transformed into the different materials – be this steel or ebony, hard or soft, silver or gold, cool or warm. Gems and precious metals are combined with cast iron, acrylic, mother of pearl and finds from nature. Industrial products are incorporated together with curios from distant countries. By preference I design brooches or pendants because they correspond most closely to the 'picture'. The basic material of each piece of jewelry should transmit as vividly as possible the contents of that picture. It must be able to contest with the meaning of the picture in its own peculiar way, so that finally it may evolve a story of its own.

233] Ulrike Bahrs
Brooch, 'Woman in a Captive Balloon'
Silver, gold, steel, ebony
5 cm (2 in.)
1973

234] Ulrike Bahrs
Brooch, 'Me in the Tower, out of the Tower a Cloud, in the Cloud the Time'
Silver, steel, enamel, acrylic
4.3 cm (1¾ in.)
1973

235] Ulrike Bahrs
Brooch, framed
Gold, steel, onyx, opal
6.5 cm (2½ in.)
1972

236] Ulrike Bahrs
Brooch, 'Dream of Death'
Gold, silver, lapis lazuli, ebony
4 cm (1½ in.)
1973

233

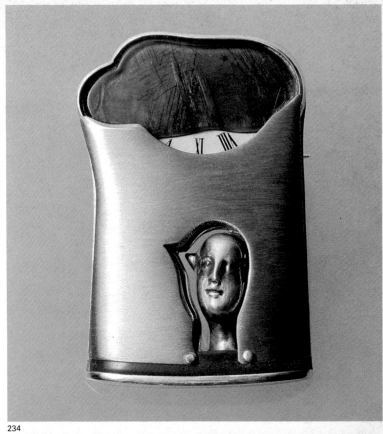

234

235

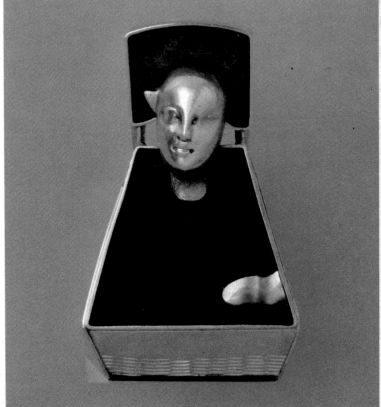

236

Meditative contemplation without intellectual reflection was important in order to reach an impalpable, non-rational dimension.

The rational, analytical dissertation was an attempt to articulate the sensual and psychical planes of experience. Conflict between conviction and doubt became the starting point of a confrontation, and a thought-process was triggered off that culminated in a probing of the question of man's purpose in the world.

Every way of life, generally speaking, is an attempt at satisfying the longing for expression, activity and gratification of desires. To this end it is important that the individual should feel at one with his environment, so that he may find suitable opportunities for expression. There is always an urge to verify observations, to heighten the sense of awareness and to reflect, modify, express and share that which has been perceived. The attempt to formulate or materialize some knowledge gained is a way of trying to assess and safeguard its quality. This urge is universal and applies to everybody. The results, however, are entirely subjective and differ from person to person.

Discussing form, Hermann Nitsch said: 'The main essence lies in the form'. First and foremost comes beauty, art must be beautiful, which means art is formal, Without form there is no art. Everything is contained in the form. The only specific message art has for mankind, is form.' Here form and content are meant to be component parts. Form without content would be formalistic nonsense.

I, as a goldsmith, face the same problem of finding the right form in my specific field. Whether it is to be a piece of jewelry for a particular person, a candlestick, a spoon or a miniature in metal, the form is all important. 'Function' is a precondition for the utilitarian object – in contrast to the 'free' object. In its function lies the aesthetic value, the sensory perception of the object – the form. The Shakers – a religious sect – have a saying which states that the object which offers the highest degree of usefulness, also possesses the highest degree of beauty.

The striving after a perfect form is an existential striving, free of materialistic tendencies, favouring non-materialistic values. The non-materialistic world is the world in which the original relationship of man to myth and magic still exists. The longing for that other world is brought about by the materialistic

orientation of mankind and the hostility of an all-powerful modern science and technology. The resulting rationalism rejects any non-rational theory of life, and this in turn creates a growing need to admit the archetypal images into our modern world of thought.

1974

Gerd Rothmann – Germany

The meaning of an action, expressed in a story from Japan; it demonstrates clearly how the essence of something spiritual, something worthy of reflection, may be communicated. An action that presents nothing immediately discernible; but is based entirely on imagination.

A friend of mine who had been invited to a tea-ceremony related: several people were sitting on the floor, forming a circle. Tea was served and the visitors chatted to each other. When the trivial topics of conversation had been exhausted, the host rose, fetched from a cupboard a smallish object he had just acquired, or perhaps found, and showed it to his guests. It went from hand to hand and was minutely examined. Each person's individual perception or impression contributed to an intense discussion. The object was used as a physical and mental stimulus.

The significance of the object lay in shape, content and experience.

Awareness of the object was achieved through the sense perceptions of touch and sight, and this in turn stimulated metaphysical and psychical reactions.

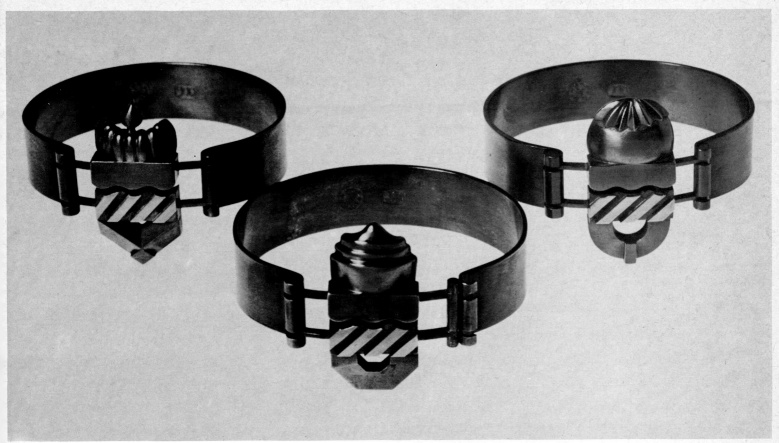

237]

238

237] Gerd Rothmann
Bracelets
Oxidized silver, gold
Limited edition of 5
6 cm (2⅜ in.)
1972
Collection: the artist

238] Gerd Rothmann
Multiple plates with bracelet and pendant
 attachments
Steel, acrylic
5.5 cm (2¼ in.)
1970–71

242

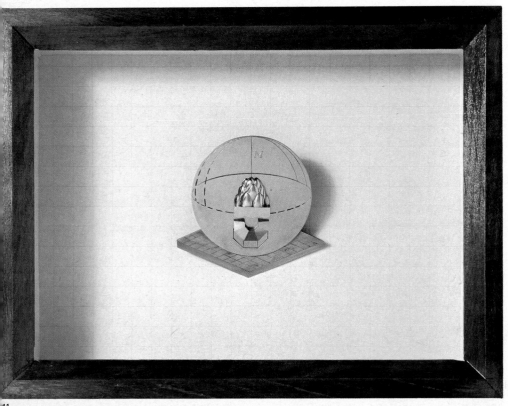

239] Gerd Rothmann
Brooch object
Steel, gold
5.5 cm (2¼ in.)
1973
Collection: the artist

240] Gerd Rothmann
Brooch object
Steel, gold, engraved
6 cm (2⅜ in.)
1974
Collection: the artist

241] Gerd Rothmann
Brooch object
Steel, gold, engraved
6.5 cm (2½ in.)
1974
Collection: the artist

242] Gerd Rothmann
Brooch object
Steel, gold
5.5 cm (2¼ in.)
1973
Collection: the artist

Friedrich Becker — Germany

Professionally speaking, my home is neither in the sphere of free artistic endeavour nor in the field of artistic craftsmanship, but rather in the world of machinery construction and aerospace technology.

Although I was designing and producing pieces of jewelry as long ago as 1938, it was not until 1947 that I finally decided to opt for the profession of goldsmith pure and simple. What fascinates me now — even more so than at that time — are the limitless possibilities offered by this profession. There is scarcely any other metier which allows you to think out, orient and produce the finest creations yourself via the stepping-stones of semi-finished goods and mechanics.

In my particular case these fantastic possibilities were supplemented by native insight into design and technological know-how which emanated from the calling referred to above.

I prefer to design jewelry from my own volition and on my own urge, that is to say, without waiting for orders to come in, and it is not primarily a matter of adornment but rather a question of delight in freedom of action, invention and creative fantasy. It should be said, however, that in my particular case, the 'playful phase' is followed by the 'industrious phase', namely, the systematics. Test series then ensue with creative

variants being checked with regards to aesthetics, functions and economy of shape. All my work is designed on the basis that it can be measured, produced and repeated. All accidental occurrences of a structural or ornamental nature are excluded.

July 1959

I have worked on kinetic jewelry since 1965. My efforts consist of pieces of jewelry which record, reinforce and transform accidental movements on the part of the wearer into new and differentiated movement configurations. This is achieved by the use of movable parts, concentric and non-concentric bearings, balances and impulse cones. (See exhibition catalogue Friedrich Becker at Goldsmiths' Hall, London.) Large kinetic reliefs and sculptures also date from the same year.

It is my purpose, with the aid of kinetic media, to discover new aesthetic shapes and manifestations, perhaps even to come across an inherent orderliness in this sphere. The onlooker is intended to participate more intensively than hitherto, a fact made possible by a certain psycho-physiological sensitivity to movement released in him by the kinetics.

1974

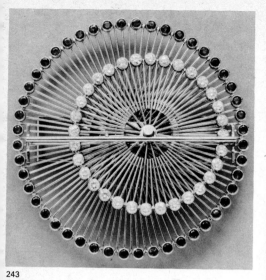

243

244

245

243] Friedrich Becker
Brooch
White gold, rubies, diamond; kinetic
6.5 cm (2½ in.)
1968
Private collection
Photo: Günter Schieder

244] Friedrich Becker
Ring
White gold; kinetic
1971
Private collection
Photo: Walter Fischer

245] Friedrich Becker
Ring
White gold; kinetic
1971
Private collection
Photo: Walter Fischer

246] Friedrich Becker
Ring
White gold; kinetic
1971
Private collection
Photo: Walter Fischer

247] Friedrich Becker
Ring
White gold; kinetic
1971
Private collection
Photo: Walter Fischer

246

247

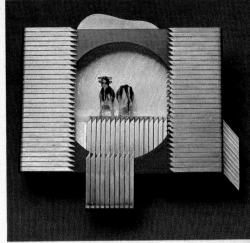

248

249

Norbert Mürrle — Germany

Since 1970 I have been working on making technical, organic affinities.

At that time I tried to achieve affinity in my drawings and then later on translate it into jewelry. Most of my pictures date from this period. From 1970 to 1972. I basically used gold combined with ivory in my jewelry. Ivory was a material that gave me the right kind of volume. I could then make my technical parts in gold and represent the connection with the organic in a change of line or volume within a certain area; i.e. my technical part was deformed from a certain point onwards, and this is where I could start to work in organic terms.

In 1972 I happened to come across some steel cramps that fascinated me in the way they lined up absolutely perfectly. They were just right for my statement, and I was going to use them. The same thing happened with the organic volumes. I simply happened to find

some plastic cows that I could also put to use.

I now did not let my drawings precede my jewelry. Instead I would now build models from the material at hand and go straight into making the three-dimensional form. My models were sketches of thoughts now partially carried out. In my last works it was important for me to utilize fully the cramps and all that they stood for. By intensifying them I could direct them in such a way that they would be right for the figurative ring now to be made. That is how my last three objects really stem from aspects of a miniature (three rings that are meant to be carried on the little finger).

The band is no longer just the carrier of the object, but a sculpture in its own right.

1974

248] Norbert Mürrle
Brooch
Gold, steel, acrylic
6.5 cm (2½ in.)
1972

249] Norbert Mürrle
Brooch
Gold, steel, acrylic
7 cm (2¾ in.)
1972

250] Norbert Mürrle
Brooch
Gold, steel, acrylic
6 cm (2⅜ in.)
1972

114

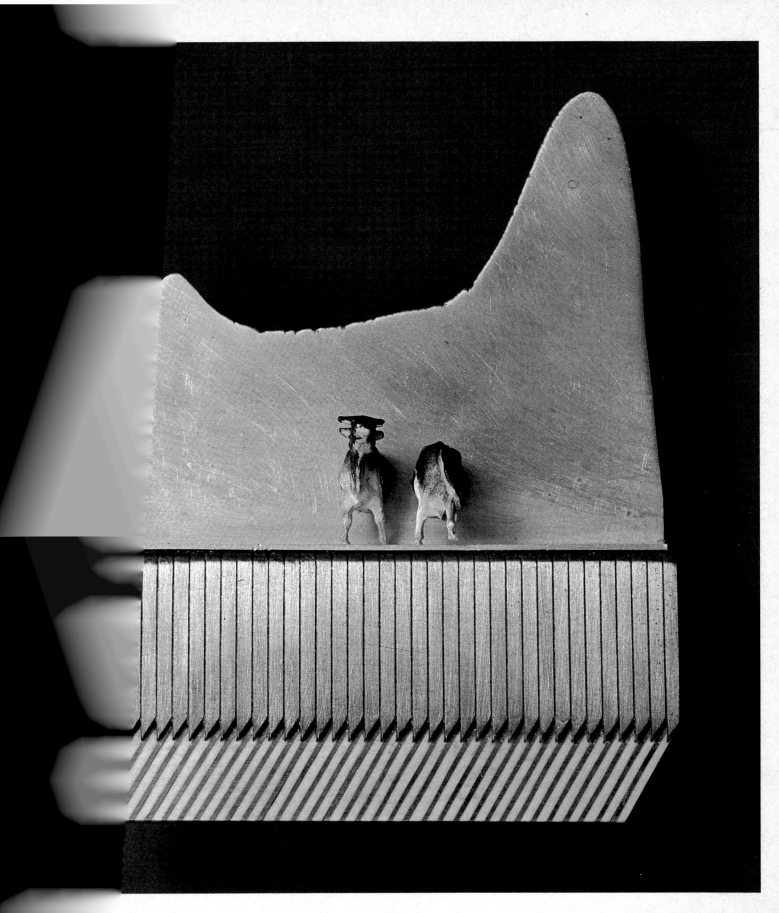

251] Norbert Mürrle
Brooch
Gold, silver, steel
6 cm (2⅜ in.)
1973

251

116

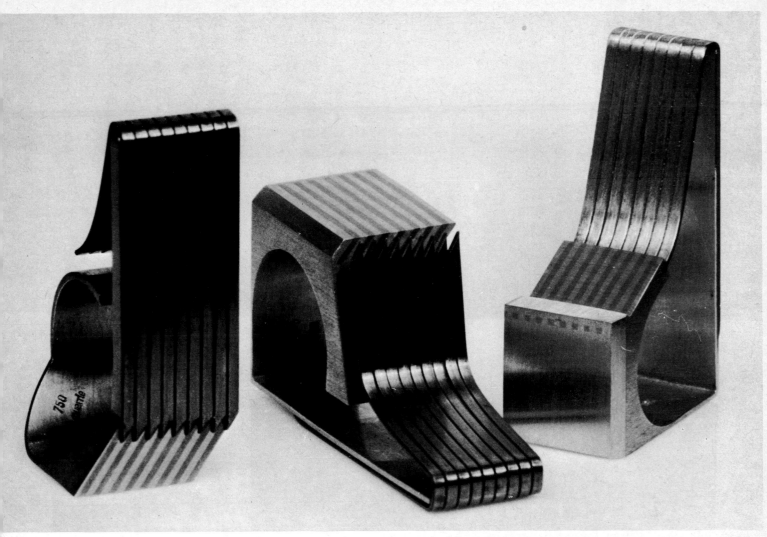

52] Norbert Mürrle
ngs
hite and yellow gold, steel
974

53] Norbert Mürrle
rooch
old, steel, ivory
cm (2 in.)
973

253

Roger Morris — England

My jewelry was initially designed around the use of agate slices combined with precious metals. Agate became in time a restricting material owing to its hardness and inflexibility. Acrylic sheet provided a freedom of design with an exciting range of colour, and enabled a wider use of selective forms.

The theme of my work is based on geometric compositions incorporating organic breakdowns and reliefs, on occasion creating three-dimensional illusions on a two-dimensional plane.

The organic themes have been influenced by my strong interest in nature. Last year a scholarship enabled me to visit the West Indies to draw and observe the birds of the region, and the exotic colour seen there influences my present work.

254] Roger Morris
Necklace
Acrylic, gold
8 cm (3¼ in.)
1974

255] Roger Morris
Brooch
Forming lid of box containing rir
Acrylic, gold
5.5 cm (2¼ in.)
1974

256] Roger Morris
Ring in box
Acrylic, gold
4 cm (1½ in.)
1974

257] Roger Morris
Ring in box
Acrylic, gold
5 cm (2 in.)
1974

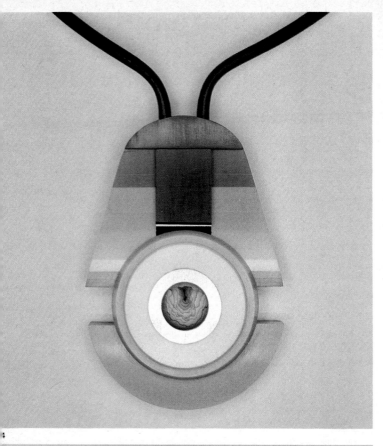

254

255

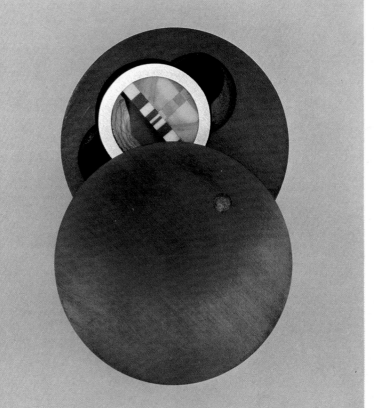

256

257

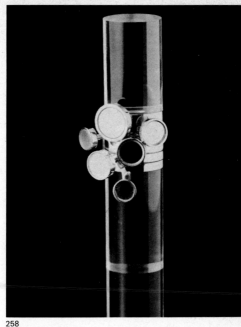

258

Wendy Ramshaw — England

I enjoy making jewelry. I enjoy looking at jewelry and I enjoy wearing jewelry. These, in simple terms, are the real reasons why I am an artist whose main means of expression has become the creation of jewels.

To be entirely successful for me a piece should function as an object in its own right, hence my involvement in the additional extension of the piece by means of what could be regarded as minor environmental mountings. The use of frames and columns to enable a piece to be temporarily free of the need for support on the human form has led me to become more and more involved with the integration of the support and the jewel. This does not mean that this aspect of the work has become overidingly important because for jewelry to fulfil its true role it must relate to the human form in some way which enhances the body and its movements. I find the attempt to fulfil both these requirements simultaneously the most challenging aspect of making jewelry.

I have not found myself limited by the concerns of functionalism as it would seem for me creatively stifling. I find no problem in making a piece which is excessively delicate or projecting, thereby requiring a commitment from the wearer in possibly practical as well as aesthetic terms. Despite the fact that I find my work related (though at first this was without my real knowledge) to the ancient and more modern traditions of jewelry, one of my conscious

aims is that my work should be deliberately related to the time in which it is made, reflecting the period in some way. I am concerned that my own work should continue to be progressive within its own context and that my ideas will continue to evolve. It is the adding to and subtracting from, developing and refining with shape, colour and balance which keep me producing one piece of jewelry out of another inrelated series. I find enjoyment in variation as well as in directions which are new to me. Watching ideas grow and change reinforces my view that even when using machine forms I am articulating them in ways which are related to structures found in nature as well as those found in the man-made world. Nothing is new and I am aware that only by delving instinctively and subconsciously amongst my visual experiences of art and non-art can I hope to make a statement with a direction which is personal enough to be regarded as an individual aesthetic expression.

A desirable artifact or object often has in it qualities which are impossible to define, i.e., when it has become much more than the sum of all its parts and ideas. There is an extra sort of magic which makes it work as a special and unique piece. I suppose like all artists I am conscious that it is this indefinable extra which I would hope to very occasionally capture in my work.

1974

258] Wendy Ramshaw
Set of six rings
Silver, mirror
3 cm (1¼ in.)
1970
Private collection, Sydney
Photo: Bob Cramp

259] Wendy Ramshaw
Necklace
Silver, gold, blue and grey enamel
20 cm (7⅞ in.)
1973
Collection: the artist
Photo: Bob Cramp

260] Wendy Ramshaw
Set of five rings
Gold, red enamel
3.5 cm (1⅜ in.)
1971
Collection: the author
Photo: David Watkins

261] Wendy Ramshaw
Set of three rings
Gold, tourmaline, agate, enamel
Dark green translucent acrylic stand
1973
Private collection, London
Photo: Bob Cramp

120

262] Wendy Ramshaw
Set of 18 rings
Gold, silver, enamel, agate, emerald, sapphire,
   tourmaline, garnet
Stand, Nicol silver set tourmaline and acrylic
1974
Collection: Elizabeth and Ian Frazer, London

263] Wendy Ramshaw
Set of 3 rings
Gold, enamel
1971
Collection: The Worshipful Company of Goldsmiths

262

Helga Zahn — England

What is jewelry?
Is jewelry important?

Of importance is the importance of the monkey
he eats every day an immense amount of bananas
a very important consumer-product
in his importance so important
he eats too many and dies
with due importance is the importance
covered with red yellow withered plastic-flowers
in plastic terms the monkey died from greed
seen with importance he died from banana-importance
a banana-hero a consumer-product
a monkey an important weight.
1969

I made my first pieces of jewelry to decorate
myself and for the sensuality which went with it.
My conscious awareness of colour, form and
space-relationships I carry as natural and
unconsciously as moving, sleeping, seeing and
laughing. And in a continuous conscious study of all
things around me I keep them alive, developing but
away from intellectual soul-destroying analysis.
I am and I work.
1974

264] Helga Zahn
Pendant
Silver, plastic, amber
44 cm (17$\frac{7}{8}$ in.)
1973
Collection: the artist
Photo: David Cripps

265] Helga Zahn
Necklace
Silver, green agate, mother of pearl; mobil
16 cm (6$\frac{5}{8}$ in.)
1966
Photo: Jorge Guerra

266] Helga Zahn
Necklace
Silver, black pebbles
14 cm (5$\frac{1}{2}$ in.)
1966
Collection: the artist
Photo: Ray Carpenter

124

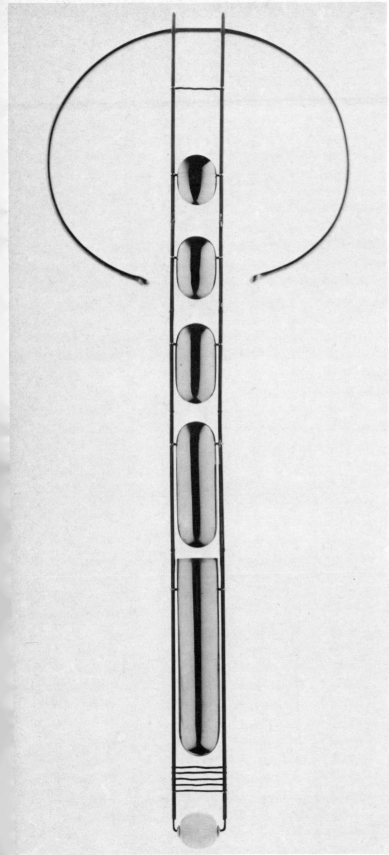

264

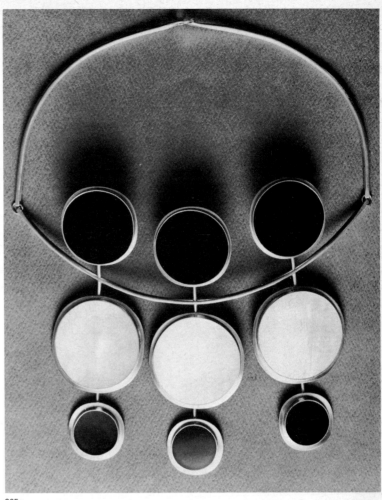

265

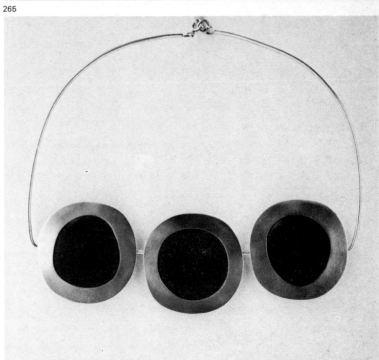

266

125

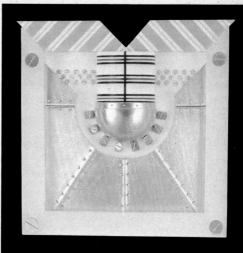

267

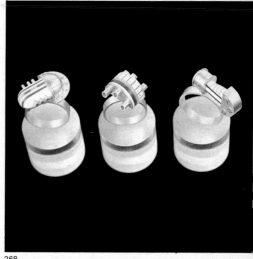

268

from it. In 1971 and 1972 I tried to express this feeling in some larger pieces (80 x 80 cm) of jewelry; a clarification of my artistic statements in relationship to the environment. In 1971 I was busy with my first wall-ornaments and other decorative objects, from which wearable pieces of jewelry could be detached. The wall-ornament remains decorative even after the wearable piece has been removed. It was important to me to achieve an active, spacial relationship between the wearer of the jewelry and my work; in other words, to create a confrontation between *me* and the wearer.

Generally speaking, I refuse to have my jewelry displayed in show-cases. This, I hate. It reminds me too much of 'valuables'. People must be able to live with my jewelry. As naturally as possible. To this end, attitude and clarification of ideas are essential. A decorative object must, like any other object, fit into its environment in a perfectly natural way.

My finished work always strikes me as too simple. I do not like to refer to it as 'objects', either. An 'object', to my mind, is something inflexible and impersonal. After having struggled with a task for a considerable period of time, it seems inappropriate to call the result an 'object'.

Each of my creations has its own little 'story of development'. It proceeds, so to speak, in three stages:

a] Mental process. An idea is born and sketched on paper.
b] Technical process. Proportions are analysed and layed down in detail. The various component parts are drawn.
c] Manual process. This is by far the most lengthy part in the process of making an imagined piece of jewelry visible and tangible.

In all three stages adjustments may become necessary. During the manual process a logical sequence is worked out and put into effect. At the same time a parallel development of smaller-detail-pieces such as multiples, super-imposed layers, etc. may take place.

My work must present a co-ordinated whole. There should be no difference in the scale of sizes. I draw no limiting boundaries. I always try to create a certain amount of tension. This is the only way in which I can move freely.

1974

Fritz Maierhofer — Austria

The works I produce are freely invented forms, evolved from the basic elements of geometry. They develop through a continuous process of labour, absorbing influences from, as well as confrontations with, the so-called fine arts. Realizations gained in daily life, and environmental influences and techniques also have their say. Technique has always played an important part in my attitude to life and work.

I try primarily to identify myself with my work — that is, to recognize myself in my creations. This led to my experimenting with acrylglass, and gave a new outlet to my strong sense of colour. A beautiful way of combining gold, silver or steel with a synthetic product, yet letting each material speak in its own expressive way. There must be clarity between each distinct type of material.

I work with conviction, and because I derive joy

267] Fritz Maierhofer
Brooch
Gold, acrylic
(mount not shown)
1973

268] Fritz Maierhofer
Rings
Gold, acrylic; movable units
1973–4

269] Fritz Maierhofer
Brooch
Gold, acrylic
(mount not shown)
1973

270

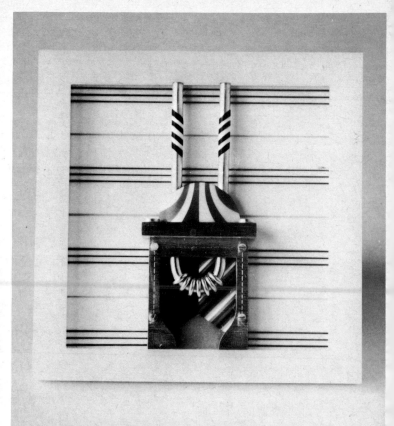

271

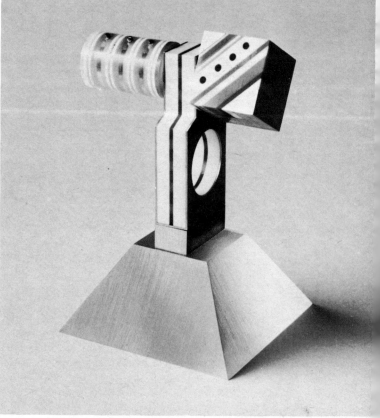

272

270] Fritz Maierhofer
Bracelet
Acrylic, gold
1974

271] Fritz Maierhofer
Brooch
Acrylic, silver
1973

272] Fritz Maierhofer
Ring
Acrylic, gold
1973

273] Fritz Maierhofer
Bracelet
Acrylic, gold
1974

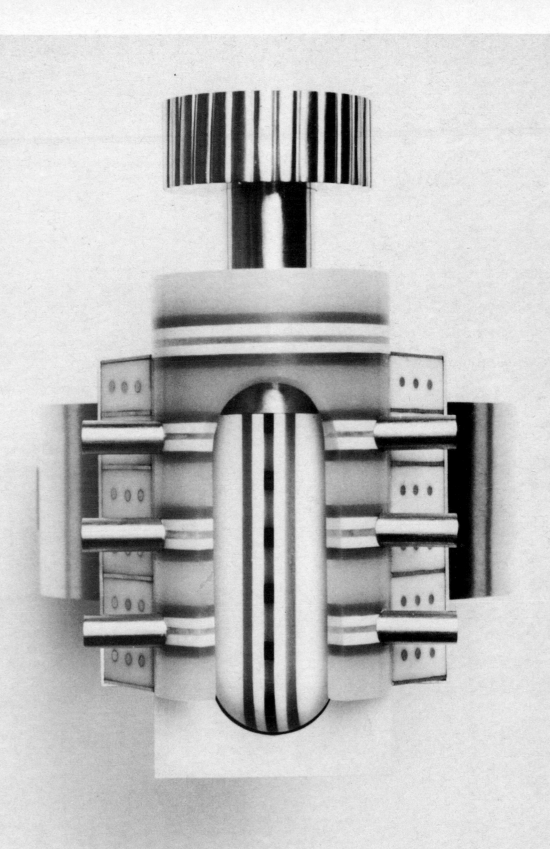

Otto Künzli — Switzerland

What I do, I do mainly because I would otherwise be bored. Since boredom has a very negative effect on me I have to keep myself busy as fully as possible with something that captures my attention completely and poses problems for me to solve. This happens to a certain degree in thinking, talking, observing, etc, but above all in doing, in making.

I am concerned with jewelry because I find it very stimulating to bring into being a form rich in charm and sensibility, in the smallest possible space using a very wide variety of plastic miniature elements. Miniature scale suits me very well and is the most easily accessible realm of experience for me. This applies as much to the design as its realization.

I make jewelry first and foremost for myself — that is, I start from the conclusions of form that come to me. These conceptions are the result of ideas of order. As order has something supra-individual in it, my conceptions of form can also be those of others. The more closely I follow them or the ideas of order, as the case may be, the more fundamentally another person can identify with a piece or, rather, the more clearly he can express himself through it. My

standpoint emerges quite naturally out of this: jewelry is less a representative object than a manifestation of individual being.

One requirement of jewelry is its wearability. For me, as with others, experimenting means taking little notice of this requirement. And so from time to time I come up against the borderlines of jewelry. Experimenting is often the most intense form of work for me.

I work out jewelry mainly on the drawing board. The design develops spontaneously and immediately. For me the design will always be the 'more personal' part, and designing the more intense experience. At the basis of the design lies the mental picture of a particular piece of jewelry. I try to make this mental picture concrete by using my skill to transfer it to a material. Unfortunately this finality is often gained at the expense of spontaneity. Only the completed piece of jewelry can prove mastery over the initial problem.

I cannot explain my efforts in their complexity. Their foundations are sensual experiences and 'sensually' is the way they should be understood.

274] Otto Künzli
Brooch
Silver, white and yellow gold, lapis lazuli
5.5 cm (2¼ in.)
1973

275] Otto Künzli
Bracelet
Oxidized silver, white and yellow gold, steel
9.5 cm (3¾ in.)
1974

276] Otto Künzli
Brooch
Silver, white and yellow gold
5.5 cm (2¼ in.)
1973

277] Otto Künzli
Bracelet
Oxidized silver, white and yellow gold
8.8 cm (3½ in.)
1974

275

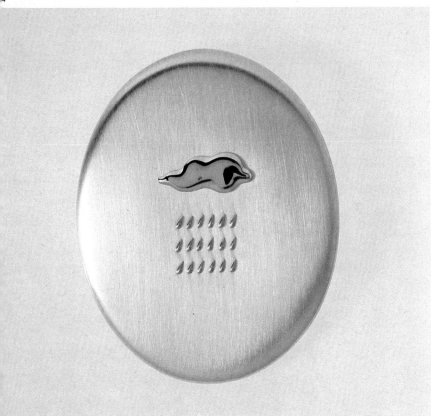

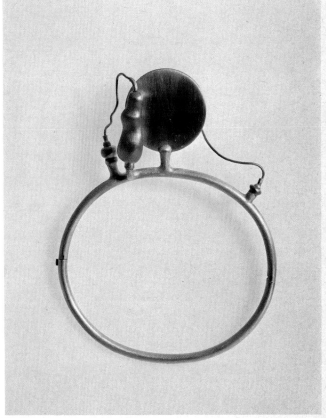

277

131

278

Svatopluk Kasaly — Czechoslovakia

I have spent nearly eleven years making jewelry,
and, as a creative artist working with glass, this
material has preoccupied my studies. By using a
non-traditional and individual method, I have
succeeded in combining glass and metal. I am
interested in carrying out research into the different
characters of these two materials and in joining them
in one organic unit. My work uses mainly (soda)
potash-glass and lead-glass, materials which have to
be shaped entirely by cutting. Stones, either coarse-
grained or fine-grained, are best for this, and
afterwards I polish the glass with pumice and oxide.
It is a rather complicated process. I always choose a
jewel to suit the particular person it is being made for.
First of all I make a plaster model of the cut glass, in
which I work out shapes and weigh up the
possibilities of the optical effects most suitable for
glass. I follow the same procedure for metal, first
making a model, designed to suit the personality of
the woman who will be wearing the finished jewel.
Then I start work on a metal. I use mainly the less
expensive metals which give me a far greater
opportunity to experiment, and I am not restricted by
any conventions, as some jewellers are when working
solely with expensive metals. I use brass, refined on
the surface with nickel and rhodium, which is quite
expensive in this country. I also sometimes use silver.

278] Svatopluk Kasaly
Bracelet
Glass crystal, rhodium-plated brass, nicol
8 cm (3¼ in.)
1972
Photo: Jiří Erml

279] Svatopluk Kasaly
Pendant (detail)
Glass, rhodium-plated brass
42 cm (16½ in.)
1972
Photo: Jirí Erml

280] Svatopluk Kasaly
Pendant
Glass, rhodium-plated brass
42 cm (16½ in.)
1972
Photo: Taras Kuščynskyj

281] Svatopluk Kasaly
Pendant
Glass crystal, rhodium-plated brass
42 cm (16½ in.)
1972
Photo: Taras Kuščynskyj

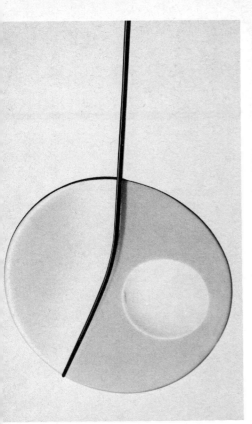

279

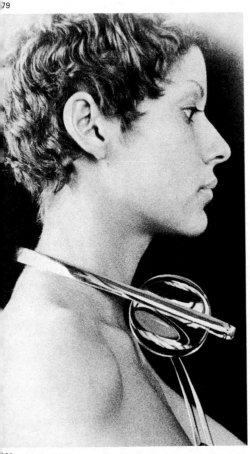

280

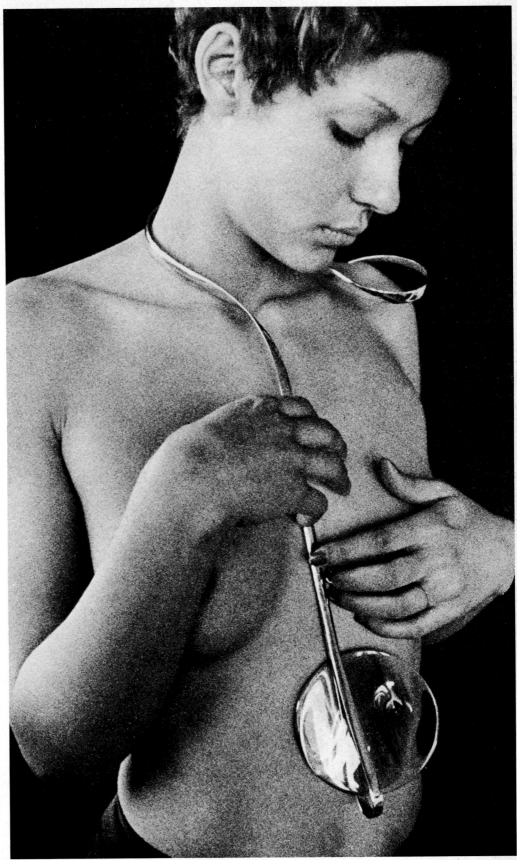

281

282

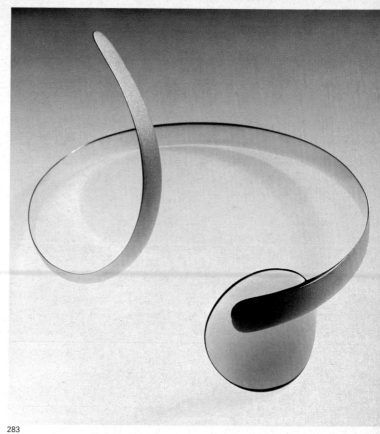

283

284

282] Svatopluk Kasaly
Bracelet
Glass, rhodium-plated brass
8 cm (3¼ in.)
1973
Photo: Jiří Erml

283] Svatopluk Kasaly
Diadem
Glass rhodium-plated brass
5 cm (2 in.)
1973
Photo: Jiří Erml

284] Svatopluk Kasaly
Sculpture
Glass
10 cm (4 in.)
1972
Photo: Jiří Erml

285] Svatopluk Kasaly
Leg bracelet
Glass, brass
7.7 cm (3 in.)
1972
Photo: Jiří Erml

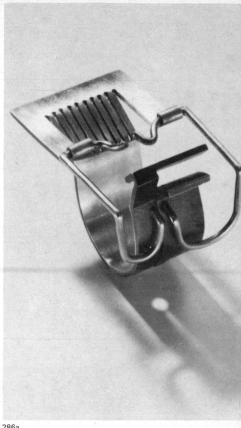

Rudiger Lorenzen — Germany

What is jewelry? The portrait of a thought? The solution of a form-problem in small dimensions? None of the various definitions clarify the matter. All leave doubt; but doubt is my working basis in all attempts to make visible my imagined forms.

Current tendencies, though minutely observed, give me no direct stimulus. The flood of general. unceasing stimulation prompts me to look for an entirely different approach to my work. What fascinates me is not the loud, obvious and immediately discernible, but rather its opposite: the quiet, the hidden, the need for searching.

My initial material is metal, with all its possibilities of absolute change of surface — particularly silver which I like best, because of its special 'depth'; there are also the many-sided but easily controllable colorations, and the plasticity which metal offers.

My work ranges from surface to relief. On the one hand detailed formulation of colour and shape — whereby the results sometimes take on the character of exchangeable sectors — on the other an attempt at reduction of colour and plasticity to a point where 'stillness continues to be, or once again starts to be, interesting'.

Contrasts in form and colour are particularly significant. Objective outer form in contrast to subjective inner shaping. Detail, contrasting with a pure plane or a colour contrast; sometimes harshly set against one another — contrast in the purest sense of the word — sometimes graduated and differentiated to a point where the purely optical is transcended.

Considering usefulness, pin-on jewelry is preferable, because of its almost universal wearability. Size, weight and technical function are minor considerations and thus allow a great measure of creative freedom. A logical development of this is the miniatures, which mark the limits of my work-area. Limits — because their size and weight make them unsuitable for wear, though the creative basis, emanating from my work-concept, remains the same.

My interest in the work is, therefore, concentrated solely on the independence and value of the result: a relief or a small scale sculpture — always bearing in mind the possibility of its being looked at or worn.

For these reasons it is no longer important to me, once I have completed a work, whether it is worn, or just looked at. Whether it is, or becomes, jewelry and is used as such, is not decided by me, but by the attitude and wish of the beholder or wearer.

1974

286a,b,c] Rudiger Lorenzen
Three rings
Silver, gold, metal paint
1971

287] Rudiger Lorenzen
Pendant
Silver, steel, gold, acrylic
13 cm (5½ in.)
1972

6b

86c

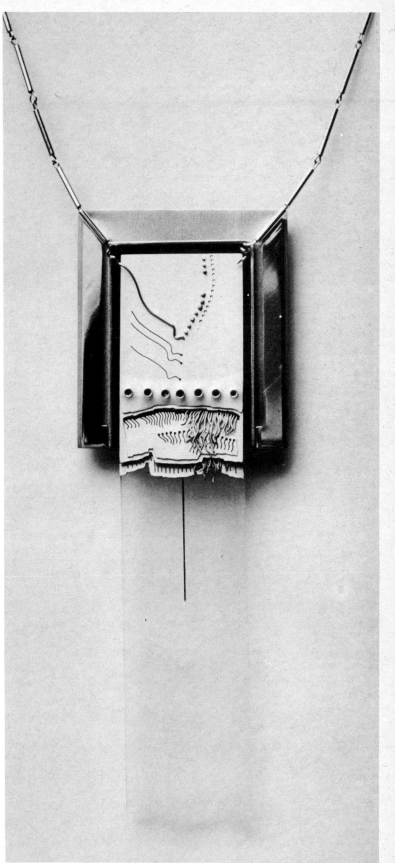

287

137

Claus Bury — Germany

If I refer to my creations as 'jewelry', it is not only because my professional training and the traditions of the goldsmith's craft have quite logically helped to open up ways of expressing my artistic ideas in that particular direction, but also because, through making my intentions visible, I draw a demarcation line against the trendy, commercial concept of jewelry as an investment, a fashion accessory, a mere object of decoration for the broad masses of consumers. To me jewelry is first and foremost an intellectual confrontation with the environment, and identification with the artistic statement expressed is a prerequisite to the correct understanding and using — that is wearing — of my jewelry.

Coming to grips with the artistic concept, right through to its realization in the object created, is therefore a primary task; thereafter 'function', meaning 'wearing' and 'adorning', becomes a much more natural and non-problematical act.

This is the only way in which I can interpret the correct meaning of jewelry. It remains jewelry (adornment) even if a direct relationship to the wearer is missing and 'use' as such never takes place. Therefore jewelry can never be a dead utilitarian thing; rather it becomes part of a personal environment, contributing just as much towards an individual life-style as furniture, pictures and photographs.

Drawings, sketches and notes on details and materials are necessary stages in the process of making my treatment of themes visible. They are just as important as the finally realized, three-dimensional object; they are integral components of a concept, facilitating identification with the created form — making visual reconstruction possible.

In this sense a mere idea, an imaginative drawing, could be perfect jewelry in itself, obviating the necessity of creating a tangible object — if I personally did not place such high value on the very use of my creative work; if I did not wish to urge the recipient to adorn himself in his environment — in joyful freedom of individual choice.

1974

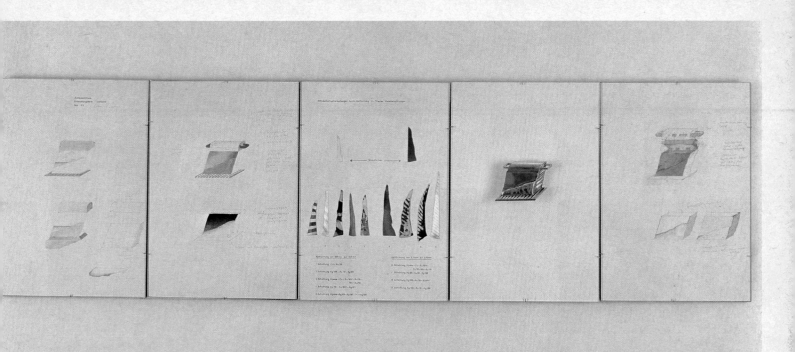

8] Claus Bury
och
ver, gold, brass, German silver, copper
cm (2¾ in.)
74

9] Claus Bury
awings
planatory notes
search into chemical and metal combinations
ished brooch
amed, signed
74

0] Claus Bury
och
ld, acrylic
cm (3⅝ in.)
72
llection: Schmuckmuseum, Pforzheim

290

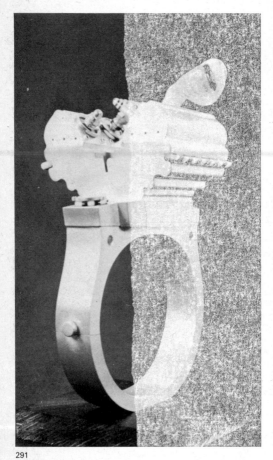

291

292

291] Claus Bury
Bracelet
Gold, acrylic; movable sections
8 cm (3¼ in.)
1971
Private collection

292] Claus Bury
Brooch
Gold
1973
Photo: Cyril Wilson

293] Claus Bury
Brooch, with separate pin
Gold
7.5 cm (3 in.)
With mounted framed drawing and explanatory notes
Signed: Hanau 1972
Private collection

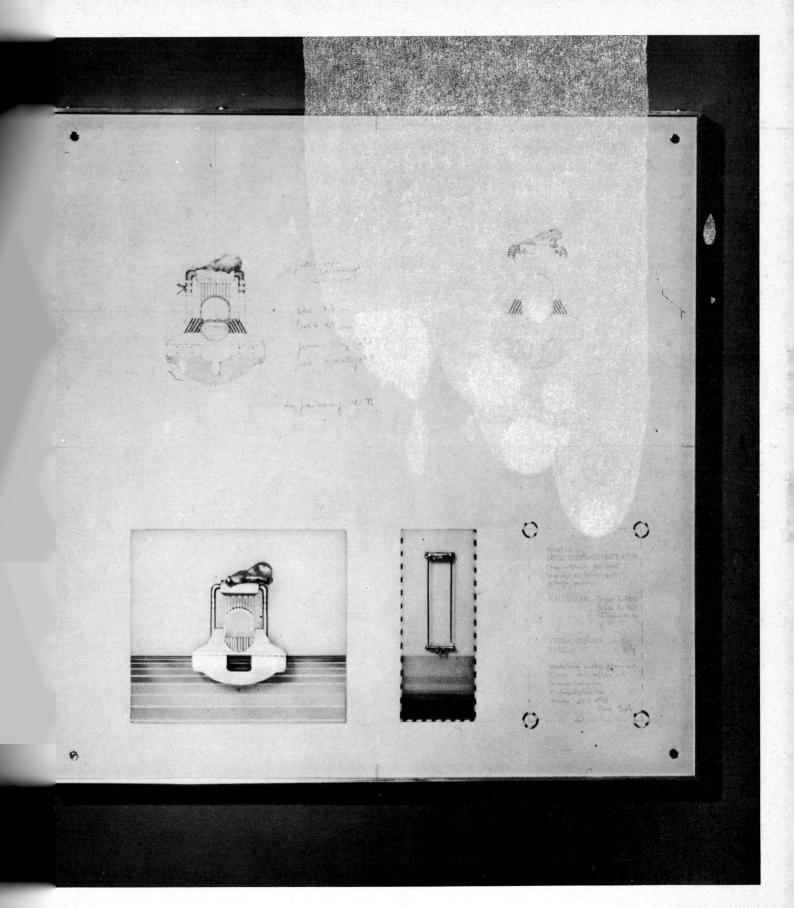

Sergi Aguilar – Spain

My work originates in the belief that jewelry today is being produced at a time which has no established creative ideals. It exists basically as a commercial entity, a means of supplying the prospective client with an object containing the correct ingredients for a good financial investment. It lacks all type of communication and purity of form and shape which responds to our present society. Today's jewelry is thus in an alienated state, smothered within our sick society which understands no other language than that of financial gain.

In the construction of my jewelry, I start from zero and I attempt to create works whose expression is inherent in the form itself and in the materials, which are used quite freely. The aim is to create a work whose total value comes from its very personality, from its intrinsic purity and from the implications — violent or pleasant — which it has for the observer.

The final result is nothing more than a small, free object which can be worn, played with, or kept in the house as just one more element of the space in which we live and communicate.

April 1971

The relation between jewelry and sculpture:
I don't believe there is a direct relationship between jewelry and sculpture. The limits within which jewelry evolves are different from those of sculpture. Why? Because things have a name and it is this name which determines what they are.

Jewelry must be a specific size and must use specific materials. It must contain a certain mystery and magic, must be shocking or pleasing and must enter into a direct relationship with the human body, because first and foremost it is jewelry.

With sculpture the size-volume of the work is indeterminate, the materials used even more so, particularly in relation to weight and usage, and the work exists in a direct relation to the space which it occupies and vacates.

They do perhaps have one point in common; that of the concept involved — the 'theme' of both jewelry and sculpture can be the same, but to discuss this would be to enter into one specific area.

Jewelry must possess a quality, a personality, and a power of its own, quite independent of its relation to sculpture.

November 1973

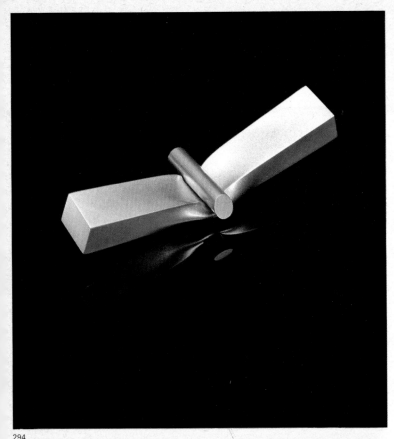

294

295

296

297

143

Bruno Martinazzi – Italy

Just as it was in its most primitive form in the early
history of man, the jewel today is the outward sign of
man's subconscious desire to transcend the limits of
physical existence. It is a symbol of the religious
feeling which establishes a link between man's
brief life span, and the endless succession of the
generations.

1970

I am looking for the whole, but all I can find is a part.
I need the whole but I can only produce a part of it.

1974

298] Bruno Martinazzi
Brooch, 'Homo Sapiens'
6.5 cm (2½ in.)
1973

299] Bruno Martinazzi
Bracelet, 'Goldfinger'
White and yellow gold
8.7 cm (3⅜ in.)
1973
Photo: Rampazzi

300] Bruno Martinazzi
Brooch, 'Dactylos'
6.5 cm (2½ in.)
1973

301] Bruno Martinazzi
Collar, 'Women's Lib'
Gold
1973

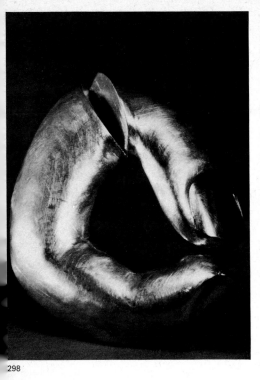

298

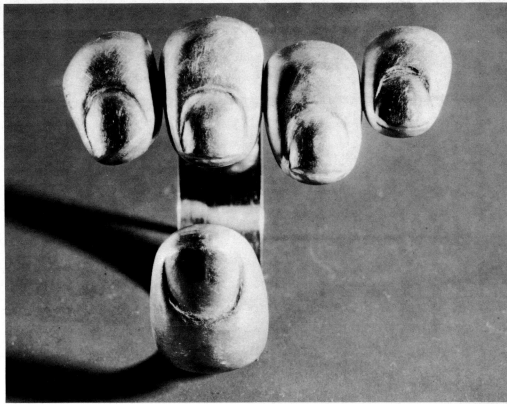

299

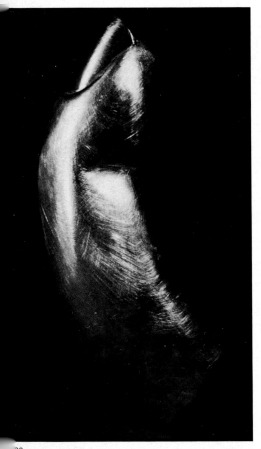

00

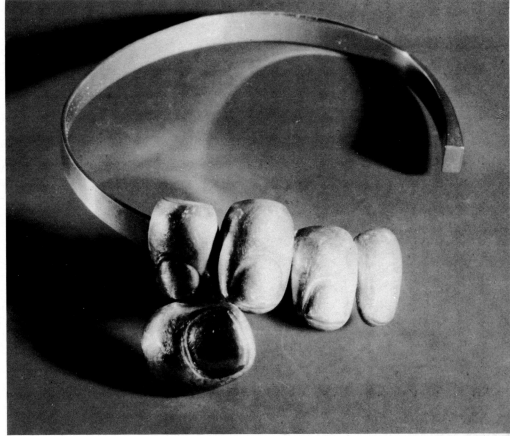

301

John Plenderleith — England

Jewelry. A discipline for creation of things to adorn the body. The choice of the individual reflects the character. Jewelry could be any material, any size, any colour. The restrictions of design are dictated primarily by the marketing channels, secondly by the customer, thirdly the materials used, fourthly the state of mind of the designer. A marriage of all these disciplines and creativity and originality is the accepted form of jewelry. The designer's job is to break these barriers. Collectively, individually or by degrees in each area.

In the final reckoning the designer is forced by the mundane realities of his existence to adhere to some or all of these disciplines. The degree and method by which it is done is the art.

Create an object which performs a function in the guise of another form is a concept that interests me. To create one thing that looks like something else. To hide in a three-dimensional object another function, to secrete its real *raison d'être*. To create a secret identity within another form becomes a personal ambiguity which questions the three-dimensional normality of your surroundings.

1974

302] John Plenderleith
Brooch, 'Toothbrush and Paste'
Silver
9.5 cm (3¾ in.)
Private collection, London
Photo: Ray Carpenter

303

303] John Plenderleith
Rings
Silver and acrylic
1971
Private collection, London
Photo: Jan Van Gaalen

304] John Plenderleith
Ring, 'Aeroplane'
Silver
1972
Private collection, London

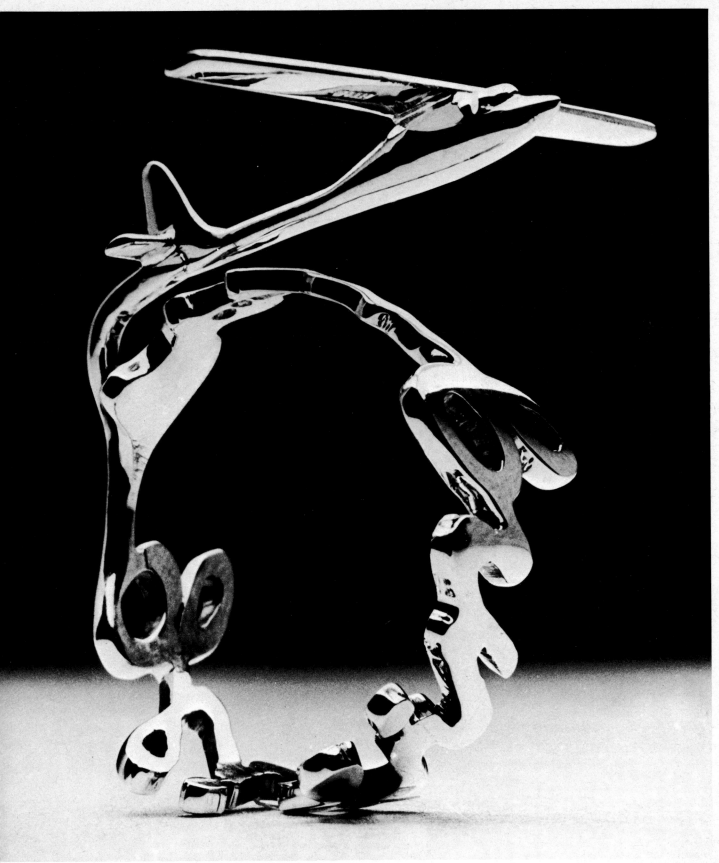

305

306

Hubertus Von Skal — Germany

Do I make jewelry? I want signs, signatures, marks to draw the eye's attention. I would like to give my objects the character of totems rather than that of mere ornamentation. Conventional jewelry is meaningless to me.

Does an ugly woman become more beautiful by wearing ornamental jewelry? She becomes uglier! Ornaments are an optical emphasis. Does a beautiful woman become more beautiful if she wears jewelry? Well, it may stress her beauty. But even that is not my aim.

I certainly do not see my task as one of creating status symbols. Why then make jewelry?

The painstakingly shaped earthenware vessels of early cultures were richly decorated. But such ornamentation did not express a taste for art; it was not meant to embellish, it was meant to emphasize. The vessel became distinct; it became a symbol, a signature — something remarkable. In that sense I agree with jewelry.

This means that jewelry should be anti-traditionalistic — not because it should adhere to principles of fashion, but because jewelry must have a certain uniqueness if it is to signify something characteristic, and if it is to be noticed at all in this era of clichés.

Such jewelry demands original thought and creativity from a goldsmith.

I feel that my task lies in optical experimentation; in creating new values; in finding new materials, new forms, new meanings, new references.

The same tasks are faced by the fine arts in their current experimental stage. That is why the work of a goldsmith and 'pure art' objects can quite easily stand side by side in an exhibition. The chasm between so-called 'applied art' and 'pure art' has vanished. The boundaries are fluid and uncertain, and I therefore see no reason why my objects should always be wearable as nose, ear or finger decorations. I find the brooch a far more intriguing theme. It has a special significance for me. One should also be able to hang my work on the wall, or lay it on a table, if one so wishes.

Experimental creativity need not concern itself with the destination of a work. All options should be left open. The prospective owner is asked to live with the objects without being given 'directions for use'.

1974

305] Hubertus von Skal
Bracelet
Oxidized silver, gold, lapis lazuli
6 cm (2⅜ in.)
1973

306] Hubertus von Skal
Brooch
Gold, steel, enamel
5 cm (2 in.)
1972
Private collection

307] Hubertus von Skal
Small sculpture
Steel, gold
30 cm (11¾ in.)
1970
Collection: the artist

150

308] Hubertus von Skal
Brooch
Iron, steel, gold, rock crystal
6.6 cm (2½ in.)
1967

309] Hubertus von Skal
Object
Steel, gold
17.2 cm (6¾ in.)
1972
Collection: the artist

153

Anton Cepka – Czechoslovakia

Silver is my favourite material.
I like to work with it.
Its excellent qualities give me many possibilities to
form it.
I respect it greatly.
I give to it as much as possible to multiply its beauty.
Clear and clean form, face, detail, space are the alpha
and omega for me.
On these principles I create the composition of jewel.
Every created thing, older or newer, holds the magic
of its era.
The fantastic precise calculations and inventions in
any scientific field of the overtechnicalized world
of today contain something special, apart from
their purpose, which we have to take for beautiful.
Computers, radar antennae, television screens, jet
planes, and the whole of space technology in a
great measure influence man.
We are in the everyday contact with it and have to
accept it as it is, precise and cold.
But also these techniques have their charm, have
their aesthetics.
All these facts are the stimuli for my work.
I try to make a jewel which is the reflection of this
world.

1974

310] Anton Cepka
Brooch
Silver, glass, lacquer
8 cm (3¼ in.)
1972

311] Anton Cepka
Brooch
Silver, lacquer
9 cm (3⅝ in.)
1970

312] Anton Cepka
Brooch
Silver, acrylic, steel, PV
Mobile
8 cm (7¼ in.)
1973

313] Anton Cepka
Brooch
Silver, acrylic
7.5 cm (3 in.)
1973

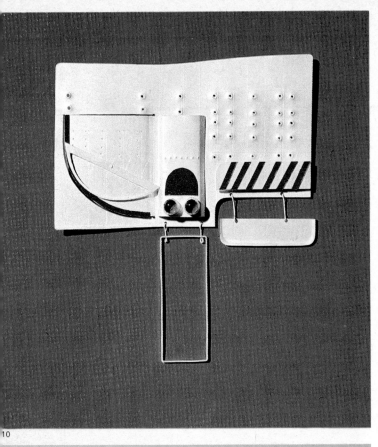

10

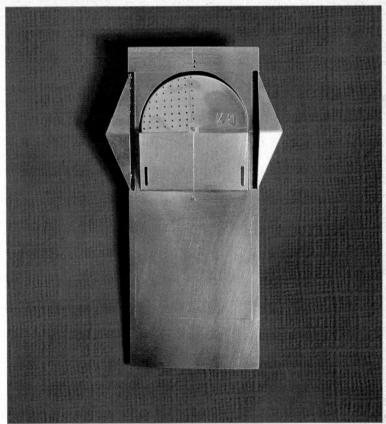

311

12

313

155

Gunilla Treen — England

I think that the best thing is to describe my work as I see it, my aims and ideas.

I cannot think of any influences that affect me consciously such as painters etc. although they must obviously exist.

I am very interested in effects obtained by using different materials, especially plastics. I enjoy using these in combination with various metals and semi-precious stones. I try to aim for a delicate effect, often using transparent materials and subtle colour combinations. The use of plastics enables the pieces to be large and yet still light to wear, this is especially true of my brooches. I am also interested in jewelry which contains elements not immediately noticeable. This is obtained by the use of mobile parts in most of the pieces. This mobility is of the simplest kind, not at all mechanical or functional.

At the moment I cannot see any firm direction in which to work, my ideas and designs usually coming out of the materials I work with, the variety of these materials being endless.

February 1974

314] Gunilla Treen
Brooch
Acrylic, ivory, agate beads; mobi
5.5 cm (2¼ in.)
1973
Collection: the author
Photo: Horst Kolo

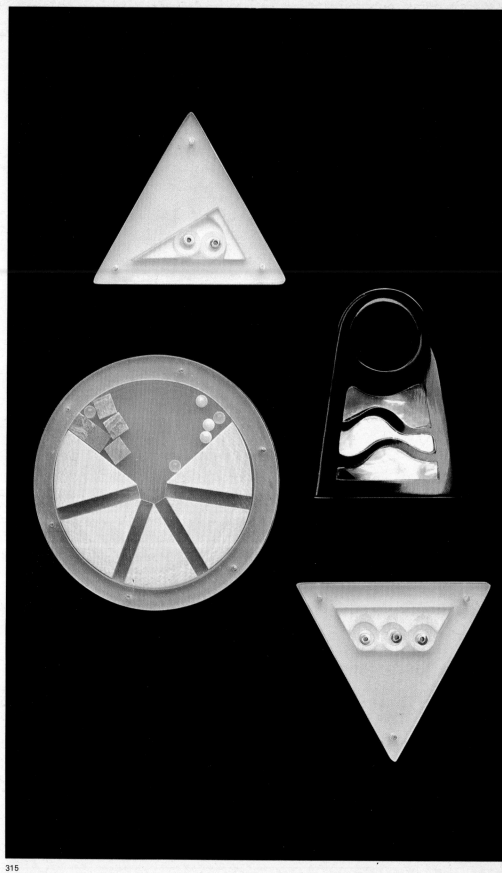

315] Gunilla Treen
Brooches and ring
Acrylic, mixed media
Mobile
5 cm (2 in.)
1974–5
Crafts Advisory Committee, London
Photo: Rob Matheson

316] Gunilla Treen
Brooches
Acrylic, silver, opal, lapis lazuli, malachite
Mobile
6.5 cm (2½ in.)
1974
Photo: Ray Carpenter

315

158

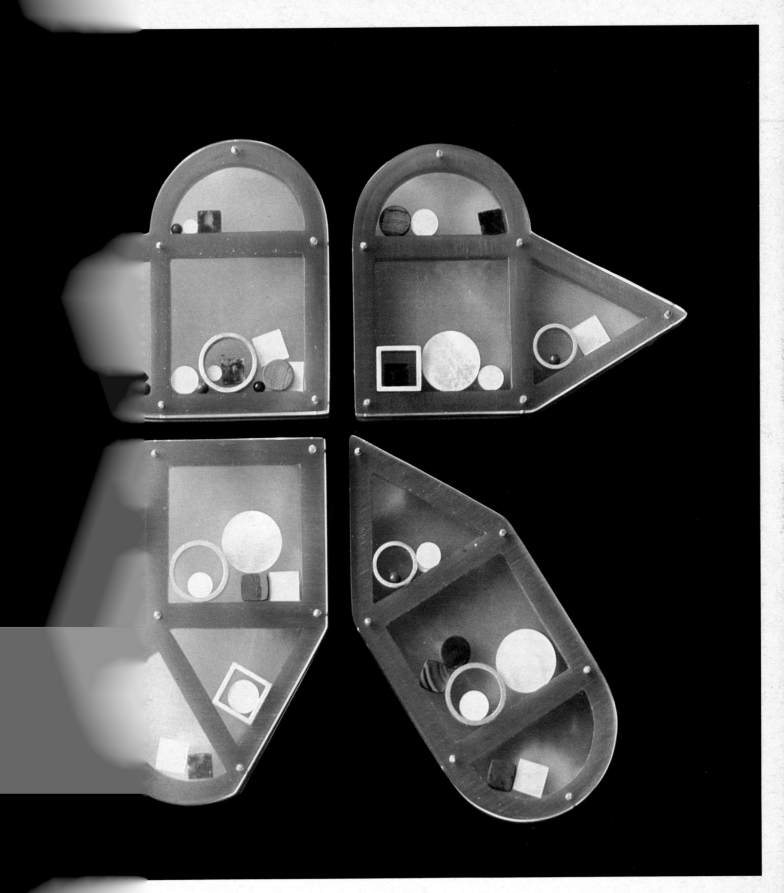

317

Gijs Bakker and
Emmy van Leersum — Holland

Gijs Bakker

The last development in my work showed that the effect from a form on the body is getting more and more my interest, more than the form in itself. I had the wish to make an invisible piece of jewelry, at last to find a form on the body which makes a change to the body. The changed body has to be more visible than the piece of jewelry.

In 1973 I made a 'bracelet' from a very thin gold wire. This gold wire was put on the arm as tight as possible until the wire disappeared into the flesh. Only an indication (marking) is visible. The attention is placed more on the body than on the object. In a next step I don't use a wire, I only show the imprint from a wire which has been there before. The imprint has the function of a piece of jewelry. One could call it an organic jewelry piece — organic in the sense that a print is a growing process with a clear course. An imprint appears or grows by an action and wanes after some time, to disappear completely. In another way I tried to make an invisible piece of jewelry by putting something under the clothing. Both ways are very different, each has its own context. The wire around the face and the stainless steel circle form around the profile are indications of the very personal face or head. It is just an idea to take away the well-known function of the face and to let people experience it in another way.

1974

Emmy van Leersum

Stainless steel is hard and stiff, it does not lose colour or rust. For me it is better than silver. I use it more together with gold. I can cut it into a steel tube and bend it together, and it will stay in the new position without the need of solder.

Especially in recent years I have been working mostly on the arm. The conic form of the arm intrigues me tremendously. The basic prefabricated tube is cylindrical, so I had to find systems to transform the cylinder into a conical form. My system had to produce the minimum of interference with the maximum result in transformation of the surface. I want the conical tube to look as if nothing special has happened, not a dramatic change, but a very small poetical event with an unexpected result.

The measures in an object are very important for me. Each chosen measure needs an explanation. That is why my work gets more and more mathematical — not as a result but as a means to reach the point.

1974

317] Gijs Bakker
Bracelet
Wood
1973

318] Emmy Van Leersum
Bracelet
Acrylic
1972

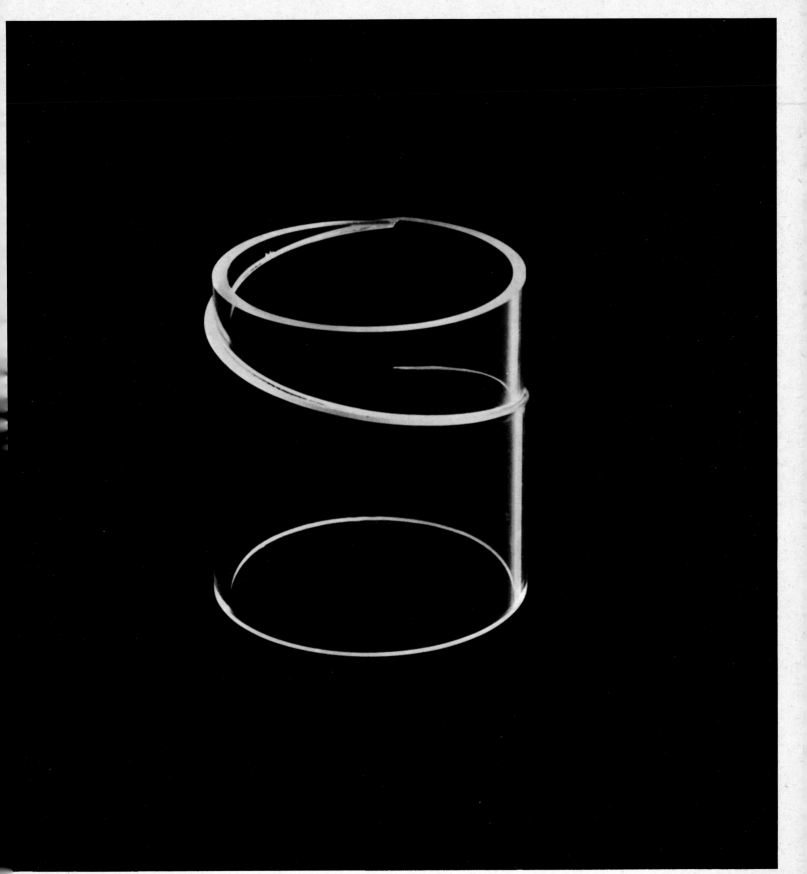

Susanna Heron — England

I think of jewelry as something which should function on a multitude of levels. Perhaps I can most easily clarify this statement by explaining some of the major considerations in my work.

From the start I am very concerned with the drawing of a piece, and draw incessantly to obtain the right line, colour and form, and the right combination of these; at the same time considering wearability to be an essential factor. I treat the figurative images in my work in a two-dimensional way. This enables me to juxtapose silver and resin inlays to create flat planes which contribute to the abstract quality of the finished pieces.

Transparency, translucency and near opacity are some of the qualities of resin that can be totally controlled and must be considered with the silver which has a colour and opacity of its own. The reaction of one colour with the next is governed by the area, the line, and the quality of the colour itself; but this reaction can be varied by altering the translucency of the resin. When a piece is held up to the light, colours will change to become bright, light

or dark, sometimes reversing the qualities they had when no light could shine through; this can change the whole appearance of the form, pinpointing new areas and masking lines (as when a colour is opaque and next to a silver line which is also opaque, thus the division disappears). As the silver also has a higher reflectivity than the resin it constitutes a further medium for change. These properties of change fully assert themselves in the jewelry that is designed to stand away from the body, two-dimensionally. Until the late sixties jewelry was predominantly three-dimensional, frequently being likened to sculpture; my work relates more directly to painting.

At one time I used a sequence of images to promote a strong sense of narrative (as in the necklace showing a bird pulling at a worm). This now seems to be resolving itself in an interest more specifically concerned with visual change and less dependent on a story line.

February 1974

319] Susanna Heron
Necklace
Silver, resin
16 cm (6¼ in.)
1974
Photo: Ray Carpenter

320] Susanna Heron
Earrings
Silver, resin
4.5 cm (1¾ in.)
1973
Private collection
Photo: Ray Carpenter

321] Susanna Heron
Brooches
Silver, opaque resin
4.5 cm (1¾ in.)
1974
Photo: Ray Carpenter

322] Susanna Heron
Bracelet
Silver, resin
11 cm (4⅜ in.)
1971
Collection: Sue Prickett, London
Photo: Ray Carpenter

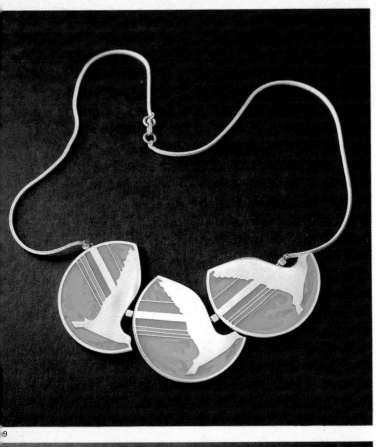

9

320

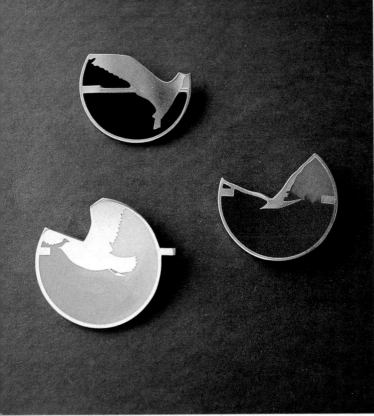

21

322

163

323

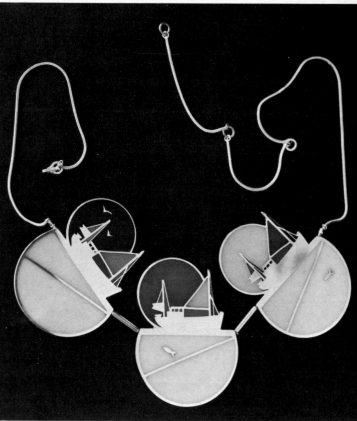

324

325

323] Susanna Heron
Earrings, 'Bird and Reeds Sequence'
Cream, burnt orange
5 cm (2 in.)
1973
Photo: Ray Carpenter

324] Susanna Heron
Rings
Silver, resin
3.5 cm (1⅜ in.)
1974
Photo: Ray Carpenter

325] Susanna Heron
Necklace, 'Trawler Sequence'
Silver, resin
17 cm (6¾ in.)
1973
Private collection, London
Photo: Ray Carpenter

326] Susanna Heron
Necklace, silver inlaid with resin
17 cm (6¾ in.)
1974
Photo: Ray Carpenter

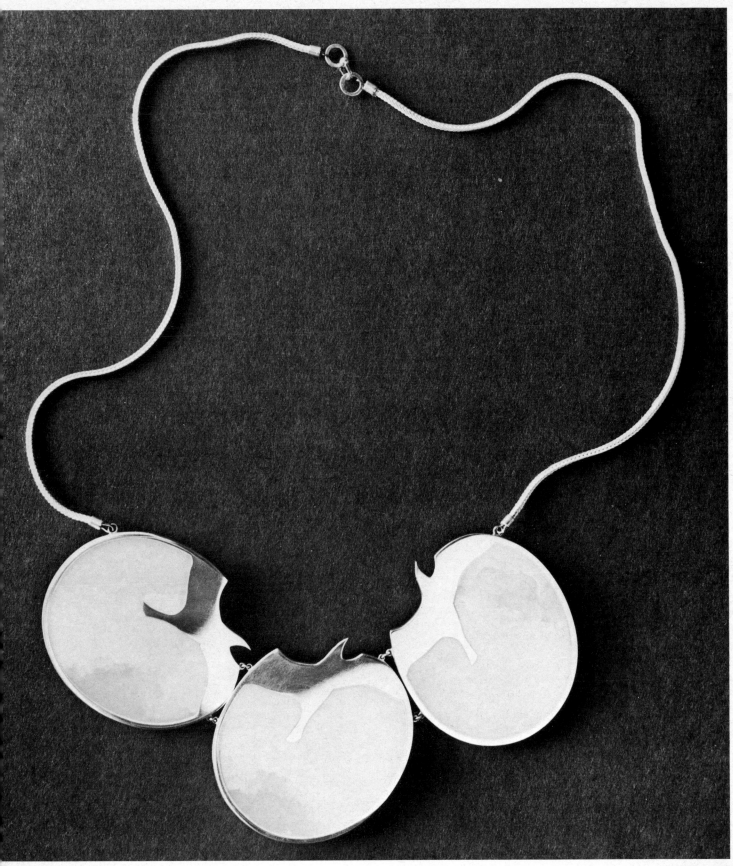

David Watkins — England

This is necessarily an interim statement. I am a comparative newcomer to the field of jewelry. I came to it by chance and am still a little surprised at my involvement. I have arrived at no clear philosophy for jewelry — no guidelines as to form and function. In some ways I hope that I may not. It is simply a means of communication.

Jewelry is interesting because people are interested in jewelry. They naturally approach it on an individual and subjective level which establishes an effective channel of communication. There is built-in magic in the scale of jewelry as there is built-in ambiguity in its effect. A jewel may stand alone, or it may be worn. The object may speak for itself, or it may articulate the body-object. Or it may not. It might transform the wearer or the wearer transform it, or they might in some way fuse. This closed/open-ended/closed situation is for me intriguing and stimulating.

I enjoy making things. But only if the making has purpose. For the moment that purpose is to give shape to my sense of form, to invent, and to develop and exercise new skills. Making jewelry satisfies such requirements very well. In addition, any piece may in the making test my patience, dexterity and cunning, my ability to formulate and co-ordinate a complex sequence of construction, and finally confront me with the need to improvise. It is a challenge. It is exacting and frustrating. But often enough it rewards me with a special pleasure: an idea, now dextrously realized in beautiful material.

I suppose that my experience in other media adds dimensions to my response to jewelry — sometimes as I work I am aware of a process of synthesis, but I have never attempted to analyse it. I am certain, however, that for me the major attraction of making jewelry is that I regard it as an activity of less than earth-shattering importance. Philosophical problems seem at a minimum, allowing a sense of liberation. The only convolutions that need concern me are those of form, and yet I find room for serious, disciplined and progressive exploration. Towards objects of conviction and (hopefully) beauty.

1974

327] David Watkins
Neckpiece
Acrylic, silver
60 cm
1974
Photo: Bob Cramp
Collection: the Scienc
Museum, London

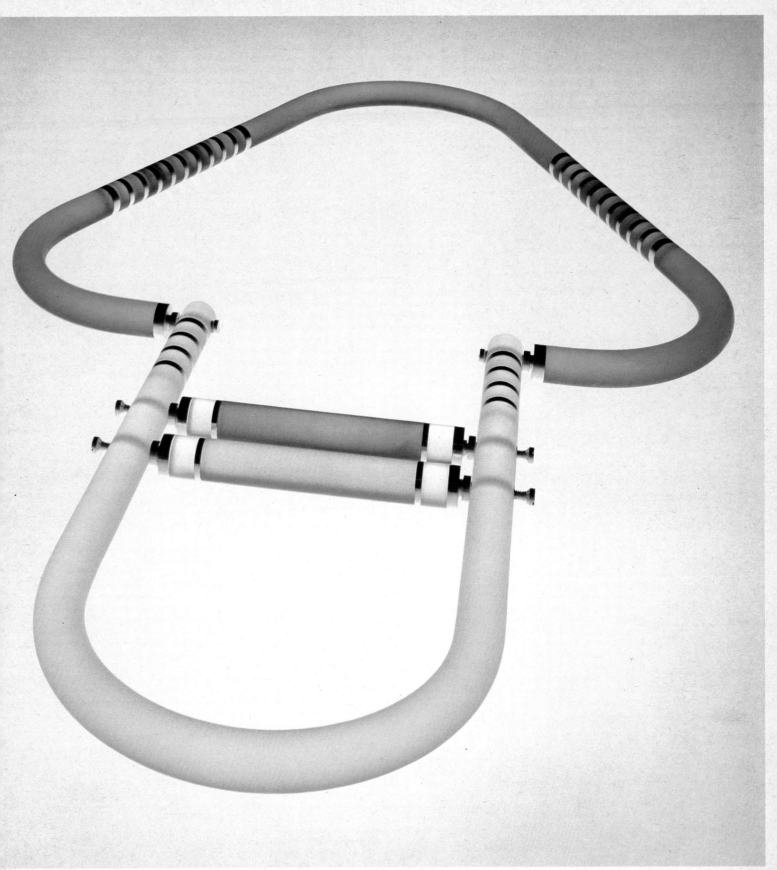

David Poston — England

Jewelry is commonly accepted as a visual
decoration of man's image of woman and man, with
the visual taste tending towards the inconsequential,
as is suitable to that conception of a person.

One of the languages of experience and expression
that is close to dying the death in our society, where
everyday manually dextrous tasks and common
physical contact almost cease to exist, is that of
touch. If touch is your experience and
communication then what you touch, handle and
wear assumes a far greater importance than that of
frivolous decoration, and the monetary value far less
importance than the physical and spiritual value.
Since my principal language is touch I am naturally
involved with jewelry, because it is the closest
touch-expression medium to things called people.
The objects I make sometimes also look decorative,
and since I enjoy colours they tend to have colour in
them, but they are primarily tactile products intended
for experience by touch, though my cerebral
conditioning continually invades.

I believe absolutely that jewelry is for the wearer, not
the spectator, since I believe it essential that people
should be involved in their own existence rather than
in the image of it.

1974

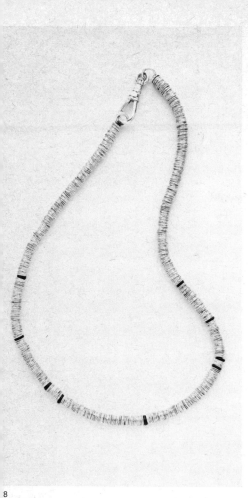

8

[28] David Poston
ecklace
ilver, azurite beads, spliced, beeswaxed, terylene,
 whipping twine
) cm (19½ in.)
974
ectrum Gallery, London
noto: Rob Matheson, *Crafts Magazine*

29] David Poston
ecklace
lver
urk's head spacers on hemp string
3 cm (16⅞ in.)
974
ollection: the author
noto: Rob Matheson, *Crafts Magazine*

329

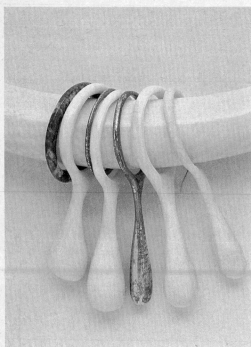

330]

330] David Poston
Neckpiece (detail)
Ivory, string, silver, lapis lazuli
10·5 cm (4½ in.)
1973
Collection: the artist
Photo: Rob Matheson, *Crafts Magazine*

331] David Poston
Necklace
Silver, hemp string, azurite beads, Turk's heads knots
45 cm (17¾ in.)
1974
Collection: Roger Gerret
Photo: Rob Matheson, *Crafts Magazine*

332] David Poston
Neckpiece
Cotton, silver
60 cm (23½ in.)
1973
Private collection, London
Photo: David Poston

331

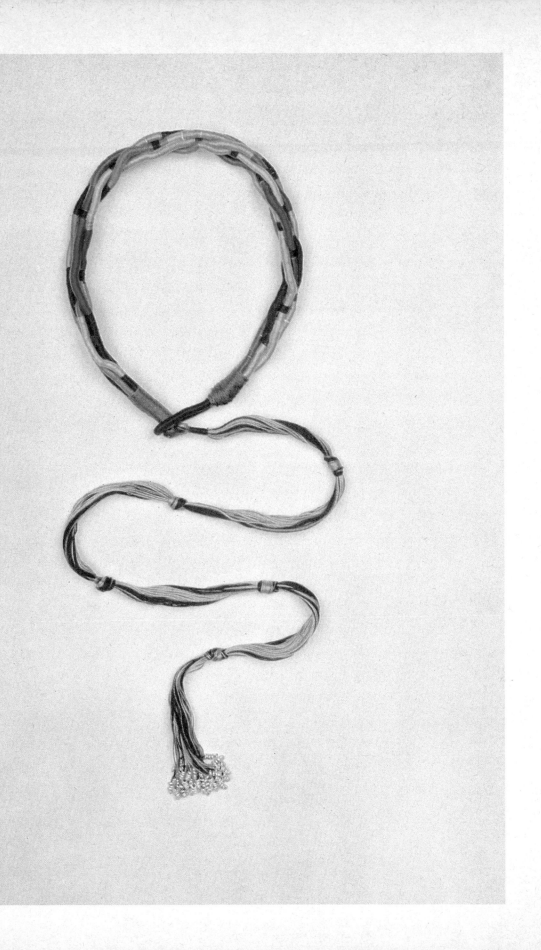

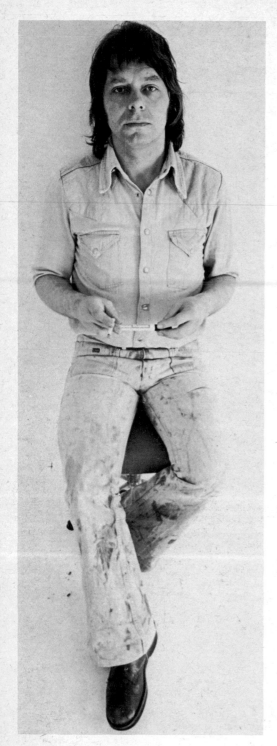

333

Robert Smit – Holland

Some Statement

In short; it all happened on a beautiful warm day in
May, Ralph, a really *great* day with a superfabulous
happening: the day I sold my goldsmith's equipment
for 2000 guilders.

333] Robert Smit
Wearable object
White gold, acrylic
10.5 × 9 cm (4¼ × 3½ in.)
1968
Photo: Chris-Paul Stapels

334] Robert Smit
Wearable object
White gold, acrylic
10 cm (4 in.)
1968
Photo: Chris-Paul Stapels

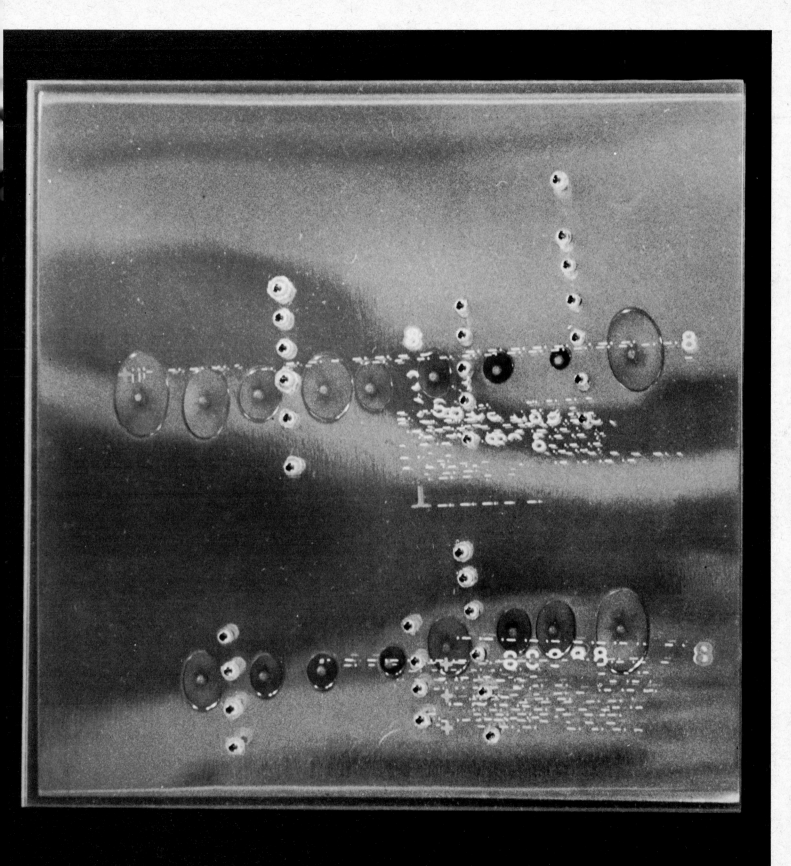

Barry Merritt – USA

Being a full-time producing goldsmith, I find the need to divide my energies into three major areas:

The first area, which is primary to me, is producing one-of-a-kind, crafted jewelry for clients.

The second area is designing and making jewelry on speculation, and this is offered for sale through Shop One Inc., which is the only gallery that I am connected with. This work, of course, leads me back to the first area, in that clients see this and may want to have something individually made.

The third area which is important to me is the exhibition area. Even though I derive a small amount of income from this type of work, the importance of it lies within the stimulus, both creative and emotional. This particular segment of my work today is most creative because I am not involved with the limitation of designing with a person in mind or with a cost factor. I am making objects for the pure pleasure of consummating an act. This, I might add, acts as a stimulus for a fourth area, which is the lecture circuit. It is a very pleasant circle that I work within because the first feeds the fourth, and the fourth feeds the third and so on, so that I never want for inspiration.

To elaborate on the exhibition area, in 1968 I started working in a less traditional way which could be classified as 'funk'. This took the form of badges because I found a very simple and child-like humor in these pieces. Many of them, of course, have *double entendres*, but for the most part they were for people to view and hopefully enjoy. At this point in time I started thinking bigness. We think of badges as being not more than three or four inches, and I was thinking in terms of a foot. This led me to another field of exploration, body coverings. They automatically jumped in size to approximately eighteen inches in length. Badges led me into a mixed media area which I have carried forth with body coverings. They include fibreglass, metal, leather, and found objects.

I perceive the day when these will cover not only the upper torso, but the shoulders, legs, back, and other parts of a person where they can slip the coverings on, and then add or subtract jewelry objects, which would be designed for these pieces, as they see fit.

I do not know where this will lead me, but as long as it means growth, then I will explore it to my limitations.

At present I am also involved with larger-than-life plastic objects with metal additives. This is merely an offshoot of the coverings, which I am sure will be combined in the near future.

1974

335] Barry Merritt
Torso piece, 'Bullet Woman'
Fibreglass, silver, copper, enamel, leather, found
    objects, lacquer, onyx
1972
Photo: John Griebsch

336] Barry Merritt
Torso piece, 'Wonder Woman'
Fibreglass, silver, enamel, chrome, bronze, lacquer,
    sardonyx
1972
Photo: John Griebsch

337] Barry Merritt
Badge, 'Merritt Badge'
Silver, bronze, brass, photograph and found object
1970
Photo: John Griebsch

338] Barry Merritt
Badge, 'Buffalo Bill Badge'
Silver, bronze, ivory and found object
8 cm (3¼ in.)
1970
Photo: John Griebsch

339] Barry Merritt
Necklace, 'Fancy Turkey Corn Necklace'
1972
Photo: John Griebsch

340] Barry Merritt
Buckle, 'Captain Marvel dime bank'
Silver, bronze, gold plate and found object
1972
Photo: John Griebsch

335

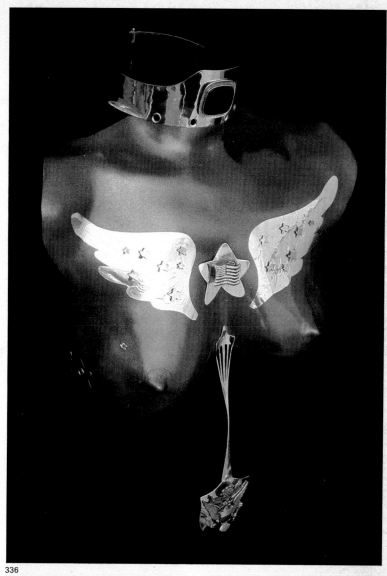

336

7

338

339

340

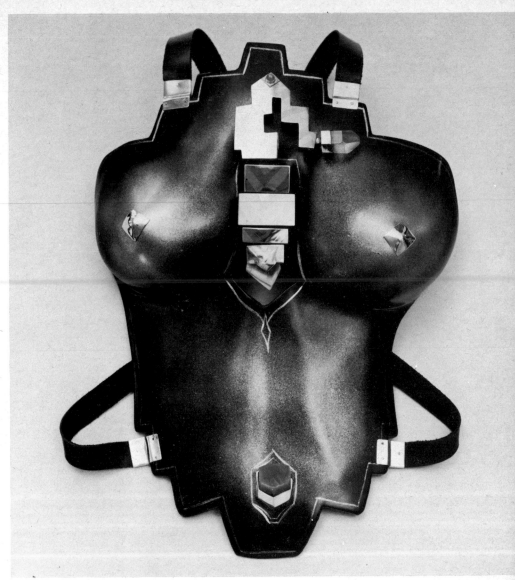

341

341] Barry Merritt
Torso piece, 'Deco Queen'
Fibreglass, silver, brass, bronze, leather, quartz,
    agate, ruby, crystal, lacquer paint
45 cm (17¾ in.)
1973
Photo: John Griebsch

Museums and Public Galleries

342

Considering the achievements that have been made by creative jewellers this century, public exhibitions of any real importance have been few and far between. Large retrospective shows at national museums and galleries throughout the world have been dominated by 'fine' artists' work, consequently the public at large is unaware of the developments that have taken place. There have been more exhibitions of late, but in general they do not attract sufficient attention, and are not selective enough in their material.

USA and Canada

As already mentioned the first *international* Exhibition of Modern Jewelry was held in London in 1961 at the Goldsmiths' Hall, organized by the Worshipful Company of Goldsmiths in association with the Victoria and Albert Museum. However, national exhibitions had been given in the USA since 1946, when the first was held at the Museum of Modern Art in New York. This was followed by similar events at the Walker Art Center in Minneapolis in the spring of 1948 directed by Hilde Reiss, and several other exhibitions devoted to jewelry from the Center. In 1959 it mounted a large collection of contemporary work fully illustrated by the *Design Quarterly*, published that year. In some cases it becomes extremely difficult to assess these events for, with few exceptions, many exhibitions concerned with jewelry in America go unrecorded and few catalogues are published. When they are, they tend to be modest with few illustrations or documentation.

However, the Museum of Contemporary Crafts in New York, under the direction of Paul Smith, has organized several important exhibitions for the American jeweller, including one-man exhibitions by John Prip, Margaret de Patta, John Paul Miller and Stanley Lechtzin. The Museum is sponsored by the American Crafts Council, which also publishes a magazine *Craft Horizons*. But, as the name of the Museum implies, it embraces a number of interests, and consequently does not have the facilities to specialize in any one.

In 1974 the Museum mounted an exhibition Baroque 74 which focused interest on American craftsmen working in a mixed media involved in heavy ornamentation. Although embracing work from numerous artists working in a variety of media, this exhibition provides a representative survey of jewelry in America during the first half of the seventies. Many familiar names in creative jewelry contributed – Bob Ebendorf, Jem Freyaldenhoven, Stanley Lechtzin, Richard Mawdsley, Eleanor Moty, Albert Paley, and Marci Zelmanoff. With little doubt, it could not have been conceived anywhere but in America at that time, for the entire concept of the show, with its self-conscious turn to the past, is peculiar to the USA.

The Society of North American Goldsmiths, whose president is Professor Robert Ebendorf, promotes the interests of its members through numerous exhibitions throughout America. Their Student

342] Goldsmiths' Hall, London
First International Exhibition of Modern Jewelry
1890–1961
Photo: Edgar Hyman

Metal Invitational exhibitions have helped to stimulate interest in the subject as have many universities and colleges in America by mounting exhibitions such as Artists in Metal presented by the California State University in 1973.

The Institute of Contemporary Art in Boston presented an exhibition in 1973 with the intriguing title Jewelry as Sculpture as Jewelry. This was arranged with the cooperation of the Sculpture to Wear Gallery, New York and Gem Montebello in Milan. An extensive exhibition, it did not assess contemporary work from America for the emphasis was on the work of painters and sculptors of repute, but it did include some work from several important jewellers, such as Hans Appenzeller, Frida Blumenberg, Françoise van den Bosch, Marion Herbst, and Fritz Maierhofer. The remainder of the collection comprised principally work from the Montebello Studio in Milan.

As already mentioned in chapter 1, the much-praised exhibition Objects USA opened at the Smithsonian Institute in Washington in 1969 before going on an extensive tour of America and Europe. It embraced various media, and jewelry played only a small part in this mammoth exhibition.

During the summer of 1973 the Metropolitan Museum of Art in New York mounted a sumptuous exhibition devoted to the art of the goldsmith aptly titled Gold. Superb examples were on display from Egyptian headdresses, Celtic torques from the third century BC, Florentine Renaissance pendants and candelabra to Greek and Roman goblets and vessels. The exhibition included a collection of contemporary work by contributors to the Leslie Rankow Gallery in New York. Again, no catalogue was available, but the museum's bulletin fully illustrates the contents of the show, at least as far as the antiquities are concerned, but no contemporary work was illustrated.

In Canada exhibitions are less frequent, but an important one was arranged by the Art Gallery of Ontario in 1971 directed by Renée Neu. It was intended to be a partial review of jewelry in North America and Canada and gave the citizens of Toronto some idea of the work that had been conceived around the states of Canada and the USA. Canada was also host to the World Crafts Council's first International exhibition under the title In Praise of Hands in Toronto in 1974, but such a varied collection of exhibits did not fit easily into one exhibition. With the large number of works exhibited a great effort was necessary if one was to draw any real conclusion. As far as the jewelry section was concerned, most of the principal talents in the world today were not to be seen at this event.

Great Britain

The medieval guild known as the Worshipful Company of Goldsmiths was originally formed over eight hundred years ago by the Livery

3] Museum of Contemporary Crafts, New York
as Wanted exhibition
72

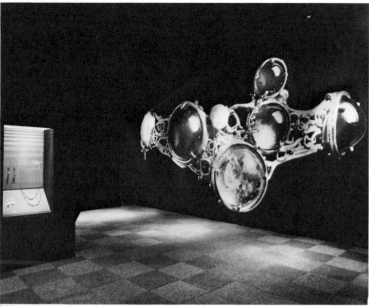

344

345

Companies of the City of London, and is a successor to the ancient craft guilds that were common to many medieval cities throughout Europe. These voluntary associations were originally founded for worship and mutual help and protection for the good of their fellow. A hall has stood on the site of the Goldsmiths' Hall since the fourteenth century, the present handsome building, designed by Phi Hardwick, dating from 1835. It provides a place for meetings and conferences connected with the work of the Company, and houses the numerous exhibitions that are mounted in their elaborate Livery Hall. The Hall's own collection is known throughout the world, primarily for its superb display of seventeenth- and eighteenth-century plate, often given by members of the Guild. Now under the artistic direction of Graham Hughes, the present collection includes contemporary jewelry by British and foreign artists. One-man exhibitions have been given by Bruno Martinazzi, Friedrich Becker, Sigurd Persson, Louis Osman, Irena Brynner, Harry Abend, Stanley Lechtzin, Wendy Ramshaw and David Watkins.

Officially sponsored jewelry exhibitions are, at last, on the increase. In 1969 the Victoria and Albert Museum in London planned a series of exhibitions in which 'the work of outstanding craftsmen would receive the emphasis more frequently accorded to the work of painters and sculptors'. That year the textiles of Peter Collingwood an the pots of Hans Coper were exhibited in the Museum. The second exhibition in this series was devoted to the jewelry of Gerda Flöckinger and the glass of Sam Herman.

In 1971 the Crafts Advisory Committee was formed with the suppor of the British Government, its aim being to promote a nationwide interest in the artist-craftsmen in Britain by promoting their activities with exhibitions and grant schemes. One of the committee's first major achievements was to arrange a large exhibition at the Victoria and Albert Museum in 1973 called The Craftsman's Art. This exhibitic was an attempt to augment many media, including book binding, ceramics, furniture, glass, woven textiles, jewelry and clockmaking. As it did not specialize in any one medium, like its American equivalent Objects USA, it is difficult to assess constructively. However, it did achieve its principal objective which was to draw the public's attention to the talents of the contributors.

Several exhibitions out of London have followed the Victoria and Albert Museum. The Welsh Arts Council organized one in 1973 whic opened at the National Museum of Wales in September and then went on tour. This exhibition was devoted to jewelry, and comprised work by Charlotte de Syllas, Gerda Flöckinger, Louis Osman and John Donald. These four jewellers were given exhibition space that included photographic and recorded material which was intended to give the visitor a more concise view of their work and environment. Included in the exhibition was work from a wide variety of different aspects of jewelry, including Victorian sentimental jewelry, Greek

344] Victoria and Albert Museum, London
Jewelry by Gerda Flöckinger, and glass by
    Sam Herman
1971
Photo mural of necklace by Gerda Flöckinger (1968)
Display by Alan Irvine
Photo: Edgar Hyman

345] Welsh Arts Council
Poster
Designed by Design Systems
Photo of Rocker by Peter Jones

fourth- and fifth-century BC, Ch'ing Dynasty, work by Jean Lurcat, nineteenth-century fans, Egyptian funerary necklaces, nineteenth-century glass beads, seventh-century Berlin iron jewelry, military regalia, etc., and contemporary work from fifteen other contributors! The idea of this exhibition must have been to show the diversity of the subject, but in fact only created confusion. Other provincial museums in Britain which have shown interest in creative jewelry, include the Bristol City Art Gallery, and the Aberdeen Art Gallery in Scotland.

Western Europe

In Europe jewelry exhibitions are rapidly becoming more and more frequent, although standards are not always as high as they could be even though the talent is undoubtedly there.

The Dutch government has given generous support to their artists in grants and financial arrangements of exhibitions that are held both within the country and outside. In Amersfoort, at the Zonnehof Museum, some miles outside of Amsterdam, an exhibition of major importance was mounted covering the entire twentieth century under the title Sieraad 1900–72. Several important artists were not represented, but the scope of the exhibition was remarkable, especially considering that this is a small provincial museum, with limited resources. The catalogue was well illustrated and documented, and acts well as an historical guide.

Recently the Stedelijk Museum in Amsterdam started to add contemporary jewelry to their acquisitions. This is what Liesbeth Crommelin, spokesman for the Museum, has to say on the subject:

In 1965 the Stedelijk Museum started a series of small exhibitions entitled Dutch Jewellery, I, II . . . For each show two artists were invited to display their ornaments in a number of showcases on the ground floor of the museum. The object was to stimulate the public's interest in ornaments whose material and shape differed from what was still generally accepted at that time. The first two exhibitions in this series were devoted to the work of Esther Swart, Joseph Citroen, Archibald Dumbar and Ton Meulendijks. Then after an interval of a year an entirely new development was observed initiated mainly by Emmy van Leersum and Gijs Bakker who took constructed elements of aluminium and steel as the basis upon which to work; building ornaments *around* the human body. Nicolaas van Beek developed his own specific way as seen in the third Dutch Jewellery exhibition.

In 1971 the Museum decided to start a collection of modern jewelry. The aim has been to seek out ideas with new material and the manner in which they are used, and also experiments with traditional materials. The collection, which is still in its infancy comprises of work from Holland and abroad.

346] Zonnehof Museum, Amersfoort
Sieraad 1900–72
Photo: Robert Schlingemann

347] Stedelijk Museum, Amsterdam
Permanent collection
1974

Italian exhibitions, including the Milan Triennale and the Venice Biennale, have held a key place in the development of jewelry design since the fifties, and provided a show place for jewellers such as Persson, Weiss-Weingart, and the Pomodoro brothers. Much the same could be said of the Hanverskmesser exhibition in Munich, which although primarily a trade fair, houses a section of creative work providing a forum for new talents. Germany, in fact, has seen much activity in establishing exhibitions and collections. Although it is a small town, Hanau, near Frankfurt, has seen many important exhibitions in its Goldschmiedehaus. Friedrich Becker, Ebbe Weiss-Weingart, Reinhold Reiling, Hermann Jünger, Rüdiger Lorenzen, Claus Bury, have all held one-man exhibitions at this museum. Unlike so many larger museums in Europe and America the Goldschmiedehaus goes to great pains to publish some of the most excellent catalogues that have been printed concerning creative jewelry. The museum is directed by Fritz Bredel.

Nuremberg staged an important exhibition of creative jewelry which was mounted and organized by the Landeseewerbe Anstalt Bayern in the Noris-Halle in 1971. It showed work from all over Europe, carefully selected and arranged, under the direction of Curt Heigl. The Hessisches Landesmuseum in Darmstadt, renowned for its collection of Art Nouveau, has also mounted international exhibitions of contemporary jewelry by notable creative jewellers. Its director is Gerhard Bott, who has written numerous books and articles on the subjects.

The Schmuckmuseum (Jewelry Museum) in Pforzheim, a small town on the edge of the Black Forest, is the only museum devoted solely to promoting the art of jewelry in the world today. The museum exists to house the town's collection of jewelry and to promote the subject by mounting exhibitions and competitions in an endeavour to stimulate public interest. Now under the directorship of Dr Fritz Falk, it is the envy of the world. Apart from its important biennales, Tendenzen, the museum holds an international competition every few years that attracts principal artists from all over the world.

Throughout the year the museum is usually open to the public, where the development of jewelry can be seen from early times with Egyptian, Grecian, Roman, Etruscan work, through to the Renaissance. The twentieth century is well represented with its collection of Art Nouveau and Art Deco. And unlike so many museum collections, the Schmuckmuseum follows a policy of collecting the work of contemporary artists and owns some of the most advanced pieces of today including work by many of the artists mentioned in this book. Consequently it is a concise collection with very few omissions.

The museum is extremely active, giving exhibitions to individual artists as well as mixed, or exhibitions with a particular theme or period. Its major drawback is that it lies tucked away and off the

348] Schmuckmuseum, Pforzheim
Photo: Sigrid Neubert

349] Schmuckmuseum, Pforzheim
Part of permanent collection
Photo: Günter Meyer

350] Gallery 'D', Prague
Jewelry by Svatopluk Kasaly, 1973
Photo: Jiří Erml

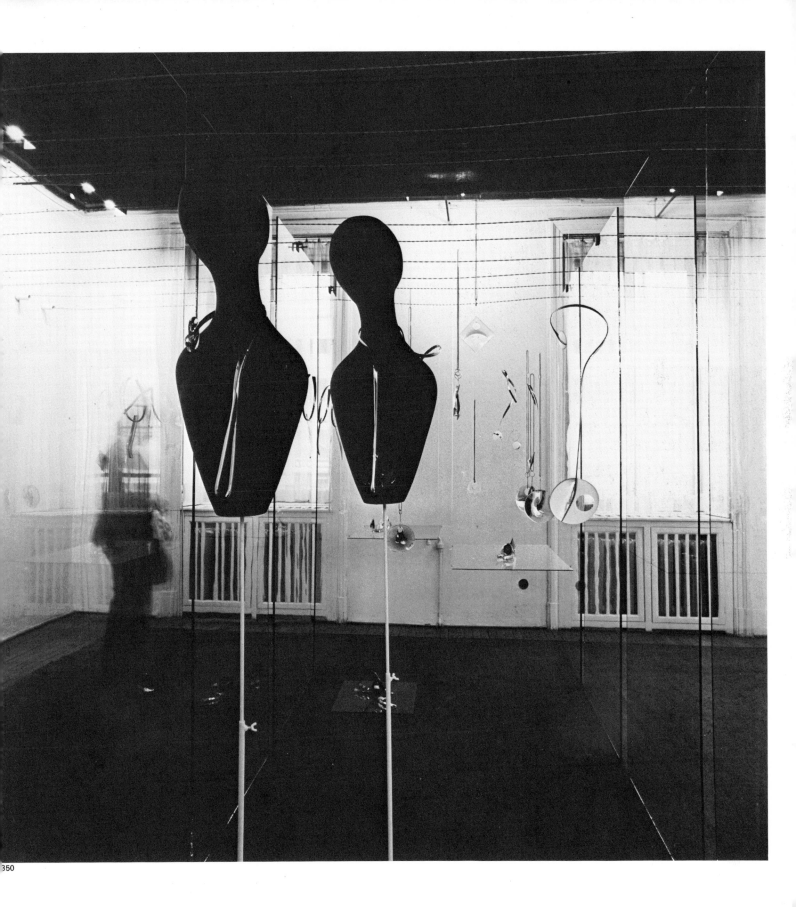

351

beaten track. The museum's work is of such importance that if it were, say, in Munich or Berlin, it could attract a far wider audience than the quite reasonable one it draws at present.

One-man exhibitions at the Schmuckmuseum have been given by Rüdiger Lorenzen, Othmar Zschaler, and the notable exhibition given to Claus Bury in 1974.

Eastern Europe

Socialist countries in general are keen supporters of art in all its forms especially Czechoslovakia. Since 1965 the Czech Government through its official office at the Museum of Applied Arts in Prague, and under the direction of Vera Nováková, has mounted a series of jewelry exhibitions. These shows are of the highest quality and are very selective in their choice of contributors.

The Union of Czechoslovak Creative Artists based in Prague is an association of professional artists who are elected by a jury which is renewed from time to time. The Union submits designs to the government and sells to the general public through the official governmental shops. Official government-directed effort of this kind is applied throughout many Eastern European countries and, certainly in Czechoslovakia, does not have the stiffling effect one might expect.

Japan

Despite the newness of Japanese interest in jewelry, the Japanese have mounted exhibitions of fine quality. Their triennales in 1970 and 1973 comprised collections of work that would do justice to any European city, owing much to the foresight and imagination of Yasuhiko Hishida, the exhibitions' chairman.

351] Nordiska Kompaniet, Stockholm
Exhibition of Sigurd Persson
1974

7

Commercial Galleries

352

Commercial art galleries, now big business, first came into being during the eighteenth and nineteenth centuries. Prior to that painters and sculptors were faced with the task of not only creating their work, but of selling it as well. Many artists still have this problem. Some are content without any commercial outlet, feeling that they can cope far better when they have direct contact with their clients, but generally speaking most artists feel it is a great advantage to have someone else looking after this aspect of their work. Apart from the obvious advantage, it also gives them a home for their work where it can be seen by the art critic, who should offer them constructive criticism. These advantages were until quite recently beyond the reach of the creative jeweller.

Like any artist's work jewelry needs special consideration. This could not be provided by the High Street jeweller — even the best of them could not be expected to provide such a service. But prior to the opening of commercial galleries for such work, jewellers sold their work privately, or were fortunate to be exhibited by the very few art galleries that did also show jewelry. A handful of commercial galleries in Britain showed some interest in what was happening in jewelry during the fifties and sixties. Without exception they all embraced other media and jewelry only had a small role to play in gallery policy. In London, the Institute of Contemporary Art primarily concerned itself with giving shows to artists who produced work of a non-commercial nature, and since the late forties and early fifties, especially under the directorship of Ewan Phillips, has shown some interest in jewelry. As we have seen, there was little happening in Britain during those years but both Alan Davie and Gerda Flöckinger contributed to the ICA's exhibitions at that time.

Perhaps it was this initial interest in jewelry that led Ewan Phillips to exhibit the work of the creative jeweller when he opened his own gallery in Maddox Street in 1964 spurred on by his wife Kathleen Grant who is a jeweller. His small gallery did much to encourage the subject but mainly dealt with nineteenth- and twentieth-century painting and sculpture, and consequently there was neither sufficient time or space to devote energy in any one direction. Much the same could be said of the tiny Pace Gallery in London that opened in 1969 (Both galleries are now closed.)

The British Crafts Centre, the Design Centre, Primavera, and Cameo Corner have all contributed to the development of creative jewelry in Britain, but only the Arnolfini Gallery in Bristol did as much as Ewan Phillips to elevate the jeweller. Since 1961 Jeremy Rees, the director of Arnolfini, has exhibited the work of numerous jewellers in an effort to get their work recognized. Now the gallery has moved to larger premises they are able to expand their activities in jewelry, films, painting and sculpture, and it is one of the major centres of contemporary art in Britain.

352] Arnolfini Gallery, Bristol

The author of this book was involved with the Ewan Phillips Gallery and Pace Gallery, and from them gained the necessary experience when planning a gallery that was to deal specifically with jewelry The Electrum Gallery was founded in 1971, but the seeds were sown for such a venture in 1964 with the opening of Ewan Phillips Gallery.

There are of course fundamental differences between a shop that sells jewelry and a commercial gallery. A gallery must be prepared to undertake far more responsibility than merely selling the goods it displays. In the first place a gallery, if it is to be worthy of the title, must be highly selective in the work it exhibits. Whereas with a normal retail outlet commercial considerations come first, a gallery should act as a place of learning, with a responsibility to the public and to the contributors whose work it handles. Like other outlets for creativity galleries are subject to commercial pressures, and it soon becomes apparent that starting such an enterprise can be hazardous. As I was extremely involved in this aspect of the subject I hope that the reader will forgive a rather lengthy diversion concerning Electrum Gallery.

When Barbara Cartlidge, who now runs the gallery alone, and I decided to open a gallery for jewelry we knew we were accepting a challenge — to create an art gallery without exhibiting painting or sculpture. As has been seen, jewelry had been shown with other forms of art and the public and critics had accepted this mixture, if in some cases with scepticism. But to get acceptance for jewelry as a valid form of expression capable of being considered seriously without the support of other forms of art, was not going to be easy.

There is very little point in reiterating the original policy of Electrum, for much of the content of this book is based on it. However, it is important to point out one or two factors that may need rather fuller explanation than has so far been given. Firstly the gallery from the outset was conceived as an international stage on which the most interesting ideas that were in progress throughout the world could be shown. Unlike the galleries mentioned, which primarily exhibited only British jewelry, Electrum was to have no frontiers. The opening exhibition showed work from Germany, Holland, Austria, Spain and Britain. The following exhibition, with the theme Erotic Jewelry, exhibited the work of Omar K. Bone and Ed Samuels from America, Hubertus von Skal from Germany, and Patricia Tormey — one of the foremost exponents of this type of work in Britain.

The artist who chooses to express himself through jewelry need not necessarily limit his talents to that medium alone. In several instances the creative jeweller also works in other media, such as graphics, film, sculpture, etc. Consequently the exhibitions given at Electrum tried whenever possible to show the creativity of the artists as a whole. For example, in the exhibition Objects to Wear we showed not only Leersum and Bakker's recent jewelry, but also their new experiments

63] Electrum Gallery, London
Revolt in Jewelry by Onno Boekhoudt,
Marion Herbst, Karel Niehorster, Berend Peter
and Françoise van der Bosch
1974
Photo: Ray Carpenter

354] Galerie Swart, Amsterdam
New Jewelry by Emmy van Leersum and Gijs
   Bakker
1971

in clothing. Claus Bury, Fritz Maierhofer and Gerd Rothmann exhibited there with an exhibition Objects and Acrylic Jewelry. To those who saw the exhibition it was an environmental experience of light, form and colour. At that time all three were intensely interested in acrylic. The large objects complemented their jewelry and gave the visitor a clearer insight into their ideas.

We found that a gallery context worked well as an international forum for students and professional artists alike. It served as a centre for the exchange of ideas, as well as a means of reaching the public. More than that it has made possible events outside the gallery in an effort to reach a wider audience beyond the London area.

In spring 1973 we mounted an exhibition of work by contributors to the gallery at the Aberdeen Art Gallery and Museum. It gave the people of Scotland an opportunity of seeing advanced work from our stable of artists drawn from Britain and several parts of Europe. It was followed in the summer with an exhibition of British Jewelry that later opened at the Goldschmiedehaus in Hanau, Western Germany, prior to its tour of museums in Karlsruhe and Frankfurt. The collection included work from students at the Royal College of Art, Central School of Art, and Hornsey College of Art, as well as our own professional artists. In both cases it was possible to publish well illustrated catalogues, giving visitors a complete document of these events.

Extending the idea of exhibiting our artists outside of the gallery we displayed a series of collections of work at the national Museum of Wales, Cardiff. These were given at fairly regular intervals throughout the year. Each artist was shown at the museum for about three months.

There are now several galleries in different parts of the world that deal with the promotion of contemporary jewelry. The policy and quality of the work exhibited varies from gallery to gallery. Some are perhaps rather obviously commercial in their approach, while others strive to promote good progressive work. As yet, the financial rewards are limited, and considerable staying power is needed to survive the commercial pressures. Often a gallery has opened with good work, and a positive creative policy, only too often to fade away into oblivion, or to lower the standard of work and pander to popular taste.

One of the first serious galleries to open in Germany was the Galerie Lalique in Berlin. While under the artistic direction of Renate Kant, this gallery had some excellent exhibitions in its early days. This was followed by the Galerie Cardillac in Munich – the gallery took its name from the possessive goldsmith who, in not wanting to part with his work, murdered his clients and then stole the pieces! Now closed it was a small gallery but in the limited amount of space available used to show some good work, primarily from German artists. In fact,

5

it would be true to say that in most cases, galleries tend to limit their horizons to their geographical position, as happens in Holland with Galerie Sierraad, mentioned in a previous chapter, and, to a large extent, with Galerie Novelles Images in the Hague.

In New York there are four such galleries, including the Fairtree, the Leslie Rankow, Lee Nordness's gallery, although they do not specialize in jewelry, and a small gallery within the Plaza Hotel which does specialize, but in jewelry by painters and sculptors. In recent years they have extended their policy to include the jeweller.

Lee Nordness, responsible for much of the organization of the Objects USA exhibition, has his own gallery. He deals in a mixture of media that include jewelry. The Leslie Rankow Gallery has a section devoted to the jeweller, called Goldsmiths' Hall after its older namesake in London. This gallery operates as a cooperative, and has a selection board that sits to decide the policy and direction of the gallery. Regrettably they have tended to be somewhat conservative in their taste, and have rejected artists whose work has not been in keeping' with the gallery's policy, although they do have some notable members, including Noma Copley and Barbara Chase Riboud.

Sven Boltenstern opened the Galerie Sven in Paris, also with a jewelry section. Galerie Sven chooses work from painters and sculptors, such as Pol Bury, Niki de Saint Phalle and César. He has also exhibited work from Maierhofer, Susanna Heron and the Pomodoro brothers. In Toulouse, Jacques Pulvermacher has opened a gallery under the intriguing title of Galerie at Home. Again he deals with art in the broadest sense, and has given exhibitions to jewellers since 1969.

In Australia the creative jeweller until very recently had to fend for himself, although the Bonython Gallery and the David Jones Gallery in Sydney have helped in showing such people as Rod Edwards, Emanuel Raft, Frank Bauer, Darwena Lewis and Helge Larsen. The Bonython Gallery is said to be the largest commercial gallery in the world and has exhibited a fair share of jewelry. In 1971 David Dunn, another jeweller from Australia, opened a gallery in Sydney's Double Bay. Like many, it was short lived and now closed. Dunn complains that too few people in Sydney at that time were prepared to support him. However, by July 1973 Dunn himself was one of the contributors to the newly opened Lord of the Rings Gallery, in Paddington, a suburb of Sydney. The directors, Mike Aisenberg, Ginette and Norma Ackermann, presented a selection of jewellers exclusively from local talent. Other contributors included Frank Bauer, Roy Lewis, Ray Norman and Albert Steen, who had worked with Patricia Tormey in London. Later, the gallery expanded its programme and included work from English, German and Austrian artists.

With the growing awareness of creative jewelry, it has been promoted as a means of expression, although often the work has in most cases

55] Galerie At Home, Toulouse
hoto: Sud Ouest

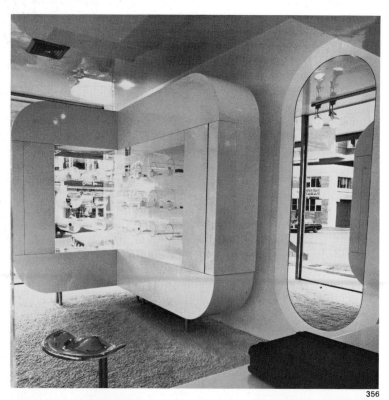

nothing whatever to do with creativity. Commercial concerns have been quick to see the value of adding the word 'art' to their campaigns. Advertisements now talk in terms of 'collections' or limited editions. Words like 'unique' or 'exhibited' crop up with regularity. Window displays depict reproductions of old master drawings or a painter's palette, planting the idea of an association with fine art. The commercial promotion of any art is a delicate business and need to be conducted with considerable care and understanding. With the art of the jeweller, because of the very word 'jewelry', the pitfalls are even more tricky. Over-exposure or any sign of real commercialism can quickly turn a talent into another consumer product. Certainly the creative jeweller needs to sell his work, but once within the grip of a business or organization that cannot respect his individuality as an artist, this turns sour and becomes fraudulent.

Very recently a few goldsmiths have indicated that a gallery specializing in jewelry is perhaps after all not the best solution to their problems. The very fact that a place has been set aside exclusively fo their work somehow indicates that what they are doing can only be considered in isolation. What is needed now is for the commercial gallery to open its doors to the jeweller, as an artist in his own right, and give him the same critical consideration and offer him the same facilities afforded to other artists.

356] David Dunn Gallery, Sydney

357] Galerie Sierraad, Amsterdam

190

8

Private Collections

The art collector is an elusive creature. Many of the finest works of art are now in private hands, shut away from the world, secretive and secluded, and often bought for their commercial value. I remember vividly the sinking feeling inside me when handing over a fine collection of Klee drawings some years ago that were doomed to a life of darkness in the vaults of a Swiss bank. Jewelry of all things should not be subjected to this internment. It is created to be worn and admired. This, the most personal of art forms, needs human contact more than any other medium; however, the collector of art is an important figure, as it is he who can act as patron to those artists who need his support. In many instances the collections are twofold. They are displayed in the collector's house and enjoyed by those privileged to see them, and by those by whom they are worn.

The serious collector of contemporary jewelry is a relatively recent phenomenon. Collectors of contemporary art are not uncommon, but the equivalent in jewelry is still as yet a rare breed.

Nearly all major collectors of modern jewelry are male, although in most cases it is the women that wear it, and by and large men usually have far better taste in jewelry than women. Perhaps because diamonds are a girl's best friend, men are usually far more adventuresome and selective in their choice of contemporary work, and women often react to jewelry in a very traditional way. However, there is an increasing number of men who wear this type of jewelry. One English collector, primarily a dealer in Art Nouveau and Art Deco, but an avid collector of contemporary jewelry, wears pieces with great style and masculinity.

As well as having one of the most generous and sympathetic governments to the arts, Holland also has a large number of private collectors. One such who has contributed a great deal to the development of contemporary art, especially jewelry, and who was largely responsible for Sieraad 1900–72 is Benno Premsala. He finds jewelry amongst the most interesting of contemporary arts:

> Within the sphere of arts and applied arts, it is the workers in fine metals who are holding my special interest, because for some considerable time a renewal has been going on that, perhaps more obviously than in any other artistic discipline, is running a parallel course with contemporary changes in society and the changing standards they bring with them.

> I would draw attention to three aspects:

> 1. Jewelry is no longer a status symbol; the value of the material used is not now important; the chosen material is only valuable according to its efficiency in communicating visual information.
> 2. Jewelry has come to stand in a definite relationship to the human body, it is never merely trivial.

3.   Men are wearing jewelry (again), which is coming to differ less and less from women's jewelry.

Reasons enough for me to follow this development closely.

One of the largest collectors of contemporary jewelry in private hands belongs to another Dutch collector, who wishes to remain anonymous. This collection in Amsterdam was started in the early sixties, and is comprised of work of many of the contributors to this book. In Brussels a fine collection of ethnological jewelry belongs to a doctor and his wife. These Belgian collectors also believe in patronizing contemporary artists and, like the Dutch collector, they are adding to their display some of the best work being produced at the moment. Both these collections are drawn from an international market, and are not restricted to their own geographical positions.

Charles Handley-Read made a superb collection of furniture, glass, silver, painting, sculpture, ceramics and jewelry from the Victorian and Edwardian periods which was shown in London in 1972. His collection was known to many, but what is perhaps not known is that Handley-Read was also slowly acquiring a collection of contemporary jewelry, prior to his tragic death in 1971. With his quiet and unassuming manner he would attend exhibitions and spend hours talking and looking before making a purchase, but when he did, he bought with great knowledge and perception. He had just begun to acquire a taste for modern jewelry during the sixties, when he added pieces by Patricia Meyerowitz, Emanuel Raft, and Helga Zahn to his collection.

9

Jewelry without Boundaries

358

This chapter is in no way intended to offer the reader any theory or idea as to how jewelry may develop in the future. No one can predict that. Rather I would like to use the few remaining pages to illustrate the diversity of the subject, and indicate some of the areas being explored at the moment.

The word jewelry in the English dictionary means: 'Ornament containing precious stone(s)'. I think we have seen that the word has a broader meaning. In German the word 'Schmuck' means:

Schmuck: ornament; decoration, adornment; trimmings, trappings pl. finery, adornment, get-up; jewel(le)ry, jewels pl; *unechter* — imitation jewel(le)ry, trinkets pl; fig.; flowers pl. (of speech etc.); . . *arbeit* f. jewel(le)ry

Perhaps these photographs are a fitting conclusion showing that jewelry has no boundaries. It all depends on how loosely or widely one interprets the word.

Wherever possible I have included brief notes by artists, but in most cases the reader is left to draw his own conclusions.

359

358] Claudio Parmiggiani
Deiscrizione
Galleria L'Uomo e L'arte
Milan
1972

359] Marc Chaimowitz
'Genug Tyrannei' (Enough Tyranny)
Random audiences in various outdoor locations
Autumn 1972
Photo: Robert Zehetleitner

360–361] Marc Chaimowitz
'Genug Tyrannei' (Enough Tyranny)
Random audiences in various outdoor locations
Photo: Robert Zehetleitner

362] Catherine Riley
'My answer to a six week "fashion project"
  completed in two days'
Grey stretch nylon tube, felt maggots beads
Aim: 'To make a non-fashionable "fashion"
  garment — also to provide drawing themes for my
  own work and development'
Manchester
1973
Photo: Jackie Ward

363] Glaudio Parmiggiani — Mario Diacono
Malanggan
Galleria L'Uomo e L'arte
Turin
1972

360

361

362

363

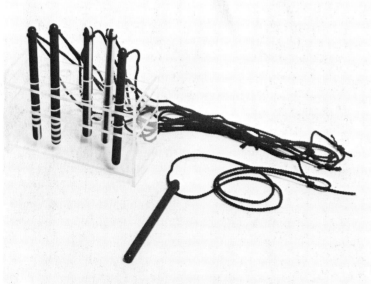

364

365

366

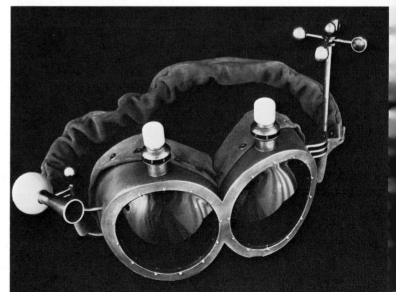

367

364] Berend Peter
Unwearable rings
Acrylic
9·5 cm (3¾ in)
1973
Photo: Berend Peter
Exhibition: Revolt in Jewelry, Electrum Gallery,
    London, 1974

365] Ballet Rambert
'Ziggurat'
Choreography: Glen Tetley
Design: Nadine Baylis
Photo: Alan Cunliffe

366] Marion Herbst
Pendants
Acrylic, silk in rack
Exhibition Revolt in Jewelry, Electrum Gallery,
    London, 1974
Photo: Berend Peter

367] Gerry Evans
'Homage to Eyes'
Bronze, brass, silver, copper, acrylic, rubber, suede
1973

368–370] Gijs Bakker
Steel profile circle
(Fritz Maierhofer is the wearer)
1974

371] Emile Souply
'Jack in the Box'
Welder's helmet
1970
Photo: Yves Auquier

368

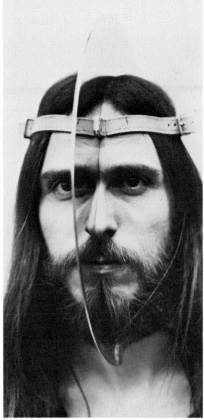

369

370

371

372

373

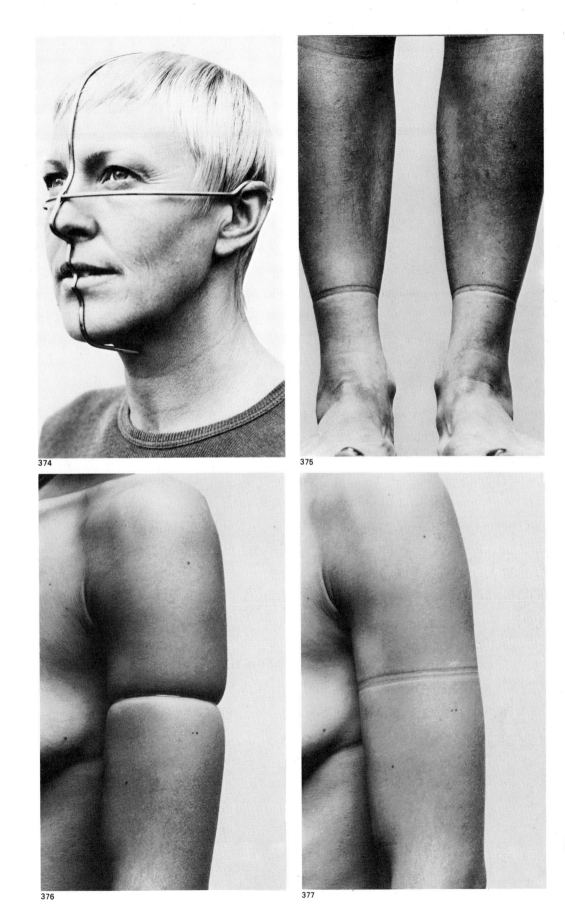

374

375

376

377

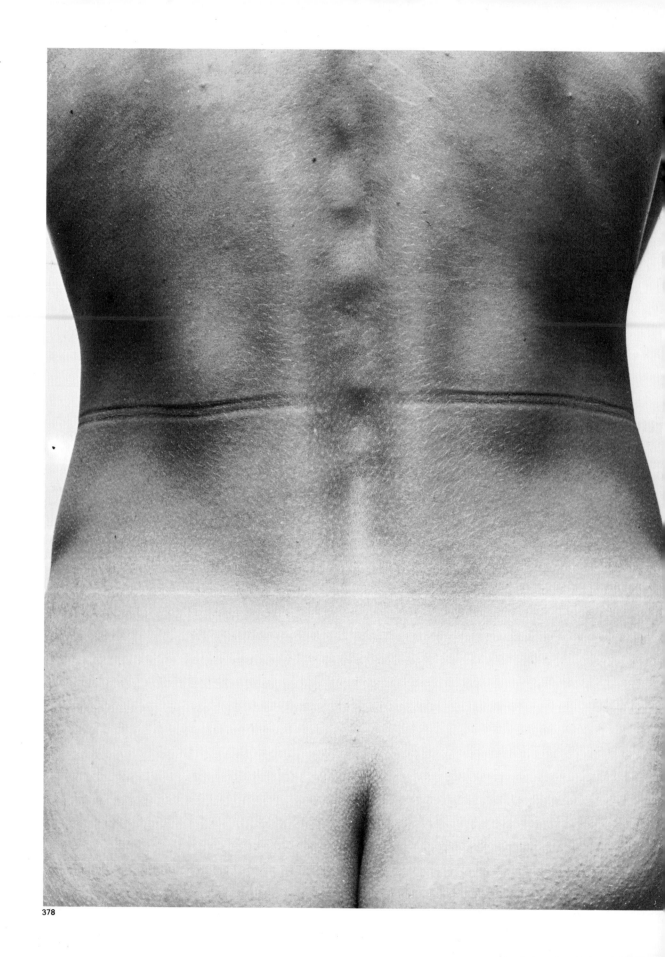

378] Gijs Bakker
Shadow jewelry and
   invisible jewelry
1973

378

Further Reading

Books

Amaya, Mario, *Art Nouveau*, Studio Vista, London; Dutton, New York, 1966

Armstrong, Nancy, *Jewellery – An Historical Survey of British Styles and Jewels*, Lutterworth Press, London, 1973

Berger, John, *Ways of Seeing*, Penguin, Harmondsworth, 1972

Bott, Gerhard, *Schmuck*, Hans Schöner, Berlin, 1971

Bott, Gerhard, *Ullstein Juwelenbuch, Abendländischer Schmuck von der Antike bis zur Gegenwart*, Verlag Ullstein, Berlin, 1972

Evans, Joan, *A History of Jewellery 1100–1870*, Faber & Faber, London, 1953; Boston Books, Boston, 1970

Gere, Charlotte, *Victorian Jewellery Design*, William Kimber, London, 1972

Gregorietti, Guido, *Jewellery through the Ages*, Paul Hamlyn, London, 1970; American Heritage, New York, 1969

Hillier, Bevis, *Art Deco*, Studio Vista, London; Dutton, New York, 1968

Hollander, Harry, *Plastics for Jewelry*, Pitman, London, 1974

Hughes, Graham, *The Art of Jewelry*, Studio Vista, 1972

Hughes, Graham, *Modern Jewelry*, Studio Vista, London; Crown, New York, 1963

Hughes, Graham, *Jewelry*, Studio Vista, 1966

Laver, James, *Concise History of Costume*, Thames & Hudson, London; Abrams, New York, 1969

Lucie-Smith, Edward, *Movements in Art Since 1945*, Thames & Hudson, London, 1969

Meyerowitz, Patricia, *Jewellery and Sculpture through Unit Construction*, Studio Vista, London, 1967

Morton, Philip, *Contemporary Jewelry, A Craftsman's Handbook*, Holt, Rinehart and Winston, New York, 1970

Naylor, Gillian, *The Arts & Crafts Movement*, Studio Vista, London; MIT, Cambridge, Mass., 1971

Neumann, Robert von, *The Design and Creation of Jewelry*, Pitman, London, 1962

Nordness, Lee, *Objects: USA*, Thames & Hudson, London; Viking, New York, 1970

Pevsner, Nikolaus, *The Sources of Modern Architecture and Design*, Thames & Hudson, London; Praeger, New York, 1968

Rowland, Kurt, *A History of the Modern Movement, Art, Architecture, Design*, Van Nostrand Reinhold, New York, 1973

Schollmayer, Karl, *Neuer Schmuck*, Verlag Ernst Wasmuth, Tubingen, 1974

Woods, Gerald, Thompson, Philip, Williams, John, *Art without Boundaries: 1950–70*, Thames & Hudson, London, 1972

Willcox, Donald, *Body Jewellery*, Pitman, London, 1973

Catalogues

Design Quarterly 45–6, Walker Art Center, Minneapolis, 1959

International Exhibition of Modern Jewellery, 1890–1961, Worshipful Company of Goldsmiths

Modern British Jewellery 1963, Worshipful Company of Goldsmiths

Internationale Ausstellung Schmuck '65, Hessisches Landesmuseum, Darmstadt

Friedrich Becker, Goldsmiths' Hall, London, 1966

Objects to Wear by 5 Dutch Jewellery Designers, Van Abbemuseum, Eindhoven; Smithsonian Institute, Washington, 1969

Herman Jünger, Deutsches Goldschmiedehaus, Hanau, 1969

Herbert Zeitner, Deutsches Goldschmiedehaus, Hanau, 1970

Stribrny Sperk Jablonec '68/71, Czechoslovakia

Flöckinger/Herman 1971, Victoria & Albert Museum, London

Gold Silber Schmuck gerat von Albrecht Dürer bis zur Gegenwart 1971

Jewelry '71, Art Gallery of Ontario

Reinhold Reiling, Deutsches Goldschmiedehaus, Hanau, 1971

Friedrich Becker, Deutsches Goldschmiedehaus, Hanau, 1972

Eberhard Burgel, Verlag Galerie Oly, 1972

Experimenta '72

Rudiger Lorenzen, Schmuckmuseum, Pforzheim, 1972

Bruno Martinazzi, Galleria la Parisina, Turin, 1972

Sieraad 1900–1972, Zonnehof Museum, Amersfoort, Holland

Third National Student Metal Invitational 1972, The Society of North American Goldsmiths

Victorian and Edwardian Decorative Art – The Handley-Read Collection 1972, Royal Academy of Arts, London

Othmar Zschaler, Schmuckmuseum, Pforzheim, 1972

Objects and Acrylic Jewellery, Claus Bury, Fritz Maierhofer, Gerd Rothman, Electrum Gallery, London, 1972

Aspects of Jewellery, 1973, Aberdeen Art Gallery, Scotland

The Arts and Crafts Movement in America 1876–1916, The Art Institute of Chicago, 1973

The Craftsman's Art 1973, Craft Advisory Committee, London

British Jewelry 1973, Deutsches Goldschmiedehaus, Hanau

Artists in Metal 1973, California State University

'73 International Jewelry Arts Exhibition, Japan Jewelry

Jewelry as Sculpture as Jewelry 1973, The Institute of Contemporary Art, Boston

The Observer Jewellery Exhibition 1973, Welsh Arts Council, Cardiff

Schmuck 70/73 Tendenzen, Schmuckmuseum, Pforzheim

Ebbe Weiss-Weingart, Deutsches Goldschmiedehaus, Hanau, 1973

Baroque '74, Museum of Contemporary Crafts, New York

Claus Bury, Schmuckmuseum, Pforzheim, 1974

18 Orfèvres d'Aujourd'hui 1974, Musée des Arts Décoratifs de la Ville de Lausanne

Magazines

Goldschmiede Zeitung

Mobilia 131/132, June/July 1966

Design 228, December 1967; 266, February 1971; 272, August 1971; 284, August 1972; 290, February 1973; 317, May 1975

Crafts, 3 July/August 1973; 9, July/August 1974; 15, July/August 1975

Craft Horizons, September/October 1965, June 1966, September/October 1968, February 1971, June 1972, April 1973

Domus

Index

Figures in heavier type indicate a major reference; italic figures refer to pages on which illustrations appear.